CU00659588

# ROGER "TWIGGY" DAY

## PIRATE OF THE AIRWAVES

All rights reserved; no part of this publication may be reproduced or transmitted by any means, electronic, mechanical, photocopying, or otherwise, without the prior permission of the author.

First published in Great Britain in 2023

Copyright © Text Roger Day 2023

ISBN 978-1-3999-4972-9

Printed and bound by CPI Books

Cover design and formatting by
Softwood Self Publishing

This book is dedicated to Ronan O´Rahilly, the man who changed British radio and my life. Not forgetting my parents, family, and listeners, who have supported me for many years and allowed me to follow the dream.

# CONTENTS

# FOREWORD

Unless you lived in the UK during the early 1960s, it would be difficult to imagine the lack of choice on your radio. The BBC provided just three channels: the Home Service was responsible for news, current affairs, and other serious speech; the Light Programme broadcast easy-listening music and light entertainment; and the Third Programme was for lovers of classical music and highbrow arts programmes.

As groups like the Beatles and Beach Boys formed the vanguard of the Swinging Sixties, if you wanted to hear their latest hits and follow your favourite groups, you were not going to find them, or much else to reflect that historically significant musical era, on the BBC. Well, not yet, anyway.

Top 40 radio, as we came to know it, evolved in the United States of America at the start of the 1950s. By the 1960s, there wasn't a city in America that didn't have multiple competing radio stations playing chart hits 24 hours a day. However, it wasn't just the music. Pivotally, the music was linked by big personality DJs whose connection with the audience was one of the biggest factors in establishing listener loyalty and, therefore, commercial success.

Those Brits, lucky enough to experience American radio at that time, wondered why they couldn't hear a similar style of radio back home in blighty. The biggest blockages included the publicly funded BBC with its radio monopoly, the control of pop music by the record companies, and the reluctance of the government to open up the airwaves to commercial radio.

In 1964, a young entrepreneur, by the name of Ronan O'Rahilly, decided to do something about it, and on March 28th of that year, just outside British territorial limits, in international waters, he launched Radio Caroline – Great Britain's first commercial radio station. And at the same time of course it became Great Britain's first pirate radio station. In doing so, Caroline, and its rapidly growing fleet of imitators and competitors, became responsible for changing the sound and structure of popular radio in the UK.

As Radio Caroline started broadcasting, a few miles back on shore down the coast, in the seaside town of Margate, the mods and rockers were rioting, and a young accountant by the name of Roger Thomas was moonlighting as a DJ at the Dreamland Ballroom. Despite knowing nothing about radio at that stage, he was offered a job on a new pirate station called Swinging Radio England ... which promptly folded six months later. But, by then, Roger Day (to use his stage name) had been heard by those in charge at Radio Caroline, and it was at this point that the 'Legend of the Thinner Record Spinner' was born. In fact, Roger 'Twiggy' Day was destined to become one of the most famous of the offshore broadcasters. The respect he earned in the music industry was such that he compèred the 1968 Beach Boys' tour of the UK.

After a period as Programme Director with Radio Northsea International (RNI), Roger joined the new onshore commercial radio scene with stints at Piccadilly Radio in Manchester, Birmingham's BRMB, Radio West in Bristol, and, for me, one of the most important gigs of all: Pirate FM in Cornwall, where, in 1992, he was the launch CEO. Roger was also the first voice heard on-air. He launched the station as the star breakfast show presenter.

At the time, Pirate FM was one of the most technologically advanced radio stations in the world – so much so that BBC television's legendary Tomorrow's World programme did a major segment on it. Starting with clips of the original pirates, the piece morphed into the modern day 'legal' Pirate radio. Roger Day was cast as the disc jockey 'with no discs to jockey' as he worked with an all-new computerised play out system – something that didn't faze him for one minute. Suffice it to say, the launch of Pirate FM was successful beyond our wildest dreams – thanks to a real pirate from the swashbuckling era when sea-based pirates truly did rule the airwaves.

They say you should never meet your heroes, but after being a long-time fan since his Caroline and RNI days, I am glad to say I had the privilege of working with Roger. A true professional.

From Pirate FM, Roger rejoined Piccadilly and then later went on to work for various other radio stations, both in the UK and in Europe.

Notably, one of the organisations that hired his unquestionable talent was the BBC. However, if you think this meant that this particular buccaneer had sold out to the establishment and resorted to the respectability of his accounting past, then I am here to assure you it was not the case. Indeed, if you are lucky enough to be in his presence when he talks about those pirate radio days, you will still see the twinkle in the eye. Once a pirate, always a pirate!

Now, at last, Roger Day has written his side of the story. I suggest that you pour yourself a glass of wine, sit in your favourite chair, stream a background of Beach Boys' music, and turn the page of the book you're holding.

You are going to be in for a treat.

*- written by Mike Powell*

I first had the pleasure of meeting Roger at Ijmuiden harbour in the Netherlands in October 1967. Bud Ballou and I had just been hired as disc-jockeys by Radio Caroline, and we were about to go out to the Mi Amigo anchored off the Essex coast. We were introduced to Roger by Nan Richardson, who ran the Radio Caroline office in Amsterdam, who immediately suggested we join him for a beer in a nearby bar. We bombarded him with questions about our impending trip across the North Sea in what looked to us to be no more than a small fishing boat. I recall Roger's words to this day: "Eat plenty of bread before you get onboard if you don't want to throw your guts up. It can get a bit rough at times!" It proved to be an understatement. As we left the comparative shelter of the harbour, we were hit head-on by a force seven gale.

To my great embarrassment, and much to the amusement of Roger, I hasten to add, I was the first person to succumb to the conditions and deposited the contents of the stomach over the side of the tender.

Roger proved to be great company on the Mi Amigo, whatever the conditions. When the sea was really rough and the tender failed to arrive, there was often an air of gloom over the ship, but Roger never let it get him down and would tell us all to cheer up, using the nicknames he had created for us all.

Stevie Merike was 'Majorie', Johnnie Walker 'Joanna', Robbie Dale 'Roberta', Carl Mitchell 'Carla', and I was 'Ada.'

One afternoon, I was scheduled to read the news on the Stevie Merike Show, who Roger was sitting-in for. Roger fired off the news introduction jingle at the top of the hour then said, "It's 5 o'clock, with the latest Radio Caroline International News." He paused then added, "Here's Ada Camp." I began to read the headlines, then after fully realising what he had said, began to cough and splutter. Somehow, I managed to get through the best part of the first story before the giggles got the better of me. I looked through the glass window, which separated the two studios, and could see and hear Roger (he had left his microphone on) weeping uncontrollably with laughter.

After I don't know how long, I composed myself enough to say something along the lines of, "I think it best I hand back to Roger Day, and I'll be back with the news at 5.30." I then looked up through the glass and, to my horror, he was nowhere to be seen. All I could hear was muffled chuckles. I stood up to get a better view: Roger was curled up on the floor in the foetal position with his fist in his mouth and wriggling around like a demented stick insect. It must have been a good minute or so before he finally got back into his seat to continue his show. In the messroom afterwards, we both thought we might get fired. but as luck would have it, Robbie Dale the Programme Director wasn't on board and obviously wasn't listening in, so we managed to get away with it.

Fast forward thirty odd years and once more we were working for the same radio station. Invicta Radio based in Whitstable. I was the programme controller of Invicta Gold, Roger was my immediate boss. Three decades had passed but Roger hadn't lost one bit of his sense of fun - or come to that, his habit of dropping one in it!

At the time, there was much talk about Capital Radio taking over the station, and those of us in the management team would be out of a job, but it didn't stop us having plenty of laughs. I recall a particular incident which gave Roger much amusement. One of my disc-jockeys had a very grand name and an equally high opinion of himself. I said to Roger that it couldn't possibly be his birth name and asked him if he had any idea what it was. Roger said the disc-jockey was very secretive about it and no-one in the office knew. What a challenge! I sent him a memo explaining that the Inland Revenue had been in touch and were demanding to know the real names of all of our radio presenters. A few days later, I received a reply from him, and I couldn't wait to tell Roger.

I walked into his little office and announced that the mystery had finally been solved. When I told him his name was '*un vendeur de fromage*', he howled so loud that people from all over the building came running in to find out what was going on. But, as you might well expect if you know Roger, it didn't end there! For days afterwards, whenever this person was in the office, Roger would come over to my desk and, in a voice perfectly audible to all, would constantly refer to the aforesaid dairy product with the likes of "Fancy a cheese sandwich, Andy?" or "Would you a like a slice of my cheesecake? It's absolutely delicious."

Roger, you are a living legend in the world of radio. I greatly enjoyed working with you on Radio Caroline, Radio Northsea International, and Invicta Radio and hope you will continue to grow old disgracefully.

- ***written by Andy Archer***

Some of my most memorable moments were when I was working on the Roger Day Show. He would be on air from 10pm until 2am weekdays, and his shows were just brilliant and lots of fun! He often used to play a very funny song called 'Blowing Off" by the Goodies, which always made me giggle. If you haven't heard this song, I'll explain that it was a very funny song that referred to the subject of...shall we say...flatulence... with sound effects! Enough said! As this funny record was playing, Roger would open the phone-in lines to do an on-air competition or such like, and I would struggle to answer the incoming calls because I would be laughing so much at this very silly song! It was very embarrassing but very funny at the same time! I can honestly say that after working with Roger, who was the ultimate professional, I realised that this was what I wanted to do, and because of him, I decided that I wanted to make working in radio my career. That lasted for forty years. I could never have envisaged that at the time! So, a big thank you to Roger!

*– written by Pat Broome in Piccadilly*

When Roger 'Twiggy' Day asked me to contribute some memories of him for his book, I was totally flabbergasted! Book? When I first met him in 1966, he could barely read and write. The only book he might have been interested in back then was a coloring book. Look at him now... all grown up and not only reading 'n riting, but I bet he does 'rithmatics, too. Seriously, I am honoured to be a small part of Roger's past, which resulted in his life-long passion ... radio.

I was the original programme director of Swinging Radio England and Britain Radio. Roger came to me at the Park Lane Hilton in London and interviewed for a job. I liked him, his personality, and his voice and saw a gem that simply needed cutting and polishing! At first, Roger was so frightened of the microphone and being 'on the air', I was afraid the audience would hear him shaking. He was scared, but he listened and he learned. He picked up the format quickly, and he started speaking to YOU instead of everybody. Roger is an icon in British broadcasting. He is a unique personality and not a mundane presenter. Thank you, Roger, for becoming what I thought you were capable of so many years ago, a pro radio legend, and for being my friend.

*- written by Ron O'Quinn*

# INTRODUCTION

For many years, people have been asking why I haven't written a book about my life. There are many reasons, I guess – laziness and a thought of who the hell would want to read it are at the top of the list. I hope you get as much pleasure out of reading about my life as I've had out of living it.

Every day, I thank God I have been able to get paid for doing a job that I love. Well, there is the problem. I don't regard it as a job; it's more a hobby I get paid for. The fact that over the years so many have found what I do worth listening to is a constant source of wonder and gratitude. My attitude to radio has always been: it's got to be fun and entertaining.

Over the years, I've been asked to describe my programme. I bring a pile of records to the studio and invite friends in to have a chat. No focus groups or consultants needed. I've always thought, if you need somebody to tell you how to do it and what to play, you're in the wrong job. That's not to say I think I'm perfect. I listen to other broadcasters I admire and learn from them; wonderful talents, like Kenny Everett, Johnnie Walker, Terry Wogan, and far too many Americans to mention. There is one exception: my first Programme Director, Ron

O'Quinn. I still broadcast from the rules he laid down back in 1966. Never use plurals, talk to one person, smile when you talk, and listen to your own programme at least once a week, because that is how you improve your skills.

One of the most frequent questions I used to get was "Why aren't you on national radio?" Of course, thanks Boom Radio, that no longer applies. But before Boom, I don't really know the answer. I've always believed I'm good enough, but I think the fact that I speak my mind might have held me back. If I think something is wrong, I'll say so, and not many managers like that. But I only ask the same high standards in others as I expect from myself. As you will see from the following stories, I have had many battles with management and authorities over the years. I probably inherited it from my wonderful father, who didn't suffer fools gladly. It may also be the reason why the radio industry has never given me an award in all my years. But does that matter when the listeners still like what I do?

It is of constant amazement that here, in year 2023 56 years after I spun my first 45 on the radio, I am still doing the job I love. I never want to retire, but if I get the hint that listeners have had enough, I'll pack it in. Hopefully, that day is a long way off.

Another frequently asked question is my opinion of modern radio. To be really honest, I'm not impressed. It is repetitious and not enough fun. It is nice to have so many stations, but I often say more stations means less choice. The biggest irony is that Radio Caroline and the other

60s offshore stations were set up to cater for the young music lovers who weren't being catered for. That same generation who have now become pensioners are mostly being ignored again. Well, until Boom Radio came along. Which I will write about later. Us oldies don't appear to matter. If I hear another programme boss say we've got to go younger, I will scream. They also say we aren't influenced by advertising. Not true, they just don't know how to make adverts aimed at us.

My story is about moving around the country to the next gig on the radio, and that, for me, has brought the only downside. It caused long periods away from my family, but I guess there are many others who can say the same.

I've been lucky enough to have worked with some wonderful people and get to meet up with so many people I admire in the music world. My periods of unemployment have been rare and short lived. I am proud of my record of 56 years broadcasting a daily programme on radio, which probably won't be beaten.

As you know, in 2008, I accepted the offer to join BBC local radio.

Joining the BBC revitalised me and reminded me why I got into radio in the first place. Who would have thought the old rebel pirate would join the establishment! I guess to some, that makes me a traitor, but I had got so bored with the commercial sector, who have forgotten what local radio should be. Small playlists, little personality, and not much local content. Indeed, most have gone national.

Anyway enjoy the ride. I know have.

*Obviously I was attracted to ships from an early age*

# CHAPTER ONE

# GROWING UP IN MARGATE

There are many reasons for not liking Adolf Hitler, but mine is very personal.

Thanks to him, I wasn't born in Kent. My parents, Bert and Dolly, had been evacuated from Margate to Cheltenham, where I was born on March 29th 1945. I'm not sure if I was planned or an accident as they were in their forties and my brother, Graham, was fourteen. I never asked them, of course, but I know nobody could have wished for a more loving or terrific mum and dad.

I don't remember anything about life in Gloucestershire as the family moved back to 27, Canterbury Road, Margate, that summer. It was an eight-bedroomed guest house that had been used by the army to billet troops before the troops were sent to Europe. It took all of that winter to get the house back in running order, as you know what happens when young men are left to their own devices. The Who's Keith Moon would have been impressed by the graffiti and mess left behind! You can understand it, as these guys didn't know if they were ever coming back home.

When we opened the next summer, I guess the last thing my mother needed was a young baby to care for as well. I do remember spending a lot of time with my father. Apparently, I was very demanding, and mum would tell my dad to get me out of the way before she did something terrible to me. Fortunately, there was a local cinema, The Classic, that showed nothing but cartoons and comedies. That gave me my love of Laurel and Hardy, plus Abbott and Costello. My father could not pass an ice cream parlour without buying one for us.

There was never much money in the house as my father had to take very menial jobs when he was forced to retire from coal mining because of lung disease from the coal dust. He later got a job on the railways as a maintenance man. It wasn't well paid but it came with free rail travel for all the family, which meant we got to travel a lot. It was the income from the guest house that subsidised the family budget.

Dad was a wonderful man, who everybody loved. Born to a large Welsh family in Ystradgynlais, Swansea valley, he was very intelligent and could have gone to university but had to go down the mines in Wales to earn money for his family. He had a brother who was killed in a mining accident. Like many of his kind, he was determined his sons wouldn't become miners. Apparently, he was a very vocal member of the trade union and was regarded by management as a real rebel. Perhaps that is where I get it from!

He used to love to sit in the window at the house in Margate looking out for people he knew, passing by. In the summer, he would sit on the front step. He just loved talking to people. I guess I'm the same.

My mother had been brought up in a large hotel in Margate - Wenhams near to Margate station- where her domineering, Victorian father made her work very hard as she was the eldest of six. He was a bit of a rogue as he had a mistress in the town with another large family. As a child, I was aware of the unofficial relatives, but it was not something we were encouraged to talk about. When my mother met my dad, it gave her the chance to escape her father, although the poor woman would end up grafting in a kitchen for most of her life.

They both instilled in me the ethic that you have to work hard to get anywhere in life and never buy anything you can't afford. How I wish I'd stuck to those principles. On, I think, my fifth birthday, my parents had written to BBC Radio's Uncle Mac for a request on his children's request show on the Light Programme. I'm not sure what the record was. Probably Mandy Millers' 'Nellie the Elephant' or the Woody Woodpecker songs. I've always liked silly records. I used to walk around making the Woodpecker noise, imitating the record. Thus, my love of radio was born. It was perhaps the most important event in my early life and could be the inspiration for how I would spend most of my grown-up years. In later years, I would play 'Nellie the Elephant' at discos and people would actually dance to it.

We didn't have a car, telephone, or TV.

In 1949, by brother, Graham, like all of his age, was called up to do national service. He joined the RAF. As soon he was demobbed, he came back home and lived there for a few years until he got married and left home, so sadly, we really didn't have a normal brotherly relationship.

My first school was Garlinge Infants, and although I don't remember much of that time, I do recall my first day, as I guess we all do. I also remember missing almost a complete winter because I got the usual childhood diseases one after the other.

I recollect much more of my junior school, hitting a cricket ball though the classroom window and Miss Sooly shouting at me that I was colour blind (which I'm not).I was quite a shy boy and had no option but to be well behaved as my aunt was the school secretary! To prove how different things were in those days, I used to walk the mile home from school on my own. Well, that's what I thought. Later, I found out mum used to follow a distance behind.

As I mentioned earlier, my father worked for the railways and we got free rail travel even abroad in Europe. So at the end of the summer when the guests had gone, we started going to mainland Europe. The first trip was in 1955 to Rimini in Italy. I am a steam train fan, so I loved the ride through France, Switzerland, and then Italy. I remember on this trip I was being an annoying little brat and a French gentleman started shouting at me. My dad was having none of it and had a goat him in Welsh. Clearly, the chap had never heard this language before and walked off, shaking his head. Just as well as dad was a good boxer.

Dad loved his tea and always took a primus stove with us so he would still get his brew. I remember one classic moment when, in the middle of Milan station, he brewed a pot of tea, much to the amusement of the Italians. Another time, he brewed up in the train compartment and decided to throw the old tea leaves out of the window. There was a lot of shouting from the people next door as the tea leaves had covered their window and spoilt their view. Those holidays got me out of two weeks of school as we could only have a holiday after the tourist season had ended. Other places we visited were Tossa, Barcelona, Yugoslavia, and Dana Marina in Italy.

My parents used to go to the Nayland Rock Hotel across the road from our house in Margate. I was allowed to go with them and have a lemonade and a packet of crisps while they danced to Edmundo Ross. In the summer, they also went to the Dog and Duck pub, where we sat in the garden.

Much to my surprise, I passed the eleven plus and was accepted into the best local school, Chatham House Grammar School in Ramsgate. The good thing was that many of my junior school chums were also there. I have to be honest and say that I struggled academically and was always in the bottom half or the bottom stream. In fact, the only subject I excelled in was Maths. It got so bad that I had to repeat a year, and to this day, I remember the shame I felt and the embarrassment when I had to start the next year with boys a year younger than me. Many of them actually became good friends. The only good thing was that I had a wonderful teacher called Mr Thomas. It might have helped that my real surname is Thomas and I had a Welsh dad, like he was. He persuaded me to achieve better marks and really have me more confidence and self-esteem. He also encouraged me to keep playing tennis as I was pretty good at it.

In my school report of 1958, it says– 'Roger is cheerful, pleasant, and reliable. His manners are first class. He continues to please with his whole-hearted efforts on the games field. His best subjects are History and Religion. That's strange. I hated both!

Former Prime Minister Edward Heath was the most

famous old boy, apart from the Olympic Gold Medal Hockey player Sean Curly. The headmaster, Mr Pearce, would often say, 'If only one of you boys could be half the man he was.' That was the days of punishment being the cane. Quite how I managed to avoid that is a mystery to me. In later years, when I was on Radio Caroline, I often used to play dedications for the school. The boys would send me letters saying how the Head hated me talking about the school. I guess being a pirate wasn't his idea of an achievement. But things changed, and I was invited back to talk at the school assembly.

During those early years of my life, rock 'n' roll started to influence my generation. I remember my brother bringing home the Bill Haley Rock Around the Clock LP, which I thought was so different and fabulous.

I think my love of pop music was one of the reasons I didn't do well at school. I cared more about buying records and listening to Radio Luxembourg, plus the rare pop programmes on the BBC, like Saturday Club and Easy Beat. In fact, my nickname at school was Juke Box Jo after one of the characters on the Jack Jackson show. If only there had been a course in pop music and radio, I would have got to university. I can remember all the names of the radio hosts. Apart from Jack Jackson, who I thought was the best, there was Sam Costa, Ray Orchard, Tony Hall (he was brilliant), Barry Aldis, Pete Murray, David Jacobs, Pete Murray, and Alan Freeman.

My list of favourites does not include Jimmy Saville, who I have always thought was rubbish, even before his behaviour was discovered. Think: because of him, we DJs got the reputation of having no brains. Very annoying as most of us are well educated.

Sunday nights were the highlight. I would sneak into my granny's room while she was at church and listen to Radio Luxembourg because she had a lovely old wooden radio set that got better reception of the station. Once, I forgot to retune it to the Home Service, and there was much discussion about how this had happened when she was sure she hadn't touched it. You see, in those days it was quite normal for elderly relatives to live with their children and grandchildren. I've always wondered when and why people decided they would shove the elderly relatives in homes.

I used to love summer in Margate. It was full of holidaymakers all of July and August. The pluses were lots of northern girls to chat up, usually at Dreamland Amusement Park or Pelosi's coffee bar, and extra money to be earned as a waiter at our guest house. Our guests were very generous with tips. The downside was the more guests in the house I had to give up my bedroom, so I had to sleep on a temporary. bed in the basement and sometimes in the bathroom. I also worked at Nayland Rock Hotel, opposite our house, in the still room or pantry.

In the winter, we hung out in the local coffee bars. One frothy coffee and a shilling for three plays on the Juke Box was the norm. To this day, I think those great rock 'n'roll records sounded as if they were made for playing on the Juke Box, particularly true of 'Way Down Yonder' by Freddy Cannon.

I was fourteen when I asked for my first record player. Like all of my generation, the reply was "You can get it when you earn the money to afford it." I did though have to get it on hire purchase, and dad of course had to guarantee the HP agreement. The owner of Henry's Shop, Henry Poopard, asked him questions about the agreement, some of which were rather over the top, and I could see my father getting agitated. Eventually, he exploded and said, "We are only wanting to buy a record player, not the whole shop." The shop owner backed down. I never saw dad lose an argument or let anybody get the better of him.

So I got a paper round, getting paid 14 shillings a week. That, together with my pocket money and working as a waiter in our guest house and the hotel, meant quite a decent income. Very soon I had enough money and bought a Ferguson. I even had enough money to buy two singles - Peter Gunn by Duane Eddy and Bobby Darin's Dream Lover. I had of course already been buying records before but had to wait until my brother went out so that I could play them on his record player. My first favourite singer was Lonnie Donegan, which then became Duane Eddy. I also loved the Everly Brothers. From that day on, all my money went on buying records, usually two a week. If you are of my generation, I'm sure, like me, you remember the thrill of going out at the weekend and heading for the local record shop, where, although you knew exactly what you would buy, you always asked to hear the B side or something you had no intention of buying. Oh, the happy hours spent in those listening booths. Then going home and playing the new records over and over until they turned white. You may remember, the record players had a stacking system so you could line up 8 or 10 records. For some reason, those on different labels would sometimes slip. Very Annoying. In Margate, we were very well served by Thornton Bobby's and Kennard's record shops, but even places like Henry's Electrical Store had a record counter.

I suppose this was the start of my disc jockey career as our front room became an unofficial disco, and every winter evening I would rush through my homework and then play the hits of the day. Even in those days I had the best record collection, which is why most evenings my friends would come to my house and listen to my records. One of my friends was Rob Wyatt, who I used to meet on the 52 bus taking me to Chatham House Grammas School. We never talked about our homework, just what records we had heard on Luxembourg. He was in a group called The Lower Third who had regular gigs at the Orchid Ballroom in Cliftonville, just above Pelosis. They would be one of David Bowie's backing groups and recorded a couple of records with him. I also remember Dutch guitarist Wout Stenhous gigging at the same venue. He lived locally and had a recording studio. The busiest vocal group were the Wedgewoods.

My record collection was supplemented by taping

BBC radio's Pick of the Pops each week on my Fidelity Tape Recorder. In Thanet, we were lucky enough to have a company called Redifusion who supplied TV and radio for rent. The bonus was that somehow the radio was in FM quality, and I attached two wires to the back of a speaker with a direct feed to the recorder. I guess that was the equivalent of today's illegal downloading and so probably my first illegal act. I used to practise being a DJ in my bedroom.

Alongside all this, I had started playing tennis at Margate Lawn Tennis Club, which was very strange as it had no grass courts. In fact, I was a very keen player. I played every summer evening and all day Saturday and Sunday. As soon as I could, I joined the adult section and played in tournaments all over Kent, including Walmer and Beckenham, getting to the semi-finals on one occasion. My brother even offered to pay for coaching lessons, which I foolishly turned down, as it coincided with the increase in hormones that all teenagers experience, and girls became a factor. So England lost out on the chance of a home-grown Wimbledon Champ! Every year when that great tournament is on, I think, what if? Still, that would have stopped me from fulfilling my destiny. Hard to play tennis on a small boat!

The tennis champ. The door on the left led to the bathroom where sometimes I had to sleep in the summer. Down the stairs was the living room where we ate and watched the TV. Above that the room where my Granny lived.

Me and My Brother

Much to my surprise, I passed five GCE O levels - in Maths (where I got 90%), English, Geography, History, and Physics with Chemistry. As Maths was my only good subject, I decided it would be pointless trying for A levels and university. I do remember the careers master asking me what I wanted to do and his disgust when I said 'Work for Radio Luxembourg'. Sadly, he didn't have any idea how that could be achieved so suggested accountancy because of my skills with figures. To this day, I can still calculate numerical problems quicker than a calculator.

# CHAPTER 2

# A PROPER JOB

In 1962, getting a job wasn't difficult, and I was taken on by The South Eastern Electricity Board in Broadstairs as a trainee accountant. Well, that was the job description, but I was actually a filing clerk. In theory, I was meant to attend evening classes to study accountancy, but after one session, I decided that would get in the way of chasing girls and listening to records. I used to cycle four miles to work every day and even went home for lunch, so kept very fit, almost twig-like!

I tried to learn ballroom dancing at the Varley School of Dancing. The main reason was that I fancied the daughter of the Dog and Duck pub and knew she went there. Sadly, she didn't want to be my girlfriend, but I did learn how to waltz. Perhaps one day I will make Strictly.

After a short time, I decided I wanted to work in London and got a new job working for the Metropolitan Water Board on Tottenham Court Road. There I was sending out and receiving payments for water rates. One thing I learnt was that the Duke of Westminster owned most of London. At first, I stayed in London during the week at a grotty youth hostel, sleeping in what was basically a cell, and went home at weekends. I got fed up with that and began commuting every day on the train. That was when I was given the nickname Juke Box Joe after a character on Jack Jackson's show by my fellow travellers as all I was interested in was pop music. I loved the buzz of working in the city, but the journey from Margate was rather tiring. I had to catch a six o'clock train and wouldn't get home until eight at night. Although I didn't realise it at the time, it would be good practice for getting up early for the breakfast radio programme.

When the travelling became too much, I came back home and worked for Kennedy Airlines at Manston Airport. I didn't stay long and was lucky enough to get a job at Pfizers in Sandwich (yes, the Viagra people) in their wages department. I say 'lucky' because they were the best local employer. American-owned, they paid higher wages than anybody else, plus bonuses. I was in charge of paying out all the weekly paid workers. The worst part of the job was having to go around the plant on a Friday to deal with the pay queries. The boiler room was the worst place to go. They used to think any under payment had gone into my pocket and it came close to them holding me upside down and shaking out the money.

The best part of the job was delivering data to the computer department, which was full of young girls. One of those girls would be responsible for me getting the job that would shape the rest of my life. She was Ann Leverington from Deal, and she chatted me up just before

Christmas 1963. In those days, they called it courting, and we eventually got engaged. She soon became aware that I was pop music mad.

Dad had a Lambretta scooter, so I passed my driving test and used it in the evenings and weekends when he didn't need it for work. I was a never a proper mod, but they attracted the best-looking girls. I then bought a second-hand Hillman Minx for £180 in 1962 from Michael Gentini in Cliftonville. The only problem was I bought it before I passed my driving test. Even though I couldn't drive it alone, my dad had a licence, so he sat with me while I practised. I remember offering a girl a lift home from Dreamland Ballroom, but yeah, you guessed it – because I still hadn't passed my test, I had to ask my father to sit in the back seat so that I could drive this girl home. It was most embarrassing and there was certainly no snogging session that night.

My teenage years were spent mostly in Pelosi's Coffee bar. A frothy coffee, and a shilling for the Juke Box. Also playing ten pin bowling. Played for the Buffalos in the Animal League. I was quite good once scoring five strikes in a row.

Dreamland Ballroom in Margate was conveniently situated just three hundred yards from my house. They had a resident band led by Tommy Martin, who played on Saturdays and Sundays, performing the hits of the day. They always ended the evening playing the Mexican Hat Dance. I got to know the manager, Derek Wright, quite well, and one night, he told me he had booked a beat group to play. The first beat group that appeared was Erkey Grant and the Tonettes, who later became the Candy Choir and would be on the Beach Boys tour in 1968. As groups started dominating the charts, the resident band disappeared and was replaced by the groups.

On Sundays, there was a Rendezvous Club, where you needed to be a member. That would be for up-and-coming groups. That included Brian Poole and the Tremeloes, who we kind of adopted as our group. They would appear about every six weeks until they hit the big time and the queue to get in would stretch along the sea front. It became a tradition that they always played the Christmas Eve dance. That was good value for two shillings and sixpence. Others who appeared regularly were Dave Dee and The Bostons, who later went by their names Dozy, Beaky, Mick, and Tich, Dean Ford and The Gaylords who became Marmalade, and Spencer Davis. They would play two-hour sessions.

Every Saturday we would get the chart acts. Just about every successful group came down there, including The Rolling Stones, The Crickets, The Hollies, The Kinks, and The Animals, all for five shillings or occasionally ten bob. The Beatles never came, although they did play a week at the Winter Gardens. I was there, three rows back, and couldn't hear a thing for the girls screaming. Billy J Kramer and the Dakotas were the support act. Cliff Richard also never played at the ballroom, but The Shadows did. When The Rolling Stones appeared there, they had only just started, but word soon got around about how good they were and the ballroom was packed. Believe it or not, they were second on the bill to The Barron Knights. I was actually in the toilet when Mick Jagger was chased in by a load of girls.

The groups on a Sunday would get paid £25 for their set. I shall always remember when The Spencer Davis Group turned up the week they got to number one with Keep On Running. I was in the manager's office when Spencer came in and told Derek that as they were top of the charts, they would only play an hour. Derek was ready for that and got out the contract, which stated they had to play two hours. To be fair, Spencer agreed. The crafty manager had increased the entrance fee to five shillings so made a lot of money.

I passed the driving test first time, which wasn't difficult because during winter in Margate there wasn't much traffic. This enabled me to visit other music venues around Kent. I drove to The Supreme at Ramsgate, Leas Cliff in Folkestone, and occasionally The Tottenham Royal in London, along with my good friend Stuart Varley.

To get access to the Rendezvous Club on Sundays, I managed to become one of the committee members, so not only got in myself but signed other people in. There was no pay, but it allowed me to get free admission for all the dances.

I remember going to the Wednesday disc sessions and looking with envy at the DJ spinning the discs, wondering how I could get to do that job. I'd have to wait three years to find out.

*My first car, the Hillman Minx. With Mum*

*On the front steps with Mum*

*The house where I grew up: 27, Canterbury Road, Margate.*

The defining moment of my youth was Easter 1964. I had discovered a Dutch Radio station called Radio Veronica, which played pop music all day. I would listen to that, then Radio Luxembourg in the evening. I had no idea Veronica was aboard a ship. On Saturday March 28th, I was retuning my radio from 190 metres to 208 when I came across pop music where previously there had been nothing. I stayed tuned in long enough to hear the immortal words, "This is a test transmission from Radio Caroline on 199 - your all-day music station." Radio Veronica had just lost a listener, and I had a new love.

The birth of Radio Caroline coincided with the mods and rocker riots in Margate. As a man of peace who has spent his whole life avoiding fist fights, I wasn't involved but was an interested spectator. I have never been able to understand why people have fights with others just because they are different. Plus, I was neither a mod nor a rocker. As Ringo Starr famously said, I was a mocker. As usual, the press were up to their usual tricks. I witnessed a reporter asking a group of mixed mod and rocker lads to act like they were fighting, when they said they were actually good friends. He persisted and they gave in, and he got his picture, which appeared on the front of the Daily Mirror the next day. It was an early lesson not to believe all you read in the press.

With all that going on, I was glued to the new radio station. At last, we had a station playing the latest chart music all day. Until then, we had to put up with the fading in and out of Radio Luxembourg 208, where they only played parts of the records or the few programmes on the BBC Light programme, like Saturday Club, Easy Beat, and Pick of the Pops. It soon became apparent that this new station was broadcasting from a ship from international waters, which added to the appeal. It also gave me a new hero -one Simon Dee. It also made me think that maybe I could achieve my ambition of being a DJ, as these new broadcasting pirates were from backgrounds similar to mine and it all seemed so accessible. Another local Thanet man was involved, by the name of Carl Conway. Very soon, I would start sending off audition tapes.

Some weeks later, another radio station began broadcasting from a ship. It was Radio Atlanta, and although I listened, I didn't think it was as good as Caroline. It was based on a ship called the Mi Amigo, and little did I know that in a few years I would spend some of my happiest times broadcasting from there.

That summer was one of the best. Caroline on the radio playing House of the Rising Sun, the Zombies, and Ready Steady Go on a Friday night. It was the best time to be a teenager. In July, the two stations joined forces. Radio Atlanta became Radio Caroline South and Radio Caroline changed to Radio Caroline North and sailed around the coast to the Isle of Man, broadcasting as she sailed. I was actually quite sad, because although Caroline South improved from Radio Atlanta, it lacked the spark of the original Caroline.

It was so exciting to listen to a station playing our music all day, even though they closed down at 6 pm in the early days.

By the end of 1964, other stations had hit the airwaves, broadcasting from disused ministry forts in the Thames Estuary. First, Radio Sutch, run by his Screaming Lordship, which soon became Radio City, and Radio Invicta, which became KING Radio and eventually the Sweet Music Station 390. The advantage of living on the coast in Margate was that I could hear them all. If only I had four pairs of ears. I think by then I had abandoned Radio Luxembourg and the BBC.

At the end of the year, while searching the dial for new stations, I came across something called Radio London testing on 266. It was a step up from Caroline as it had slick American jingles and much better DJs. I soon became a huge fan of Big L or Wonderful Radio London, as it became known. I still spared some of my listening time for Caroline as they had started it all. My favourite DJ was a nutter from Liverpool called Kenny Everett, who did a show with Dave Cash. Dave would feature quite often in the future.

By then, I had changed cars to a lovely little Austin Mini. Needless to say, I had a portable radio with an aerial that I'd attach to the window for better reception. The only problem was the radio was on the parcel shelf at the back and every time the car went round a corner it slid to one side and reception was lost, so I had to keep stopping the car and putting it back in place!

Then, in late summer of 1965, completely out of the blue, I got a letter saying I had been selected for an audition to the Southern TV programme 'Pop the Question'. This was a quiz show with two panels pitting their wits against each other on pop music. It was hosted by the legendary Muriel Young, and each team consisted of one celebrity and two punters. I have to say, it was a surprise as I hadn't sent an application for the show. Without my knowledge, Ann had applied on my behalf. I attended the audition in the Dover studios and was selected. The show was recorded at the Winter Gardens, Margate, in October 1965. On my team was Chris Andrews, and we won quite convincingly. The reward was two LPs, but the real bonus and prize was soon to come. During an interval, the guest group playing were the Fortunes, famous for the Radio Caroline theme tune.

# CHAPTER 3

# SPINNING
# THE DISCS

Now to the best bit!

A few days after the recording of Pop the Question, I got a call from Derek Davies, the assistant manager at the Dreamland Ballroom, Margate. I knew Derek from his time at Pfizers in the boiler room. When he left Pfizers, as a joke, I said if ever you need a DJ, call me. He had seen me on the TV programme and said he was so impressed he would like me to spin the discs at the Wednesday Disc Sessions at the Dreamland Ballroom. At last, it was the break I had been seeking.

**ROGER IS NEW DISC JOCKEY**

After seeing an advertisement on Southern Television, for contestants for a new pop quiz "Pop the Question," Roger Thomas, age 20, of 27 Canterbury Road, Margate, went for a trial recording. Much to his surprise, he was selected.

Since his appearance on the programme on Tuesday night he has been appointed disc jockey at Dreamland, Margate, and is now spinning the discs at the Wednesday record session.

Roger has been concerned with the pop industry for some years and is also the road manager for the local group The Secrets. His ambition is to become a professional disc jockey.

Several hundred young people applied to appear on the programme, to answer questions on pop records and pop stars. Two boys and two girls from Margate were among the five selected.

Victors were the boys' team, but they started with an advantage, for guest celebrity, Chris Andrews, who has a current record, "Yesterday Man," in the number three position in the latest charts, and is the recording manager for Sandie Shaw, was in their team.

The programme will be broadcast every Tuesday, with a different guest, and compered by Muriel Young.

*My first press release in The Isle of Thanet Gazette*

Of course, come the first Wednesday, I was rather nervous and had to have a couple of drinks to settle down. But my determination to make the most of this opportunity overcame the nerves. I loved it and remember the first two records I played were 123 by Len Barry and A Lover's Concerto by The Toys. I had to pinch myself to believe I was actually appearing on the stage where I had seen many of my chart heroes perform. Manager Derek Wright liked what I did, and I became the resident DJ, also spinning the tunes at the Rendezvous Club on a Sunday. I got to appear with some groups who would later become famous. Dave Dee and the Bostons and Dean Ford and the Gaylords, who became Marmalade, were just two. The pay was the princely sum of £3 a session.

Very soon, I added the Starlite Ballroom in Herne Bay to my rota, but the pay there was only £2 a session! Among the performing groups during that time were Unit Four Plus Two and The Moody Blues. Many groups didn't make it big but were still very good, like Grant Tracey and the Sunsets, Wayne Gibson and the Dynamic Sounds, Robb Storme and the Whispers.

The DJ equipment was pretty basic. There was no cueing facility, so you had to guess when the record started. I actually worked some places where all they had was one ordinary record player.

I was working as a club DJ while still doing the day job at Pfizers, so I was earning a decent amount. It meant I could upgrade my car to a Ford Cortina. Rather foolishly, I put 'Roger Day DJ' on the sides as a bit of publicity. I say 'foolishly' now looking back, but at the time it seemed a good idea. It's no wonder my fiancée didn't enjoy riding in that car!

My next significant step forward came in March 1966, and again it was a surprise. Dave Cash on his Big L breakfast programme played a record for my 21st birthday on March 29th. Apparently, my fiancée had written to him.

The next weekend for my birthday bash, I decided to go and see the Big L roadshow at the Marquee in London. Well, guess who the guest DJ was? None other than Dave Cash! As luck would have it, I managed to track him down at the bar and thanked him for playing my dedication. I don't expect he remembered the request, but being the supreme pro he is, he acted like he did. I asked him what the chances were of getting a job at Radio London. His reply was that there were not any vacancies but that there were some guys from America who were going to start a new station. Dave told me they were looking for DJs new to radio and had flown in that day so I could be the first in line. He also told me they were staying at the Hilton.

I never stayed for the end of the roadshow. Instead, I went hot foot to the Hilton and straight to reception, where I asked to speak to Don Pierson. The reception clerk told me the room number and pointed me in the direction of the internal phones. I can remember exactly what I said: "Hi, Mr Pierson, I'm a DJ and I want to be on your new radio station."

*My first publicity picture*

*I couldn't afford a personalised number plate so just stuck my name on the door.*

**THE GREAT BALLROOM**

**Gayest Dancing in Thanet!**

*Margate. Where it all started. Love the description on the right*

*On the decks. Why a lady's bloomers are hanging over the front, I don't know*

# CHAPTER 4

# SWINGING RADIO ENGLAND

" "Come on up," replied Don Pierson. Up I went and met Don for the first time, along with his Programme Director, Ron O'Quinn. Apart from the people I'd seen in films and on television, these were the first Americans I had ever met. I think I talked with them for way over an hour, during which they described their plans for the new radio station and asked me questions about my life and ambitions. They described how they would put two stations on one ship, one broadcasting Top 40 radio and the other MOR music.

I didn't realise at the time that I was the first job applicant, which would prove very significant. It was the usual "we'll be in touch" end to the interview.

I drove back home, very excited about what I had heard and hoping that this was the opportunity I had been seeking. So imagine my surprise when I was greeted by my parents, who said that Ron O'Quinn had phoned and wanted me to call when I could. The very next day,

I was back in the Hilton, where I was offered the position of DJ on the new station to be called Swinging Radio England. It was very strange as they hadn't heard any of my demo tapes. I was to discover that the reason I was offered the gig was my lack of radio experience. They wanted to hire three English people to work alongside experienced US DJs. They hadn't been impressed with the DJs on other stations and wanted newcomers who could be trained in their style.

The only problem was that the ship was still in America, and they couldn't give me a starting date. In the next few weeks, I would spend many hours journeying up to London. I would phone to get progress reports, which they would never give me on the phone. It was always "Pop in for a coffee and we'll talk about it." It was a four-hour round trip to be told "No news yet." Seventy miles is no distance to a Texan. But after a few weeks, the ship did eventually arrive via Portugal, and at last I was given a starting date.

I couldn't wait for Monday morning to hand in my notice at Pfizers. I shall always remember the look on the face of my boss, Keith Burville. When I said I was resigning, he asked what accountants I was joining. I thought he was probably a BBC Home Service listener, and when I explained I was joining a new station broadcasting from a ship, he looked like I had stabbed him through the heart. "What about your pension?" was his retort. At 21, you never think you're going to live long enough to get one of those, so it didn't affect my decision. At the end of the week, I said my farewells to my colleagues in the wages office and also did my last gig at Dreamland. My radio adventure was about to start.

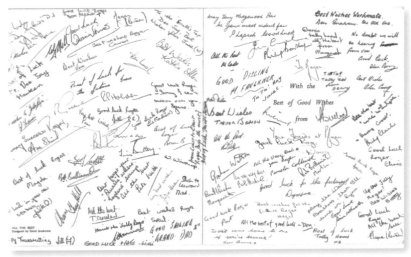

*My leaving card at Pfizers*

# MARGATE DISC JOCKEY FOR PIRATE RADIO

TWENTY-ONE-YEAR-OLD Roger Day, of 27 Canterbury Road, Margate, is expecting to be "called up" any moment now as one of four record spinners on Radio England, which will broadcast from a ship off Harwich.

"There will be two stations operating from the same vessel, which is now on its way from Lisbon," said Roger. "I shall be working with Radio England, which will transmit pop records 24 hours a day, and the other station, Radio Britain, will concern itself with music from the shows."

Roger's lucky break came when he went prospecting for a job in the music world in London recently.

"I went round the agencies and happened to hear about the new station," he explained. "After a four hour conversation with two men concerned with its promotion I got the job."

Transmissions from the ship are expected to start soon.

Roger started disc jockeying at Dreamland Ballroom, Margate. The man in charge of the turntable left and Roger, a keen pop music fan, happened to be on the spot and willing to take

He has also been spinning the turntable at the Starlight Ballroom, Herne Bay.

He keeps himself up to date with the ever-changed pop music scene and has a collection of about 1,000 records. His favourite recording groups? The Beach Boys, the Moody Blues and the Beatles.

# ENTER A TEXAN WITH TWO MORE PIRATE RADIOS

JACK NIXON, at five foot eight the skinniest Texan you're likely to meet, flew into London this week with peace in his heart and an offering of goodwill to Postmaster-General Anthony Wedgwood Benn.

An unlikely combination of virtues in the circumstances. With sixteen unnamed British, US and Canadian backers he is entering the pirate radio business.

He is floating two stations in one—Radio England and Britain Radio—beyond the three-mile limit off Harwich.

He claimed they will cover the whole of England, twenty-four hours a day.

And with characteristic Texan understatement he promises that they will be "the biggest and bestest of them all."

## Money

"We are agreeable to abide with whatever your Queen or Government decides about offshore stations," he says respectfully.

"We have put over a million pounds in this project and we know we are taking a risk."

In fact, this highly-organised project could turn out to be the ultimate in commercial radio services.

The transmitting ship Olga Patricia, fitted out in Florida and insured by Lloyd's, is air-conditioned and fully equipped to accommodate a crew of 10 and nine disc-jockeys.

It will operate on a power of 55 kilowatts—five kilowatts stronger than any other ship. Running costs will be around £1,000 a week.

The rest should be plain sailing.

## Backers

Radio England ("Swinging Radio England") will provide round-the-clock pop music for teenagers.

Britain Radio ("The hallmark of quality listening") playing romantic and light music for the middlebrow in-betweens.

Advertising will be restricted to 10 per cent of air-time.

Those mysterious backers?

"[...] Nixon "[...]

are doctors, lawyers and professional men from all fields among them.

"For obvious reasons they want to remain anonymous."

---

## THANET MAN IS 'PIRATE' SHIP DEEJAY

FORMER Chatham House, Ramsgate, pupil Roger Day is a disc jockey on the latest and biggest 'pirate' radio ship to transmit off the coast of Britain.

The ship is the Olga Patricia, a former American liberty boat now on her way from Lisbon to the sea off Harwich where she will begin transmitting this weekend.

Twenty-one-year-old Roger, who lives at Canterbury-road, Margate, started his career as a disc jockey at Dreamland Ballroom, Margate, just over a year ago.

He moved on to Herne Bay but, as he put it, decided to "go for the big time" and started hunting down agencies in London.

He spoke to a lot of people in the business and eventually succeeded in getting an interview which landed him a job with Radio England, the new pirate ship.

Besides transmitting pop music, Radio England will provide family music over Radio Britain, their second station aboard the vessel.

---

# RADIOVISION BROADCASTS INTERNATIONAL LTD

Special issue offshore stations Radio England Britain Radio

| Pirate radio will reach every home | 2 more pirate radios on the air soon |
| --- | --- |

NEW RADIO SHIP OFF HARWICH

ANOTHER POP PIRATE

ROUND-THE-CLOCK RADIO SHIP SAILS IN

Another 'Pirate' Radio to Operate Off Britain

---

TELEGRAM

"LET'S get cosy," said American businessman Jack Nixon in the Café Royal yesterday, sending shivers of apprehension down the spines of his audience while a team of fast-talking American "disc-jockeys" sailed from Miami towards international waters off Harwich.

In front of an apparently washed-out Union Jack—yellow where it ought to have been scarlet—he fended off questions about the mysterious backers of Radio England and Britain Radio who are "anonymous for tax reasons which are totally legal."

The two stations will begin broadcasting before the end of the month from the same Panama-registered ship, the Olga Patricia, whose name the owners intend to change to Laissez-Faire.

One April day, I drove my car to Harwich and met up with my new colleagues at the Harcourt Shipping company office, based in a caravan. They arranged all the supplies and tendering for the radio ships. The other new recruits for Swinging Radio England were Mecca bingo caller Brian Tylney, Aussie Colin Nichol, who I had listened to on Radio Caroline, and a used car salesman and Top Rank DJ from Birmingham named Peter Dee, who, it turned out, was the second English DJ they had hired. This fact would be very significant.

We all piled on to Offshore Three for the hour-long trip to the ship. On the way, we passed the Galaxy, home of Big L, and the Mi Amigo, where Radio Caroline South was based. Eventually, we reached the Olga Patricia, which had been renamed the Laissez Faire, which would be my floating home for the next few months. The crew of the tender were all Dutch and took great delight in telling us that any mistake in transferring us to the ship could result in us getting crushed between the two vessels. Although this was good advice, I soon learnt that part of the Dutch crew's character is to have a joke at your expense and not all advice was to be taken seriously.

We were welcomed aboard by Ron O'Quinn and the other American DJs, Larry Dean and Jerry Smithwick, along with Rick Randell, who had actually travelled across the Atlantic on board the ship. The first bad news was that the living accommodation wasn't ready. We were issued with sleeping bags and told we would have to sleep on the floor area outside the freezers. These were large freezers because the ship had been used to ferry the bodies of US servicemen killed in the Vietnam War. It was a good job I don't believe in ghosts! What was a lot worse were the cockroaches scuttling around. They were the size of small mammals.

I had never been in a radio studio before, and I headed to them straight away so I could get some experience before my first broadcast. They turned out to be far from ready, but to me that didn't matter. For the next week or so, we all took turns in learning how to operate the studio desk. Even when I wasn't on rota, I just sat in the studio and watched the US radio pros, who blew my mind with their slick operating skills. There were no gaps or stumbles like listeners were used to hearing from British DJs. It was just one seamless wall of radio sound: song, jingle, song, with no dead air. This was true rock 'n' roll ballet. I had never heard American Radio but knew this was the style I wanted to adapt.

There were few rules - just smile, keep it brief and if possible funny, and never use plurals. Ron used to say he'd kick our butts if he ever heard us say "Hello Everyone!"

"Remember," he said, "you are talking to one person." It's good advice, which I have stuck to throughout my career. The format was simple - three sections of most popular to new songs, with occasional gold classics. You took from the front of the box and put to the back so that all songs had to be played before one was repeated, well, apart from the big hits obviously.

We were to be known as 'Boss Jocks', which had been

taken from a radio format in the United States. I shall always remember the incredible jingle that sang 'The Boss Jocks Play More Music'.

The first play through of the new jingles made by the legendary Pams session singers of Dallas just blew my mind. Of course, Radio London had been broadcasting a similar style since they started, but ours took the sound to a new level. We all had our own personal jingles and show openers. It was then that a certain Peter Dee was told he had to change his name because it was too similar to mine and as I was hired before him, he was the one who had to change. Fortunately, there was a DJ ident in the set for a Johnnie Walker, which was apparently a name frequently used in American radio. I often wonder if our lives would have been different. If Johnnie had got to the Hilton before me, would I have become Johnnie Walker?

During the test transmissions, we foolishly played the new jingles. Little did we know that Radio Caroline were taping them, edited out Swinging Radio England, and playing them on air. Pretty quickly, we had a new set of jingles made - the Thatman series based on Batman, which was big at the time. That's how I got that great jingle - It's That Man Roger Day.

The highlight of any day was the arrival of the daily tender boat from Felixstowe. We were usually supplied by Offshore Twoas Offshore One was used by Caroline and Big L. It brought us fresh water, diesel oil for the generators, and letters, plus of course visitors, some from the London Office or the press.

The crew were mainly Cubans who had sailed the ship over from Texas, and the food was very spicy. There were also technicians from Continental Electronics whose job was to get the stations on air. The idea was for Swinging Radio England to be the top forty station and Britain Radio for MOR music as a rival to Radio 390. The difficulty was getting two stations operating from one antenna, which had never been achieved on a ship. I remember the many times the engineers tried to fire up the transmitters usually to end with a huge electrical crack and a lot of swearing from the technicians. These guys used swear words I had never heard before.

Eventually, all was ready, and on May 3rd, we started test transmissions. Swinging Radio England started on 355 and Britain Radio on 227. When told I would be on at six that evening, I was filled with excitement and nerves. I spent hours in and out of the toilet. Once on air though, I felt totally at ease and loved every second. I didn't even have any technical problems with the mixing panel. I guess mostly this was down to the skill of Ron and the other Americans who had shown me the ropes.

The pay was good - £30 a week paid in cash when we came ashore to the Harcourt Shipping Agency in Harwich. They were happy days and a lot better than my wages at Pfizers.

The first song I played was That's Nice by Neil Christian. One of the best things about SRE was the number of US records we played. We used to get them way before the other stations, mostly because of the contacts of our American DJs, particularly Motown records, which made us very popular with teenage listeners. The music of 1966 I consider to be among the best of the 60s. It was a joy to be getting paid for spinning those tunes.

Of course we had no idea who, if anybody, was listening until a few days after we went on air when the tender arrived with sacks full of mail from all over Europe. And some were addressed to me! I sat in the lounge and read every one of them. Crikey, I thought - people actually liked what I was doing. I also replied to every letter, a policy I have stuck to throughout my career.

The euphoria didn't last long though. There were still problems getting two stations transmitting through one aerial. It was decided that as Britain Radio would pull more advertising, it should transmit on 355 and SRE would have to wait until 227 was ready. It was a double blow because coverage was far better on 355, so good in fact that we had received a complaint of interference from Vatican Radio. It wasn't a good idea to upset the Catholic Church.

It was when I was on shore leave, while waiting at the shipping agents' office in Felixstowe for my pay cheque, that I was pleasantly surprised when a certain Tony Blackburn arrived. I introduced myself and told him how much I admired his programme on Big L. I was somewhat taken aback when his reply was to tell me how many letters he received each week.

I used that shore leave to head home to Margate for the first time since I'd joined Swinging Radio England. For the first time I realised what an impact playing records on the radio had on people. Everywhere I went, everyone wanted to talk about what I had been doing, even people I didn't even know. I didn't pay for a drink all that week. (No change there I hear my friends say!)

Our shift pattern was two weeks on and one week off. As a man with no commitments, this meant I had £90 to enjoy myself. So the clubs of London and the Carnaby Street shops saw a lot of me. The Cromwellian in London

# ROGER PLAYS HOST TO MILLIONS

TWENTY-ONE-YEAR-OLD ROGER DAY, who lives with his family at Canterbury Road, Margate, is, perhaps, the happiest person in the town this week, for his career has snowballed over the past three months to put him well on the road to fame as a top-line dee-jay on Radio England, one of Britain's pirate radio stations.

Roger, who is currently in the town on a week's leave from the good ship England, told me how he was finding life as a "pirate."

"It's tough work, and it's not as glamorous as some people make it out to be, but I enjoy it tremendously," he said.

It was a big scoop for Roger when he got the job on Radio England — Britain's most powerful pirate radio station — for it meant an astronomical leap in wages and prestige from his old job as a ballroom dee-jay at local dance centres.

His dream came true on 3 May, when he travelled across the North Sea to join the staff on Radio England, who were then preparing to begin test transmissions.

"There was a surprising amount of behind-the-scenes work to be done before we could get on the air," he said. "Records had to be filed and there was also the preparation of jingles."

### FAN MAIL

A little more than two weeks later everything was ready, and Roger, along with the rest of the dee-jays, had a half-hour spot during the test transmissions.

"That was my big test in a way," he said. "It seemed very strange at first, but I find now that it comes easily. The biggest fear I have always had is that there would be no one listening in at the other end."

Roger said that dee-jays, like himself, relied upon their weekly fan mail to prove that there were enthusiastic fans receiving the programmes.

"It's very encouraging when we receive letters from girls — and even boys — asking for autographs and photos. I get about 100 letters a week and I make a point of answering each one, whether it be just an acknowledgement or a longer letter," he added.

Including Roger, there are 11 dee-jays on the station altogether. Three are British, two are Australians, and six come from America.

They line-up as follows: Larry Dee, Ron O'Quinn (programme director) and Jerry Smethwick, plus three newcomers, are the American representatives; Colin Nichol and Graham Gill are the two Australians; and Brian Tylney and Johnny (hic, hic) Walker are the two remaining British.

Average age of the staff is 23, which makes Roger second youngest dee-jay, being senior only to Johnny Walker, whose birthday falls one day after that of Roger's!

Each dee-jay works two weeks on board the ship and one week off. At present, they have no duties on the week off, but with the probability of an increase in popularity for Radio England, it seems almost certain that jobs will be lined-up on land.

### NEWS CASTER

Local teenagers — for those remaining who don't already know — can hear Roger in his own four-hour programme between the hours of six and 10 every evening. His show, like the rest of the round-the-clock entertainment, caters strictly for pop lovers, with Top 10 discs, pick hits, sure shots, boss tunes and flash-backs.

You might also hear him during the daytime giving news bulletins.

How does Roger spend his day when he is not on the air? "There's always something to do," he said. "I get up at about 10 o'clock each morning and until my show starts at six I keep busy checking the record library, tidying the various files we keep and pottering about on our other radio station—Britain Radio."

For Roger, life on the ocean is always active. His two weeks at sea passes quickly, but when he does return home he admits to cramming as much as possible into that week with late nights very much on the cards.

"First thing I do when I reach home is to have a good cup of tea," he said. "I spend about three-and-a-half hours travelling from Harwich to Margate — a journey which I make by car."

Finally, he looked towards the future. "I think I will always stay in show business, and my progress may lie optimistically towards tele-vision. I wouldn't mind going into the advertising side of things, though, if I ever did leave the dee-jay business," he said.

Asked whether he thought pirate radio stations might ever go off the air, he optimistically replied: "No, I don't think we will ever be troubled by the Government at least, not unless a suitable alternative was found, but I think it would have to be an all-day pop music, land-based station.

"There was some talk about banning British firms from advertising with us, but we could most probably manage to sur-vive on American advertising even if they did this," he declared.

was one of my favourites, where all the stars would go, and I rubbed shoulders with most of them. If only digital cameras had been available then! The chap behind the bar was a very camp character called Harry. He was known as Harry Heart because of his catchphrase "Thank you, darling heart." When he gave you your change, he would always grab your hand and look longingly into your eyes.

After two weeks on a boat, there is nothing quite like your own bed. I also took my parents out for nice meals. It was a wonderful feeling having the cash to be able to do that after all the wonderful years they had spent bringing me up and supporting me. Not once did they ever ask if I thought I was doing the right thing, although in the next few years, I would ask myself that question on more than one occasion.

While my life was changing, my fiancée, Anne, who had been responsible for me getting on the road to radio, was still living in Deal in Kent. I realised I hadn't paid her as much attention as I should have throughout that year. She was still working at Pfizers in Sandwich so could obviously only see me at weekends when I was on shore.

Shore leave soon flew by, and I was back at Felixstowe, ready to get back to being a Boss Jock. I used to drive my Ford Cortina all the way and then leave it in a garage for two weeks. Why on earth I didn't use the train I shall never know.

Swinging Radio England put on a party at the Hilton for advertisers and invited many pop stars. It was quite a line up! Dusty Springfield, Mike D'Abo, Spencer Davis,

Chris Farlowe, Tom Jones, Manfred Mann, The Moody Blues, The Merseys, Alan Price, Paul and Barry Ryan, Helen Shapiro, Jackie Trent, The Small Faces, Sandie Shaw, The Mojos, The Zombies, Zoot Money, Benny Hill, Sir Donald Woolfit, Jon Pertwee, Edmundo Ros, Dora Bryan, Ronnie Barker, Nicholas Parsons, Patrick Wymark, Anita Harris, and many, many more. The only trouble was they never paid the bill and I wasn't there because I was on the ship.

At last, the shared aerial problems were solved, and we were ready to rock on 227. I was allocated the 6 pm to 10 pm show. We also had a news shift plus, occasionally, a programme to present on Britain Radio. I took like a duck to water on the SRE show, but the news reading left a lot to be desired. We just copied the news off the BBC, taking an hour to type out the stories for the hourly bulletin. On Swinging Radio England, we had a rather splendid and brash news sequence. It was all done on echo with the headline emphasised by full reverb to give it gravitas, all introduced by a yank with the deepest voice I have ever heard and lots of sound effects between each story. So from a voice of a bloke with a very deep voice., you had Roger Day with his high-pitched and very agitated delivery, sounding like Mickey Mouse on speed! There is no way words can describe how ridiculous I sounded. Have a listen on the various websites that feature old pirate radio recordings, including my own - RogerDay. co.uk. The intro went something like: This is Radio England Banner line news with news of what's happening around the world, followed by a drum roll, and then big balls saying The Big Story. The weather sequence was also something else. It was meant to be read over a ten to one countdown with a sting at the end. I usually read so fast I had finished by the time it got to six, so I had to sit there while the jingle continued. Fortunately, I was pulled from the news shifts very quickly, thank God.

It was much the same for the Britain Radio shifts. I found it very difficult changing my style from the raving Boss Jock to the style of David Jacobs. Thankfully, there aren't many surviving tapes of my broadcasts on that station. Again, my appearances were soon curtailed when real presenters arrived to take over, leaving me free to do what I loved doing.

I remember one of the proper announcers on Britain Radio was Gary Kemp, who lived near me at Monkton in Kent. His house was called Caroline Cottage, after the good ship Mi Amigo. He'd worked for Caroline but was sacked for coughing after a cigarette commercial. He also worked for the BBC every Tuesday on Pop Inn, hosted by Keith Fordyce. So he had gone on air under another name - Gordon Bennett. Yes, really! He would go off the ship on Monday and return on the Wednesday. On the rare occasion rough weather kept him on the boat, his wife would phone the BBC and say he was sick. I never understood how he was never rumbled, or perhaps they knew and turned a blind eye.

Others from Britain Radio were John Ross Barnard, who I dubbed John Boss Farmyard, Alan Black, Graham

Gill, and Colin Nichol. Plus, of course, there was the one and only Phil Martin. It was Phil who was the recipient of one of my infamous practical jokes. He used to do the early shift on Britain Radio and loved his sleep. So I altered all the clocks around the ship and waited until he had been asleep for about an hour then set his alarm off. I had even gone to the extreme of making sure the overnight presenter was in the studio so that he wouldn't smell a rat. Well, very shortly, he arrived in the galley to make his cup of coffee and asked why we were all up so late and observing that the nights appeared to be getting shorter. At that point, we couldn't help ourselves from convulsing with laughter and the wind up was discovered. He knew it was me and chased me around the ship. It was all very childish, but when you are stuck on a boat for two weeks, you make your own entertainment. Remember, this was before the days of daytime TV and video recorders.

Another trick we used to play on the crew was holding a neon electric tube up on deck and the power coming from the mast would light it up. They thought it was black magic.

People often ask me what we did to pass the time. As I did 18.00 - 22.00, I used to watch some TV after the show then have a few beers with the other DJs, engineers, and crew who were around. We were given a crate of beer and cola each week, plus a pack of cigarettes. As a non-smoker, I swapped my fags for beer. I'd go to bed at about 2 am and then rise at about 10 am. The highlight of the day was the arrival of the daily tender with fresh supplies of water, the daily papers, and diesel. Also on board would come sacks of mail and usually somebody from the London office with guests from the pop world, record companies, or advertisers and sometimes the press. They usually arrived about midday. After lunch, I would usually read the letters and send personal replies and sort out the ones who wanted dedications, which were actually most of them. I do still hear from people who I sent autograph photos to. The problem with the mail was that myself and Johnnie Walker were pulling more than the America guys. It wasn't because we were better. They were streets ahead of us in radio technique. The reason was because we were home grown English boys and the audience identified with us. But there were letters came from across Europe and people were so kind with the lovely comments they made.

1966 of course was famous for England winning the world cup. I was on board for the final, and we all sat around to watch it. The Panamanian crew were cheering for the Germans, which didn't please me. But we had the last laugh.

Ron O'Quinn had the honour of touring with the Beatles in the US on their last tour that August and sent back reports. But on returning to England, the customs gave him a real hard time, and due to this, together with certain promises from management not being met, Ron decided to quit. I was shocked and upset at this as he had been my inspiration and had taught me everything I knew about radio presentation. He said that I could go back to the United States with him and that he would get me a good gig as he thought I would go down a storm. I don't know why, but I turned the offer down. I suppose I had only just started and wanted to see where the journey would take me in the UK. I often wonder how different my life would have been had I gone. When Ron left, his friends, Larry Dean and Jerry Smithwick, also departed. They were great buddies and had worked together before. For some reason, we called them the Moultrie trio, as I think they had worked for a station there at some time.

They were replaced by other American broadcasters - Jack Curtis, Bill Berry, Boom Boom Brannegan, Chuck Blair, Errol Bruce, Bruce Wayne, Tom Cooper, and Mark Stevens. I loved the station and to this day think it was way ahead of its time. It was high tempo presentation with jingles and drop-ins and wall-to-wall music. At no time was there dead air. The trouble was that London and Caroline were so established and loved that it was difficult to get listeners away from them. We were very brash, and Britain wasn't ready for that style of presentation then. Years later, Laser 558 Radio would have an identical format. It would always amuse me when comments were made about how new and exciting they were. I couldn't resist pointing out that we had been doing it 20 years earlier

Sadly, Swinging Radio England closed in November 1966. We only found out by reading it in one of the local papers that had been brought out to the ship. Johnnie Walker immediately jumped on the tender never to return back on board but to appear very soon on Radio Caroline South. I decided to stay as I was loving what the station did and wanted to enjoy every moment, including the last. I became the only original Boss Jock left and had the honour of presenting the last programme on the station. It was the first and last time I've shut down a radio station.

I still, to this day, meet people who loved SRE, and it will always have a special place in my heart for giving me the opportunity to live my dream. I know I am biased, but the music of 1966 was the best ever. From the autumn of that year was the best Top 3 ever – The Beach Boys' *Good Vibrations, Reach Out I'll Be There* by The Four Tops, and The Spencer Davis Group's *Gimme Some Lovin'*.

*The Lasissez Faire (Olga Patricia)*

Approaching on the tender

Offshore 2

The leap of faith on Offshore 2

*In my cabin reading the Ipcress File*

*Left to Right: Ron O'Quinn, Brian Tylney, Colin Nicholl, below him Jerry Smithwick, Larry Dean, Rick Randall, Johnny Walker, Me*

*On the deck*

*The automation system in the
Britain Radio studio*

*The studio wall*

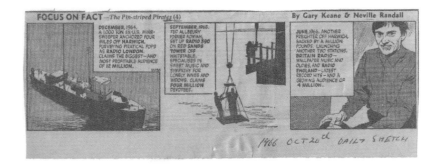

**FOCUS ON FACT** —*The Pin-striped Pirates (4)*          By Gary Keane & Neville Randall

DECEMBER, 1964. A 1,000 TON EX-U.S. MINE-SWEEPER ANCHORED FOUR MILES OFF HARWICH, PURVEYING PIRATICAL POPS AS RADIO LONDON. CLAIMS THE BIGGEST—AND MOST PROFITABLE AUDIENCE OF 12 MILLION.

SEPTEMBER, 1965. TED ALLBEURY FORMER ADMAN, SET UP RADIO 390 ON RED SANDS TOWER OFF WHITSTABLE. SPECIALISES IN SWEET MUSIC AND SYMPATHY FOR LONELY WIVES AND WIDOWS. CLAIMS FOUR MILLION DEVOTEES.

JUNE, 1966. ANOTHER FREIGHTER OFF HARWICH, BACKED BY A MILLION POUNDS, LAUNCHING ANOTHER TWO STATIONS. BRITAIN RADIO—WALLPAPER MUSIC AND OLDIES, AND RADIO ENGLAND—LATEST RECORD HITS—AND A GROWING AUDIENCE OF 4 MILLION.

1966 OCT 20th  DAILY SKETCH

## OLGA PATRICA
### PANAMA

M/V Olga patricia  August 3, 1966

From: Chief Mate A. Cacicedo

To: Harcourt Shipping Agency

     Sirs:

          Please pay to bearer of this letter Roger Thomas the amount

of pounds 86.10.0 for period of work from 17 july 1966, thru 7 august 1966.

Rate paye as follows:

3 weeks at pounds 28.0.0:  weekly:  84.0.0

Travel expenses:                         2.10.0

-------------------------------------------------

     Total pounds                  86.10.0

The above statement is true and correct as presented to me by Mr. O' Quinn

                     A. Cacicedo
                     Chief Mate

                     Antonio Cacicedo

     Reived the above amount

## SCENE

DISC & MUSIC ECHO   6 AUG 66

MAYBE the Government had brought out its beat-the-pirates bill the same afternoon, but it didn't dampen the fun at Radio England—Britain Radio's swinging "Party of the Year" at London's Hilton Hotel last Thursday.

The champagne bubbled until 3 a.m. and dancing, drinking and eating away to the tune of a £10,000 bill were ... (deep breath) ... DUSTY, JOE BROWN, MIKE d'ABO, SPENCER DAVIS group, CHRIS FARLOWE, TOM JONES, SAMMY JUSTE, MANFRED MANN, TOM McGUINNESS, MERSEYS, MOODY BLUES, ALAN PRICE, RYAN TWINS, HELEN SHAPIRO, DANNY WILLIAMS, JACKIE TRENT, SMALL FACES, SANDIE, TWICE AS MUCH, KLAUS VOORMAN, GORDON WALLER ... to name but

There was a SRE Reunion in 2006 at 32 Curzon Street with Phil Martin and me.

Rick Randal, wife Joy, and Larry Dean

Johnnie, Ron O´Quinn, and Me

# CHAPTER 5

# TOURING WITH THE SMALL FACES.

In August 1966, Swinging Radio England organised the Swinging '66 Tour with The Small Faces, Crispian St Peters, Dave Berry, Wayne Fontana, The Koobas, Neil Christian and The Crusaders (with Richie Blackmore), The Limeys, and Genevieve. I was chosen to compere the show around Britain. The London dates were sold out, but when we got outside the listening area of the station, the show was playing to half empty theatres, which was disappointing given that The Small Faces' All Or Nothing was Number One in the charts.

It was my first experience of introducing live acts in a theatre. I was nervous but very excited. One incident stands out in my memory. We were due on stage at the Odeon Birmingham and sat around in the hotel. There had been rumblings from the band backing the solo artists. They hadn't been paid and were threatening

Left to Right: Back: Kenny Jones, Crispian St Peters, Ian Maclagan, Wayne Fontana, Steve Marriot, Neil Christian, Ronnie Lane. Front: Me, Larry Dean, Jerry Smithwick, The Koobas.

DISC & MUSIC ECHO 20/8/66

## OOPS! IS NEIL DOING A PROBY?

ON SATURDAY night at Finsbury Park Astoria, the second night of the Radio England tour, Steve Marriott sang "Watcha Gonna Do About It" and tore into the stage like a demented urchin in a lilac shirt.

Two Germans in the seat next to mine said it was "Wunderbar," but they wished the girls would stop screaming.

The girls didn't. They screamed, ran down the aisle, danced on their seats—and had their Small Faces banners taken away as punishment.

Small Faces closed in near riots a show which proved two things. That it is possible to get a decent sound balance—you could actually HEAR the singers—and that Radio England may well have found the secret of success for quick presentation. The acts moved slickly, the comperes—three England DJ's—were fast and competent.

### Wayne steals show

Geneveve did well opening—always a hard job—in sparkly trousers which drew a lot of wolf whistles. Koobas were very good and reproduced their sound well, bobbing about in their dark velvet tight trousers and funny tassel-off ties.

Neil Christian looked as though he owed a lot to P. J. Proby, especially when it came to some of his microphone and hip combinations.

A nice controlled performance from Crispian St Peters who

# THE BOSS JOCKS ON STAGE

**ROGER DAY**

21 years old. Born in Cheltenham, Gloucester, England. He was educated at Chatham House Grammar School in Ramsgate, leaving to take up a position as a clerk with a city office. This however was not quite what he wanted to do, so he moved into the music world and set up his own recording studio. He became resident D.J. at several ballrooms. He applied to join Radio England soon after the station was established despite his limited experience.

His hobbies are - Driving, Swimming, dancing, meeting people and buying mod clothes. He is a fan of Brunettes, Blondes and Redheads, likes listening to the Beach Boys, The Beatles, the Tamla-Motown sound. He is very interested in food.

Roger's main ambition is however to become a top line D.J. and to make a career in films.

# THE BOSS JOCKS ON STAGE

22 years old. Born in Moultrie, Georgia, U.S.A. Brought up on a farm in Moultrie, Georgia. Jerry went to a local school, to graduate to Norman College, Moultrie, Georgia. Favourite subjects included History and Literature. He left college and joined the Army for six months service training.

After the Army he went into radio, joining station W.M.T.M. as an announcer. He later joined station W.D.U.N. at Gainsville, Georgia where he was a D.J. and Announcer before joining Radio England. When in the U.S.A. he drove a 1965 Chevrolet Malibu and competed successfully on the Drag Racing Tracks in a 1940 Chevrolet Coupe powered by a 1960 Chevrolet Corvette engine. He won five trophies. His recreational activities include reading (Historical), music both popular and classical.

His favourite artists are The Beatles and Sandie Shaw. He also listens to other stations to see how his programmes compare.

**JERRY SMITHWICK**

not to appear that night. The Small Faces said that they would also refuse to go on in support of the guys. That all changed when their notorious manager, Don Arden, arrived and ordered them into a meeting. They emerged very shortly after, looking like naughty schoolboys who had been thrashed by the headmaster. When I approached them and asked if they were still refusing to go on stage that night, a barrage of swearing was their response. Needless to say, they all appeared that night.

The venues from August 12th to 25th were Lewisham Odeon, Finsbury Park Astoria, Birmingham Odeon, Sheffield Gaumont, Leeds Odeon, Glasgow Odeon, Newcastle Odeon, Liverpool Odeon, Manchester Odeon, Cardiff Capitol, Exeter Odeon, and Southampton Odeon.

# CHAPTER 6

# THE UPPERCUT CLUB

S winging Radio England had shut down, and I had nothing lined up and wasn't really sure what to do. I contacted all the other stations, but there were no jobs. Luckily, somebody I knew from SRE told me that the boxer Billy Walker was to open a new club at a converted skating rink in Forest Gate in London's east end and needed a resident DJ. I met with the management and got the gig. It was called The Upper Cut for obvious reasons.

For the next six months, I worked every Friday, Saturday, and Sunday playing the records and introducing the stars of the day.

THANET TIMES

## Roger lands plum job in London

REGAINING his land legs after six months on the 24-hours-a-day pirate radio ship Radio England, broadcasting off the Essex coast, is Margate's deo-jay Roger Day, who led the opening show for boxer Billy Walker's Upper Cut Club in Forest Gate, London, on Wednesday, 21 December.

Roger is to continue working for this well-known British heavyweight boxer, but will still retain his titles from Radio England and will carry on with the occasional shows he now runs.

Billy Walker's club, with its plush dance floor and surrounding legs, is one of the best now open in the London area. It has accommodation for about 2,000 a private members' bar and every imaginable amenity.

Roger, a 25-year-old former Chatham House schoolboy, of Canterbury Road, Margate, compered and spun the discs on the opening night, and has continued working at the club for four nights a week.

Topping the bill was the great sound of The Who, with resident group originally from the States, The Mack Sound, Freddie Mack, a massive South American negro also has connections in the world of boxing. He is a former sparring partner of Billy's.

The following night saw another up-and-coming name, The Easy Beats, followed by Dave Dee, Dozy, Beaky, Mick and Tich on Christmas Eve the star attraction was Eric Burdon and The Animals — introduced by deo-jay Roger Day.

Forest Gate Centre, Woodgrange Road
London, E.7 Tel. (01) 534 6578/9

# BILLY WALKER'S FABULOUS OPENING WEEK

GRAND OPENING NIGHT          Wednesday, December 21

## THE WHO

7.30—11.30 p.m.               Gentlemen 17/6      Ladies 15/-

Thursday, December 22

## THE EASYBEATS

7.30—11.30 p.m.               Gentlemen 12/6      Ladies 10/-

Friday, December 23

## DAVE DEE, DOZY, BEAKY, MICK & TICH

7.30—11.30 p.m.               Gentlemen 15/-      Ladies 12/6

GALA CHRISTMAS EVE            Saturday, December 24

## ERIC BURDON & THE ANIMALS

7.30—Midnight                 Gentlemen 20/-      Ladies 20/-

BOXING DAY FOR ALL THE FAMILY   Monday Afternoon, Dec. 26

## THE JIMMY HENDRIX EXPERIENCE

2.30—5.30 p.m.                Gentlemen 5/-       Ladies 5/-

Monday Evening, December 26

## THE PRETTY THINGS

7.30—11.30 p.m.               Gentlemen 12/6      Ladies 10/-

Friday, December 30

## THE SPENCER DAVIS GROUP

7.30—11.30 p.m.               Gentlemen 15/-      Ladies 12/6

NEW YEAR'S EVE SPECTACULAR     Saturday, December 31

## GENO WASHINGTON & THE RAM JAM BAND

7.30 p.m.—1.00 a.m.           Gentlemen 25/-      Ladies 20/-

and with all this — EVERY NIGHT

## THE MACK SOUND

15-piece band show with FREDDY MACK

supported by **BRITAIN RADIO** Top Disc Jockeys

## BOOK NOW ! BOOK NOW !! BOOK NOW !!!

To the Secretary, THE UPPER CUT, Forest Gate Centre, Woodgrange Road,
London, E.7

PLEASE SEND ME ................... Tickets at ................., each for the
evening of ....................................................................................
Name (Blocks) ..............................................................................
Address ........................................................................................
......................................................................................................
Please find enclosed MO/PO/Cheque for ......................., NME/2
(Subject to G.L.C. Licence)          NOT OPEN ON CHRISTMAS DAY

*Look at this list and I think you'll be impressed*

For me, the highlight was introducing Jimi Hendrix on stage on Boxing Day afternoon. I think this was only his second live concert in England, so nobody knew what he was like. It was advertised as a children's party, so there were families with kids in their party frocks. You can imagine the reaction when I introduced – Live from America - Jimi Hendrix. I can still see the parents' reaction when this wild man launched into his act with all his signature theatrics. The parents shielded their children's eyes from this man making love to his guitar. It was in the dressing room at The Upper Cut that very day that Jimi wrote Purple Haze, which would make the Top 3 the following March.

I told The Upper Cut's manager that this fellow was going to be a big star and he should book him again for an evening session. He took my advice, and when Jimi returned, the queue to get in was hundreds of yards long down the road. Word had got around!

Here's a list of the gigs I compered; I did discos at The Upper Cut in E7, Caesar's in Dunstable, The Corn Exchange in Maidstone, The Witchdoctor Club above the Savoy Rooms in Catford, The Dreamland Ballroom in Margate, the Starlight Ballroom in Herne Bay, and The Cavern Lido in Margate.

**The Upper Cut:**
Friday December 30th 1966 - The Spencer Davis Group
Saturday 31st - Geno Washington
Sunday January 1st 1967 - The Move

Friday 6th - The Small Faces

Saturday 7th - Bitter End Singers

Sunday 8th - The Mindbenders

Friday 13th - The Four Pennies

Saturday 14th - Terry Lightfoot's Jazzmen

Tuesday 17th - Caesar's Club: Dunstable

Guitarist Mick Abrahams used to pop in, and he told me he was forming a new group called Jethro Tull. Silly name I thought.

The Upper Cut

Friday 20th January 1967 - Sounds Incorporated

Saturday 21st - The Fourmost

Friday 27th - Jimmy James & The Vagabonds

Saturday 28th - Jimi Hendrix. This time the place was packed

Sunday 29th - Freddy Mack

Friday February 3rd - Winston's Fumbs

Saturday 4th - Herbie Goin

Friday 10th – The Rockin' Brries

Saturday 11th - Episode Six

Thursday 16th Caesar's Club

The Upper Cut

Saturday 18th - The Honeycombs

Monday 20th - Corn Exchange. Maidstone

Upper Cut

Saturday 25th - Maxine Brown

Thursday March 2nd - Caesar's Club

Upper Cut

Friday March 3rd - The Barron Knights

Saturday 4th - The She Trinity

Monday 6th - Corn Exchange

Upper Cut

Saturday 11th - The Lounge Lizards

Thursday 16th - Caesar's Club

Upper Cut

Frida 17th - Episode Six

Saturdy 18th - The Stax Show with Otis Redding (I wrote in my diary: 'Sensatonal')

Friday 2nd - Eric Winstone

Saturday March 25th - Lord Sutch

Monday 27th - Corn Exchange

Upper Cut

Saturday April 1st - Dave Berry

Sunday 2n - Warren Davis Monday Band

Friday 7th - Witchdoctor, Catford -The Washington DCs

Upper Cut

Friday 14th - The Symbols

Saturday 15th - The Alan Price Set

Monday 17th - Corn Exchange

Friday 21st - The Witchdoctor-The Creation

Upper Cut

Saturday 22nd - Nina Simone

Monday 24th - Corn Exchange

Upper Cut

Friday 28th - Jeff Beck

Saturday 29th - Prince Buster

Sunday 30th - Joyce Bond

Friday May 5th - Freddy Mack

Saturday 6th - Waye Fontana

Friday 12th - The Meseys plus Warm Sounds

Saturday 13th - Peter Jay & the Jaywalkers with Terry Reid

Friday 19th - Sounds Incorporated

Saturday 20th - The Kinks

Friday 26th - The Graham Bond Organisation

Saturday 27th - The Troggs

Wednesday May 31st - Dreamland Ballroom, Margate

Disco dancers, Carole Moore and Suzette Lofts, joined my act and then appeared at all my future gigs. They called themselves The Go Go Girls.

## Roger plans to introduce 'little bit of London'

DISC-JOCKEY ROGER DAY, the 22-year-old whiz-kid of the pop scene who lives at Canterbury Road, Margate, returns to the place where he first found fame and fortune tonight (Wednesday)—Margate's Dreamland Ballroom.

He will be in charge of the entertainments on Wednesday nights for the next three weeks and his plan is to introduce "A little bit of London to Thanet."

He will be billed as "Roger Day and the Soul Sensation"—which is exactly what he has been at Billy Walker's Uppercut Club in London, where he appears regularly on Friday, Saturday and Sunday nights.

During the show, Roger will bring on stage two Go-Go dancers, Carol and Jackie.

"This is something completely new in Thanet," said Roger, "but it has gone down like a bomb in town. It's a sound idea, really. After all, two nice blonde girls give the guys something to look at during the show."

Both Carol and Jackie are local girls. They won their stage debut after Roger had auditioned hundreds of Thanet girls.

"I found that we have nicer looking girls down here than the ones I have seen in London," he added.

Today Roger is as much a comedian as he is a disc-jockey and this whole style is laced with sophistication.

He gained much of his experience from his days in the pirate ship, Radio England, but his more recent appearances at the Uppercut Club have helped him to develop as a showman.

ROGER DAY

Go Go girls Suzette Lofts (left) and Carole Moore, have returned to Thanet after dancing in London.  C. 7331.

## THE GO GO DANCERS RETURN TO THANET 26/12/68

THE "DAY GO" dancers. That's the name of the two, sprightly 21-year-olds, pictured 'above', who have recently returned to their Thanet homes after making a name for themselves in London. The next step is to carve their niche in Thanet.

Carol Moore, of Marswood Road, Sandwich, and Suzette Lofts, of Northdown Avenue, Margate, won a dancing competition organised by Roger "Twiggy" Day, just over a year ago.

They then learned the "Go Go" dancing, to go with Roger's disc jockey act, and became a popular feature at the Dreamland Ballroom whenever Roger was playing the records.

When Roger Day left the ballrooms for radio station work, and eventually Radio Luxembourg, the two lovelies became freelance dancers, and continued working in the London area.

They appeared in Maidstone on a number of occasions, and were one of the attractions at the recent Inter Temple Ball for law students.

They have appeared in dozens of dancehalls, and are well known on the London circuit — but they are relatively unknown to Thanet audiences.

"We would like to get established in Thanet," said Carol. "There are quite a lot of dances and other teenage functions, but unlike towns, they never have any dancers."

Obviously they are no longer with Roger, the girls are keeping the name "Day Go", as, in actual fact, they were all born and brought up in Margate.

"We will probably be dancing at Dreamland on a monthly basis in the near future, and if it is another of our gigs here it is possible."

**My Go Go Dancers**
Upper Cut
Friday June 2nd - Herbie Goins
Saturday 3rd - The Turtles
Wednesday 7th - Dreamland Ballroom
Upper Cut
Friday 9th - The Fortunes
Saturday 10th - The Drifters
Friday 16th - Mike Cotton Sound
Saturday 17th - Zoot Money
Wednesday 21st - Starlight Ballroom: Herne Bay
Friday 23rd - The Action
Saturday 24th - The Toys plus The Chiffons
Friday June 30th - Chris Farlowe
Saturday July 1st - Cream
Monday 3rd - The Lido Cavern, Margate, and every
lunchtime
Wednesday 5th - Caesar's Club
Upper Cut
Saturday 8th - The Small Faces
Monday 10th - Corn Exchange
Wednesday 12th - Caeser's Club
Upper Cut
Saturday 15th - Wynder K Frog
Monday 17th - Corn Exchange

# CHAPTER 7

# RADIO ANDORRA

During the spring of 1967, I was approached by a company, Ross Radio, who wanted to start a radio station broadcasting from Andorra. They wanted it to be similar to Radio Luxembourg. The people behind it were Mark Kelly and Monty Bailey-Watson, with Michael Shrimpton as the Station Manager.

On Thursday 13th April, I recorded a programme, along with Paul Kramer from Radio City and Roger Scott aka Arnold Layne of Radio Essex for a test transmission. The wavelength was 417 metres. Ben Healey was also involved.

They were due to be broadcast from midnight on April 19th, 20th, and 21stbut got postponed until Wednesday April 26th. Sadly, the tests were not audible in the UK and as a result the finance couldn't be raised.

MARK KELLY

16, ST. GEORGES COURT,
258 BROMPTON ROAD,
LONDON, S.W. 3.

KNIGHTSBRIDGE 5716

Mr. Roger Day,
27, Canterbury Road,
Margate,
Kent.

30th. March, 1967.

Dear Roger,

     As I mentioned to you, we have several tests to do from
Radio Andorra before we commence our official broadcasts and the
first and most important of these is on April 5th. starting at
midnight. I wondered if you would care to help us out with the
monitoring of the signal and so I've enclosed the leaflet which is
being sent to all the Medium Wave Circle people and our other
monitoring people. The test will be on 417 metres and we would
appreciate a postcard from you if you've time to listen on the 5th
saying on the postcard what the signal was like in your area...weak,
strong, better than Radio Luxemburg etc.. also what type of radio
you listened on...transistor, valve or whatever.

     When we have received all the postcards and gained an
idea of the pattern of the signal strength we will then be in a
better position to know about staff so it will help to have your
reply if you've time. Don't send the card to me directly, but to the
address on the leaflet. Thank you.

     Thank you also for your phone call saying that you are
interested in the idea of working with us on this project, it's nice
to know. Hope to see you soon,

          Yours,

          Mark. Kelly.

# MARK KELLY LTD.

Mr. Roger Day,
27, Canterbury Road,
Margate,
Kent.

16 ST. GEORGES COURT,
258 BROMPTON ROAD,
LONDON, S.W.3.

KNightsbridge 5716

Friday, 14th. April, 1967.

Dear Roger,

We were all very pleased with the hard work and enthusiasm shown yesterday at the recording, and I'm most grateful to you in particular, for the fun hour which came out of your work. It was professional and exciting.

The tests will be broadcast from Andorra as follows:-
April 19th. midnight until one a.m. ROGER DAY.
April 20th. from one a.m. until two a.m. PAUL KRAMER.
April 20th. from midnight until one a.m. on April 21st. ROGER SCOTT.
April 21st. from one a.m. until two a.m. Tape from previous test.
The first hour of these tests is the most important and we will have gained a lot by having your tape Roger. Thank you again.

After we've been in touch with our Ad. Agency bods and the Record company people, we'll be in a better position to offer you something more concrete, but I would ask that you might contact me if you're offered anything permanent. It will be at least two weeks bfore we reach any decision, but I assure you that you are rated very highly by us all.

Looking foreward to seeing you again soon,

Best wishes,

Mark Kelly.

P.S. I've had to delay sending this to you Roger, as there has had to be a little postponement on the tests and I wanted to make sure that you knew. They will now be held from Midnight on Wednesday 26th April. Also I've had a few words with our station controller for Andorra and although you've met him briefly, he would like the chance to meet you again over a beer or something. If we can make it sometime towards next Friday it would be good. Look ing foreward to seeing you soon, regards
m.

DIRECTOR: MARK T. KELLY
REGISTERED OFFICE: 46 OLD BOND STREET, LONDON. W.1

# MARK KELLY LTD.

16 ST. GEORGES COURT,
258 BROMPTON ROAD,
LONDON, S.W.3.

KNightsbridge 5716

Mr. Roger Day,
27, Canterbury Road,
Margate,
Kent.

Tuesday 9th. May, 1967.

Dear Roger,

This is a letter which I've dreaded writing, but it's got to be done - so here we go. We are going to have to postpone our plans for the English side of Radio Andorra as we've struck some financial difficulty. It is a postponement only though NOT a cancellation. But I wanted to make sure that you were aware of the situation as we have been very pleased with your enthusiasm towards the project and I personally was looking foreward to having you on the staff in the near future.

We had hoped that some of the capitol this deal is taking could be obtained from either E.M.I. or Decca in the form of an advance from them on the time we were asking them to buy..that is to say that we are asking for one hundred pounds per hour per night. On this basis we asked those two companies would they buy one hour per night (£ 36,500 per annum) and could we have an advance of thirty thousand in exchange for their being able to have first choice of time. While they are anxious to support us it seems, they aren't prepared to assist the launch of the new station by giving this advance. I feel that they've gotten to-gether and decided to make it a policy so that in this way they avoid having opposition to Radio Luxemburg where they now almost control the station.

We have been offered outside capitol, but this means that we lose a certain amount of the control of the company and also have to award Equity (shares) for the amount invested and I frankly don't find this attractive. However we're going to have to accept it and will do so. What we do now is look around for the people who want to invest in the station and who'll want least return for their investment - and this takes time; a long time. So I'm afraid that I've got to say to you "If you get another offer, then take it. We can't be sure if or when we're starting." I hate to say this but its only fair for you as we may be three months or maybe six months and I don't want to feel that you're waiting around refusing any work which might come your way.

.../...

DIRECTOR : MARK T. KELLY
REGISTERED OFFICE : 44 OLD BOND STREET, LONDON. W.1

.../...                    2.

There is one thing which I would like to ask of you Roger and it's this: if you are going to take any other offer which will preclude your working with us, then will you please let me know? We definitely do want you to wrok with us and I'm so very dissappointed that we have to write this letter at this stage when all seemed to be going so well.

I'm writing a similar letter to Ben Healy and Alison Brown and I've written to all the other applicants saying that we'd chosen our staff...I was on the last letter when we received the news from E.M.I. and Decca.! But I do want to stress to you and Ben that we were most excited with the talent side of things and I was busy congratulating myself on what a great team we had, and I'd like to feel that we're able to come back to you at a future date with the same proposition - meantime I'm afraid that you'll just have to regard it as "fallen through".

May I thank you again Roger, for all the help you've given us and for your enthusiasm; and that thanks comes not only from me but also from my fellow Director of Radio Andorra, Monty Bailey-Watson and also the station manager Michael Shrimpton.

In closing I'd like to ask that you keep this letter as confidential information and in particular regard the financial side as being something known only to you and very few other people. Only yourself and Ben outside of our organisation are aware of the present circumstances. We all wish you the very best of luck Roger for what we're all sure will be a brilliant career in radio with I'm sure telev-ision to follow.

Thanking you once again, Yours faithfully,

Mark Kelly.

# CHAPTER 8

# RADIO CAROLINE SOUTH

On the afternoon of July 17th 1967, I had just got back home after a lunch time disc session at the Cavern in Margate. My mother told me that a Terry Bate from Radio Caroline had called, wanting to speak to me. I, of course, knew Terry as the man who sold advertising for the station and was responsible for the extremely popular Caroline Cash Casino. I called him back, and he asked if I would be interested in joining Radio Caroline. It was like Matt Busby phoning a footballer and asking him if he wanted to play for Manchester United! He suggested we meet up. I replied, "Yeah, sure," right away.

I hopped on a train to London and met Terry at Radio Caroline's offices in Chesterfield Gardens. He explained that many of the Caroline DJs were leaving the station because the government had passed the Marine Offences Act, which made it illegal for British people to work for the station or for companies to buy commercials on air. The government thought this would force the closure of the stations. Radio Caroline, therefore, needed new people who were prepared to break the law. I think Johnnie Walker had suggested my name to Terry.

He told me that if I was arrested, I could be fined and given a two-year jail sentence and asked if I was still interested. The warnings didn't deter me, and I was pleased to accept the offer and asked when he wanted me to start. "As soon as possible," was the reply, so I asked for one day to inform all my disco gig organisers that I wouldn't be working with them anymore.

That Friday, July 20th, I reported to Offshore 1 – the supply ship for Radio Caroline. Onboard was another new DJ, Kerry Juby, who was also new to broadcasting. One hour later, we were alongside the Mi Amigo, the home of Radio Caroline. I know most people will think I'm mad, but the first time I stepped on board the Mi Amigo, I felt it was where I belonged.

A 21-year-old Margate disc-jockey is all set to defy the Government when legislation against pirate radio stations becomes effective on 15 August. With the rest of the staff on board Radio Caroline, he will continue to broadcast pop music programmes and shows.

Roger Day, who lives in Margate, is an ex-Radio England disc jockey, and has often worked at Dreamland. He joined the "pirates" on 21 July, and his first programme went over the air that night.

Roger, who is at present four miles off the Essex coast in the 470-ton ex-Swedish ship, has offered to help continue broadcasting after the Government legislation takes effect.

Radio Caroline Press Officer, Mrs. Francis Vanstaden, said that Roger Day had been selected from the many hundreds of applications received for jobs on Caroline, because of his previous experience.

"At present, he has not got his own programme, but he has been helping with the staff in running what she said.

*Photo for German Newspaper. L to R, Freddie Bear, Me, Kilroy, Keith Hampshire, Engineer Trevor*

# Caroline dig at Mr. Wilson

*DISC & MUSIC ECHO 5 Aug 67*

RADIO CAROLINE, the only pirate station to continue broadcasting after the Government's Bill becomes law on August 15, is to cock a snook at the Prime Minister with a programme on 'The Private Life Of Harold Wilson.'

Ronan O'Rahilly, the man behind Caroline's lone fight against the Government, told Disc on Tuesday: "I cannot say what content this programme will take or who prepared the material. We are simply going to broadcast private facts about his life.

"I can say, though, that Radio Caroline—both North and South ships—will continue. We are carrying on indefinitely—forever. We have offices in Paris, Amsterdam, America, Canada and Germany. We have sufficient international advertising accounts, although there'll be a bit of a squeeze for all of us."

Rival pirate stations, all of which are closing down, are sceptical of O'Rahilly's intentions. Some suggest he will stay on the air for only one day as a token gesture. "That is quite untrue—we carry on indefinitely," says O'Rahilly.

Others openly regard O'Rahilly as "a nut" in carrying on against seemingly insurmountable odds. "They thought I was a nut when Caroline first went on the air to pioneer pirate stations. Then they changed their minds. Now we're back to square one with people thinking I'm a nut again. But I've no time for anybody who doesn't stand up for his rights."

Elsewhere, however, the pirate stations are planning their farewells. Radio Scotland is staging a "Sunset Clan Ball" at Glasgow Locarno on August 14. It ends at midnight, when the Bill takes effect.

Radio 270 is staging a few farewell dances and Radio 355 (whose Dutch language station is also closing) plans "to give the boys a farewell party."

### SIRA Summer Magazine.

The Worlds Largest Free Radio Magazine! As usual approx. 36 pages packed with articles, news, comments, photos and special offers! Roger Twiggy Day, Cris St. John, Mark Stuart, John Peel, Martin Kayne, Ric Jonathan, Caroline. Dick Palmer (ex-Radio Essex). Cut clovens & Worldwide DX Club, all combining to bring you the best ever radio publication! Did you know that Roger Day and C.S.J. may be back on your radio soon? Find out where and when only in SIRA mag. — price 25p from Southern Independent Radio Association, 91 Park Street, Horsham, Sussex.

### FREE RADIO

SIRA SUMMER MAGAZINE. The world's largest Free Radio magazine! Approx. 36 pages and all your favourites Twiggy Day, C.S.J., Mark Stuart, John Peel, Martin Kayne, Ric Jonas (ex Caroline) plus contributions from Cat Stevens and Worldwide DX Club! Is Radio Scotland to be the next offshore station? When can you hear Big Bad Roger on Radio Sweden? What did the GPO tell C.S.J? All this and much more in the world's top radio publication — 25 pence from Southern Independent Radio Association, 91 Park Street, Horsham, Sussex.

## PIRATE RADIO PLANS TO BREAK LAW

By KENNETH CLARKE

RADIO CAROLINE, Britain's first pirate radio station, is preparing a campaign in reply to the Marine Offences Act which becomes law in about six weeks.

The new law is to be broken on the first day by a newscaster, a disc jockey and a religious broadcaster, all British subjects. The rest will carry on with their normal jobs.

The Bill, passed in Parliament last Friday, makes it an offence for British subjects to supply, or work for, a pirate station. It will also cut off British advertising sources and force the stations to take their administrative headquarters abroad.

Caroline's managing director, Mr. Ronan O'Rahilly, 27, told me yesterday he was ready to fight. "Each broadcaster breaking the law will have to be prosecuted.

"They will have made broadcasts knowing them to be for the use of Caroline and they will have to be arrested. I want this to happen because I am going to take each case to the Court of Human Rights, whose jurisdiction Britain accepts.

### "Morally right"

"I am morally right in this. Harold Wilson is morally wrong. What are people going to think if ordinary British people are put in prison for working for a legal radio station?"

Also liable to prosecution will be Ronald Duncan, the poet, dramatist and founder of the English Stage Company. He has been broadcasting over Caroline against the Bill, and has offered to write scripts "for Ad" when it becomes illegal to do so.

Mr. Duncan has appealed to other writers to write for pirate stations in support of their freedom to work for whom they like.

He said last night: "I shall provide Caroline with a nominal script or sign a contract with them and I hope I am prosecuted. I feel this is the thin end of the wedge."

Radio Caroline, started three and a half years ago, is beamed from two ships, in extra-territorial waters off the Isle of Man and Frinton, Essex. When the Bill becomes law, Caroline's administrative headquarters will be moved to Amsterdam.

*My first view of the ship.*

Below the 'Caroline' sign was the vent for the library, then the news studio, which was also used for production. To the right of the Caroline Bell, you can see the On Air studio. The open door led to the transmitters.

*The Studio.*

*Offshore One*

*We had to jump from the tender to the ship, and nobody ever fell in.*

*Offshore One Leaving*

*Our view of Frinton*

I was greeted by Radio Caroline DJ Robbie Dale, who showed me around, settled me in a cabin, and told me I would be presenting at midnight that day. I went directly to the studio, looking at the on air DJ, who I think was 'Tatty' Tom Edwards, so that I was familiar with the studio controls. Strangely, I wasn't nervous at all, even though I was broadcasting to a much larger audience than Swinging Radio England. It just felt so right. It was hard for me to believe that I was now sitting in the studio of the station I had listened to since 1964.

My first record of the week – the Sureshot - was the Spencer Davis Group's Time Seller.

Having proved I could do it at midnight, Robbie said I would be on air at 9 am. The pressure was now on, as there was a full load of commercials to play, including the legendary Cash Casino. Fortunately, the lovely Keith Hampshire – 'Keefers' –stayed with me to see if I pressed all the right buttons. There was a real family atmosphere about the crew on board the ship. It was so different to what I had experienced before.

On air that day, Tom Edwards had overheard one of the Dutch crew saying I was as thin as Twiggy the model. He told listeners that Twiggy Day would be on, sitting in for The Admiral at six.

Some days, I did one 3-hour show, but on others it was two 3-hour shows.

I was actually on air when the Viking Saga made its daily trip to the ship full of listeners to have a look at us. There were lots of people shouting, "Where is Twiggy

Day?" I thought, if that is the reaction from one mention on the radio, this might be a good nickname to adopt. So from that day, I have been Roger 'Twiggy' Day. And, of course, from that came the 'Thinner Record Spinner'.

Those weeks before the Marine Offences Act were very strange. I was sad for the guys who were leaving, and for those of us staying, it was a worry of the unknown. We had daily tenders bringing fuel and water, plus DJs and engineers, sacks full of mail, records, and so many

*The Viking Saga*

journalists from the newspapers and TV. This was via Offshore 1, which was a much larger vessel than the smaller Offshore 2 that had supplied SRE. It usually arrived either late morning or early afternoon and was the highlight of the day. Everyone would assemble on deck to see who was coming out to see us. An average trip from Felixstowe would take 1hour.

The studio was quite different to Swinging Radio England's. It was much smaller and positioned across the ship with a porthole in front of you and one behind. On SRE, the studios were below deck so you had no idea of the current weather situation. It was lovely to be able to walk out on deck while a record was playing. Cabins were also much better equipped and more comfortable. Each cabin had two bunks, two wardrobes, and a table.

Each week we were given a crate of Dutch Lager, a large pack of Coca Cola, and 200 cigarettes. As a non-smoker, I traded mine for cola or beer.

The food was very good and prepared by the Dutch chef. Because the Dutch had a lot of Indonesian colonies, I was introduced to some very spicy meals. The entire crew was Dutch, and there was much mickey taking between them and the mainly English presenters, all in very good humour. There were drinking contests to see which country's nationals could handle alcohol the best. The answer was inconclusive. After that, I didn't want to drink Geneva, a very strong Dutch gin, ever again. I do drink a lot of tea when I broadcast but obviously couldn't make it in the studio so had to brew it in the mess room next door.

Sometimes, it would taste of fish, and one day I discovered why - the Dutch crew had put a fish in the kettle.

What shocked me was the liberal use of marijuana. It wasn't smoked by everybody though, including me. My motto has always been 'drugs are for mugs'. There appears to be a train of thought that cannabis, a soft drug, is harmless. All I will say is that I have seen many cases where it certainly isn't and has led to lives destroyed.

One rule strictly adhered to was 'no women on board'. So forget the scenes in 'The Boat That Rocked'; that never happened. I shall always remember my first mail bag delivery. Swinging Radio England had had a pretty good response, but this was a different level. I had a sack of letters addressed to little old me.

On Monday July 31st 1967, I came ashore for what was meant to be my last shore leave in England. If ever I had any doubt about the popularity of Radio Caroline, it was the two discos I appeared at that week that proved it. They were packed out and everybody was wishing us the best after August 14th. Even in the pubs back home in Margate the support was unbelievable.

After a great week, it was time to head back to sea. I left my old Ford Cortina at home to be sold, as I knew I wouldn't be needing it anymore. To this day, I will always remember the conversation I had with my dad on Margate Station before I caught the train. He sensed a certain apprehension and asked what was bothering me. I asked him, "Do you think I'm doing the right thing?"

"Why not?" he replied.

"Well, the government could send a gunboat out and take us off air," I said.

"So what?" he said. "Life is full of risks, and if you really believe in what you're doing, then go for it. If you don't. you will always wonder 'what if'." It was great advice, the kind any parent should give.

I arrived in Harwich and boarded Offshore 1. There was no sign of Kerry Juby, who was due back on board with me. Obviously, he got cold feet, I thought to myself. I never heard from him again until he appeared on Capital Radio in London in the mid-seventies.

Back on board, I was still just sitting in for the established DJs but loving every minute. Things were getting very frantic with supplies being increased in readiness for life with no regular supply tenders.

The fateful day, August 14th, arrived. The day the Marine Offences Act became law. I had one big problem. My passport was due to expire and my new one hadn't arrived. I had no problem with being a fugitive living abroad, but I had no desire to do it without a passport. So I jumped on the tender with all the others who were leaving for good, to go ashore and sort it out. Now, I know a lot of listeners and indeed JW and the Admiral thought I had got cold feet. Also on the tender were Keefers, who was going back to Canada, the lovely Steve Young (The Curly Haired Kid in the Front Row), and Tom Edwards, who I hoped would return to the ship. On arrival at Harwich, there were huge crowds of people waiting for us to come ashore, and when the train pulled into Liverpool

Street, I couldn't believe the size of the crowd. In all honesty, they were waiting for the Radio London DJs who would be arriving later.

On that last tender trip, I was surprised to see my old friend from Margate, Morris Brown. I asked him, "What on earth are you doing here?" He replied that he had been hired as a radio engineer. Bearing in mind he had wanted to become a priest, I asked if he was sure he wanted to work with us idiots. I found out later that it was a friend of his who'd got the job but his mother had stopped him accepting, so Morris took his place.

I think Chris Cary, a Midlands club DJ, who used the on air name Spangles Muldoon, arrived later that day with Ross Brown.

Like so many millions, I listened with great sadness to the closedown of Big L. Although I didn't work for them, I was an admirer of the station and was sorry to see them close. We were quite surprised actually, as for a long time they had indicated that they would continue. I suspect a deal was done with the government, but I've no proof. With the number of listeners they had and the professional way they operated, they might have made a difference if they'd continued. But there, of course, was the difference between Radio Caroline and Big L. Big L was a business out to make money, but Caroline was in it for very different reasons. Hence the decision to continue broadcasting.

*Me surrounded by some listeners at Felixstowe.*

*L to R. Tatty Tom Edwards, Keith Keefers Hampshire, me.*

IT ALL STARTED THREE YEARS AGO WITH RADIO CAROLINE, AND CAROLINE IS

GOING TO HAVE THE LAST WORD, TOO

# The pop pirates sign off —but the melody lingers on

### by RAY CONNOLLY

SIMON DEE
An Easter "first"

TOMORROW, after three and a half years of radio a-go-go, the Fab Forty, climbers, sure shots, blasts from the past, spiky electronic jingles and station identifications, transistorised ear drums, golden oldies and general non-stop-pop, the pirate radio stations will be silenced—all but two, anyway.

Tomorrow the Marine Broadcasting (Offences) Act comes into force, to the great chagrin of a substantial section of the population and a few small, but active, independent record companies, and to the undisguised delight of most Labour MPs, the BBC and the Musicians' Union.

Only Radio Caroline with her two ships, one of the Isle of Man and the other off Essex, intends to carry on broadcasting. And how long Caroline can survive, with all links with the United Kingdom cut, is a matter of dubious conjecture.

But the offshore stations will not necessarily be sunk without trace. The ramifications of their broadcasting policy will be felt throughout the BBC and the British recording industry for years. At the Government's request the BBC are to start a special pop channel on 247 metres medium wave (Radio 1) as a replacement for the pirates. September 30, and several Big 1, and Radio Caroline disc jockeys have already agreed to join.

### Compliment

"Radio 1 will be like a commercial station without the commercials." That's how Robin Scott, the head of the BBC's Radio 1 and 2, describes his new service. Quite a step for Auntie; quite a compliment for the offshore brigade.

In three years pop music has become part of the social fabric of the country in a way that has never before been possible since Don did his first broadcast from Radio Caroline on Easter Saturday 1964.

A bishop, a priest and the Editor of The Times hang reverently to Mick Jagger's every word during World In Action; an outraged Alice Bacon casti-

gates a Beatle in the House for his views on drugs; and Cliff Richard and Paul Jones debate religious issues during a Sunday television programme.

The Beatles started the nation's fascination with all things pop. The pirates consolidated it.

But there is more to the pirates' achievements than having nudged BBC radio into the second half of the twentieth century. They've also dealt a pretty hefty blow at the small oligarchy that used to control the country's record producing industry, chiefly EMI and Decca, and to a lesser extent Pye and Philips.

In the limited needle-time available, BBC producers have always had their work cut out finding sufficient time to play the new releases from catalogued artists. For the 79 or 80 records that are issued every week by unknown artists there has been precious little hope of more than a single play.

When Caroline and London started broadcasting, however, they had all the needle time they could have wanted. (They

ignored the outcry from the Musicians' Union.) Suddenly a whole new generation of artists could get their records played more or less on merit. They name didn't have to be Presley or Richard or McCartney any time was no object. The charts became full of new names.

Then seeing their chance astute managers began setting up their own record companies recording and issuing their own artists and by-passing the major combines.

### Example

Track Records, the company formed by Chris Stamp and Kit Lambert, managers of The Who, is a good example. Since they started operating earlier this year they have had five records in the Top Ten.

"Radio London was the first station to plug The Who's Can't Explain when it was released on the Decca subsidiary Brunswick. Now we issue their records ourselves, together with those by Jimi Hendrix. It would have been much more difficult to

Hendrix, known without the pirates," said a spokesman.

Rolling Stones' manager Andrew Oldham and his Immediate label have won more success with records on The Small Faces, P. P. Arnold and The Warm Sounds.

Pyramid's Desmond Dekker blue-beat record, 007, is another example. Independent promotion man Tony Hall heard it at a party, recognised some commercial potential and spent two days tracking down the label direct. A few days later Radio London and a record which had been selling slowly, if steadily, to the country's West Indian communities, jumped into the Top Twenty.

"The pirates have helped the small labels tremendously," says Hall. "They've been forcing monopolies, whether in the form of the BBC or the major record companies."

As an independent production

company Island Records made all the Spencer Davis hits, which were then released through the Philips group. Encouraged by their success they began to release their own pop material last year.

It would not be economically viable for us to buy even 15 minutes a week of air space on Radio Luxembourg, said Chris Peers, a director of Island. (The major groups each buy several hours a week.) "We could never have become established as a nil-making concern without London and Caroline."

Meanwhile the attitude of the major companies has been, to say the least, hypocritical. But it's common knowledge that ever, one of them has co-operated with the offshore stations, sending them records, and wining and dining the disc jockeys.

### Grouse

The biggest grouse that the big companies have is that sales are down considerably. Four years ago a Number One record would have sold about half a million copies. Today sales would be nearer to 350,000, but records in the lower regions of the charts are selling better than they did before the pirates. The fact, as it were, is more evenly distributed.

Only Decca of all the big firms is prepared to give an approximate estimate of how sales have been affected—down by 25 per cent in the areas served by the pirates. But might net sales have dropped by this amount as a result of the ending of the Restilements pop boom?

If they are right, we can now expect a resurgence in sales. The major companies with their Luxembourg programmes are sure to get their slice of the market whatever happens. The independents may be less fortunate.

"We hope to be able to buy air time for two records a night on Luxembourg," say Island. "It will be much harder to introduce new artists now," say Immediate.

Tomorrow will be pretty quiet on the medium wave. Radio 270 and 355 went off the air on Saturday; Radio London on 266 ends at 3 p.m. today; 390 closed a couple of weeks ago, and Radio 370 and Radio Scotland finish at midnight tonight. Only Caroline will be left. The first and the last of the pop pirates.

---

# THE No 1 POP PIRATE IS ALONE ONCE AGAIN

By Mirror TV Reporter JACK BELL

THE party is over for the pop pirates . . . or nearly over.

At midnight tonight, after six months of virtually non-stop programmes, the stations will be outlawed by the Marine Broadcasting Offences Act.

Once there were ten "Jolly Roger" stations around Britain's coast.

But yesterday only four—Radio Scotland, Radio London, Caroline North and Caroline South—were operating.

### Survivor

And by tomorrow both Radio London and Radio Scotland will have shut down.

Caroline, the station that started pirate radio, will be the only survivor. Its headquarters have been transferred to Amsterdam—out of the reach of the Postmaster-General, Mr. Edward Short.

Caroline's boss, Ronan O'Rahilly, told me last night: "I am more committed to Caroline than ever.

"It's not just pop music any more. Every time I look at the Marine Broadcasting Offences Bill I am amazed that it has been let through."

And he added: "We want to bring this matter before the United Nations and before the

Commission on Human Rights at Strasbourg."

The new Act prohibits British firms from advertising on pirate radio—but Mr. O'Rahilly says he has enough international orders to keep Caroline on the air for a year.

About ten English disc jockeys are leaving Caroline.

Mr. O'Rahilly said: "They're a bit worried that they might go to jail. But I can't blame them.

"But we've got others joining—from Australia, South Africa, Canada and America.

"Two English disc jockeys are also staying. They say they are prepared to go ashore and see if they are prosecuted."

### 'Anarchy'

The Postmaster-General attacked the pirate stations because, he said, he wanted to end anarchy in the air.

There have been complaints that the pirate programmes interfered with ship-to-shore messages and broadcasting on the Continent in areas far apart as Sweden and Yugoslavia.

Three stations—Radio 390, Radio Essex,

pleas for police protection.

Rough seas occasionally cut off the stations' supplies, and some of the disc jockeys gave up trying to sound cheery as instantaneous waves rocked the ships.

### Legacy

Now, with most of the pop pirates off the air, their legacy is handed to the BBC.

When Radio One, the new BBC pop channel, comes on the air next month it will imitate many of their brash technique—and some of the disc jockeys will be ex-pirates.

---

# Caroline 'Plugs' Army Dance

SUNDAY TELEGRAPH REPORTER

RADIO CAROLINE, the outlawed radio station now operating from headquarters in Holland, broadcast a free advertisement for an Army dance yesterday. Roger Day, 21, a disc jockey, announced the dance, at the Royal Horse Artillery barracks, Colchester, next Tuesday, and urged all the local girls to go along and meet the soldiers.

An Eastern Command spokesman said later: "There is bound to be an inquiry.

### LAW BROKEN

"Whoever seems to hear people about the dance has broken not only civil law, but military law as well.

"There is a Part One order specifically forbidding soldiers from contacting Radio Caroline." A Part One order is an order published to the troops as a direct instruction at their level. They are originated by the Defence Council and promulgated to units.

### QUITE FANTASTIC

The spokesman added that the order was issued in July—about a month before the Marine Broadcasting (Offences) Act came into force. But Mr. Rubble Dale, a Radio Caroline official, said from his office in Amsterdam last night: "Some of the soldiers wrote to us asking for a free 'plug' for their regimental dance."

of it. We think it really is quite fantastic, absolutely ridiculous.

"We are not going to give the names of the soldiers who told us about the dance. They could only get us into a charge and probably in the 'guardhouse' or on 'jankers'."

The R.H.A. at Colchester has about 800 men. Any investigation into the advertisements would be started by the commanding officer but could be conducted by the Special Investigation Branch of the Royal Military Police.

The civil police are also entitled to take action under the new Act, although I gather they are unlikely to do so in this case.

By that evening, I was back home in Margate and, at midnight with millions of others, was listening to Johnnie Walker and Robbie Dale taking Caroline into a new era. It is one of the biggest regrets in my career that I wasn't there with them. What a wonderful job they did. It was one of the most memorable broadcasts ever.

Ironically, I sorted the passport problem out the next day. I must admit, I often wonder if the authorities had delayed my passport knowing I was a Radio Caroline DJ. My next job was to get back on the ship. After contacting Jimmy Houlihan, owner Ronan O'Rahilly's right-hand man, he arranged for me to catch a plane from Heathrow to Amsterdam. I was quite nervous as I had never flown before. It didn't help that the taxi taking me to the airport crashed! Thankfully, I caught the plane and arrived for the first time in Holland and made my way to the new Radio Caroline offices at Singel 160. They arranged for a hotel that night and told me to be at the port of Ijmuiden to catch the tender the next morning.

The tender trip from Harwich to Mi Amigo was just one hour and never really that rough. From Holland, it took 18 hours minimum, and the middle of the North Sea is not usually flat. In fact, it can get damn choppy. Fortunately, I never get seasick, but for me, boredom was the major problem. Occasionally, they let us steer the boat if it was safe to do so. And trust me, it isn't as easy as you would think. The tender usually left at 10am and arrived about 4 am the next day. It was very strange to arrive off the English coast in darkness with the lights of the Mi

Amigo shining over the water. I was so glad to be back and got a great reception, because, since I'd left, they only had four DJs on board. It was straight in at the deep end and onto the breakfast show at 6 am.

There was a big difference now. There weren't many commercials, but instead there were many plug records to play. For £100, a record got five plays a day. Half the records were ok, but the others were complete rubbish, including those on the Major Minor record label. It was owned by Philip Solomon, who was also, in reality, the man in charge of the station. But we had little choice - either play the records or go out of business. Listening back to those programmes, I am amazed anybody listened, but I think listeners knew the situation and were prepared to put up with anything to support the station.

They were amazing times. For six glorious weeks, we probably had the largest radio audience of any radio station there has ever been. Radio One hadn't started, and we were the only English music station on the air. I certainly don't think the government's threat to arrest anybody found listening made any difference. It was quite the opposite. I think that made the listeners more determined. Most were so angry that the politicians had tried to stop something that was so good and not doing any harm. Certainly the post response indicated the feelings of the wonderful British public. They sent presents, mostly sweets (in my case Twiglets and Smarties), and money too. I got a letter from a chap who cooked for Harold Wilson, who told me the PM got more letters about banning the offshore stations than any other subject. It proved that politicians ignoring the will of the people was nothing new. I'll never forgive Harold Wilson's Labour government for stopping what we did. You won't be surprised to know that since then I have never voted Labour and never will. Even my dad, a former coal miner and a staunch socialist, stopped supporting them.

The engineers on board Radio Caroline at the time were Morris and American Don Ricardson who used to turn the transmitter on in the middle of the night to send messages to his wife. Nobody found out about this until many years later. Another engineer was Ray Glennister. When he came into the studio, he was so smelly I used to have to open the port holes, even if a storm was raging! He never took any notice of our attempts to ask him to shower more often, so one day, we filled his bunk with soap suds and bars of soap.

During that time, we used to get many small boats from the Essex coast paying us a visit. The crews were never allowed on board but used to deliver things like newspapers and fresh milk. The milk was particularly welcome, as anyone who has tried cornflakes with long life milk will testify. Their visits were always a lovely break from the daily routine.

We kept in touch with dry land by a daily short wave call to Percy Scadden in Frinton-on-Sea. It was totally against the law, and he was a retired policeman!

I shall always remember my first trip to stay in Holland for my shore leave. Foolishly, I had asked a

Dutch crewman to teach me a phrase that would help me pick up a girl. He said that they all speak English, so it wasn't necessary. I persisted, and he gave me a phrase. So, I arrived at this club and used the words for the first time. There wasn't a good reaction. The girl walked off in a strop. The second attempt had the same effect, so I smelt a rat. I got chatting to a third girl and explained my story, saying it didn't have the desired reaction. "Please tell me what the phrase actually means," I asked her. She just laughed and told me the crewman was having a joke at my expense. The words meant "I want to make love to you but not pay for it". I did have a few words with the chap when I got back, and, of course, the rest of the crew were in on it.

Another time, I was on leave with Johnnie Walker and our usual hotel was full, so they recommended one next door. We dumped our bags and headed off for a night out. The next day at breakfast, I pointed out to JW that there weren't any women around. When we mentioned this to the desk clerk at our usual hotel, we realised it was another Dutch joke at our expense. What he failed to tell us was that the hotel was for gays!

It was very strange broadcasting to a country that was only three miles away but not being able to go there. At night, you could even see cars driving along Frinton-on-Sea front.

As it was summer, there were still a lot of yachts and boats from the coast who came out to see us. Sometimes bring us treats like Daily Papers.

*RTD in the Studio. Dig the groovy shirt and cravat.*

*Listeners sent us lots of presents. I adopted this giraffe as a mascot.*

*All ready to go onshore. Colour coordinated. From Take 6 in Carnaby Street.*

*The cover for my record of the week. Johnnie Walker did the writing.*

*One of the cooks, Tex*

One of the most frequently asked questions I get asked is how we passed the time on Radio Caroline when we weren't on air.

Here's a typical day:

05.00 – The alarm goes off. Head for the shower room to wash and shave, then the kitchen to eat some cereal and maybe some toast.

05.30 - To the studio and press the start button on the cart containing the Caroline Theme tune.

05.32 - Play Green Grass by the Ventures and welcome listeners to the show.

09.00 - Off air and have breakfast with whoever is up and about. Then, if it isn't a sunny day, go back to bed for a couple of hours.

13.00 – Up for lunch, followed by replying to my mail. I always thought if people took the trouble to write, they deserved a reply. After that, I picked the oldies (including songs for the Beach Boys and Beatles spots) for the next day's show and sorted out listeners requests and dedications.

Quite often, I would have another show to host for a DJ on shore leave. That was usually either 15.00-18.00 or 18.00 -21.00.

If it was the afternoon, I'd have dinner at 18.00. That was always the best attended meal as usually nobody was sleeping then.

In the evening, we'd sit in the lounge watching TV. Remember, in 1967, there was no daytime TV and there were no video players. The worst thing about that was having to keep going onto the top deck and rotating the TV aerial to shore when the ship turned around and we lost reception. It could be rather dangerous in a force 8 gale!

I used any spare time doing production for jingles and promos. I think that was what made the DJs sound so good. All we were concentrating on was making great radio with no distractions. We were always discussing how we could improve the output.

In all honesty, I was never bored.

The highlight of the week was the arrival of the supply tenders from Holland with a change of crew and DJs, plus water and fuel and sacks of listeners' mail. Johnnie Walker had the most fan mail, but we all did very well. I used to read every letter and replied to most of them. The lovely thing is that so many from those days still write to me, although now it tends to be email. I am so lucky to have such loyal listeners who have stuck by me over the years. I regard them as friends rather than fans.

Probably the best thing to raise our spirits was Frinton Flashing. Being so cut off from land, sometimes we wondered how many people were listening. So Johnnie used to do Frinton Flashing every night. The entire coastline filled with listeners' cars flashing their headlights as he asked questions live on air. For example, he might ask, "Flash if you're alone in your car. Okay, flash twice if there are two of you in your car." And so on. He ended up having a conversation with his audience via the listeners' car headlights, and often it was very funny the way the conversations developed. It certainly boosted morale.

My first week off came at the beginning of September, and I decided to go to Spain for some sun. It was the resort of Calella, 40miles or so up the coast from Barcelona. While there, I experienced a most amusing situation. One night in the bar, there was the usual 'what do you do for a living?' routine. I'd drunk too much San Miguel, which loosened my tongue, and when I revealed what I did and who I was, one of the group said he had been to a local disco where there was a DJ called Roger Day from Radio Caroline. The next night, I thought it would be fun to check it out, and after a few beers, I found the disco and approached the other Roger Day and asked him to play me a record. I can still see the look on his face when he asked me my name. The next night, he was using a different identity.

Back on Radio Caroline, the staffing problems were gradually improving. We were joined by Carl Mitchell from New York, a draft dodger who didn't want to go to fight in Vietnam. He had no radio experience but took to broadcasting like a natural and hosted the after midnight show. Known as the Weird Beard. 'Bud' Ballou did have US radio experience. A Kiwi, Glenn Adams joined us from a San Francisco broadcasting school. Others who came on board but left very quickly were Stevie Gee and Ray Cooper.

Spangles Muldoon was an outrageous character. He'd once changed his name to Herb Oscar Anderson because he had heard a radio jingle with that name on it. That didn't last long, but it was typical of a man who was always coming up with crazy ideas. One time, he decided to take a shortcut to the ship after a week's shore leave, stole a rowing boat from Clacton-on-Sea, and rowed out to the ship. The captain was less than pleased and wanted to send him back. Fortunately, we persuaded him that it wasn't a good idea. My favourite Spangles story was when we had our regular visit from the Viking Saga boat full of Caroline fans. He decided to swim to the boat. Now, the only time when it was safe to swim off the Mi Amigo was when the tide direction was changing and there was no current. When Spangles dived in, the sea was doing something completely different, and soon he was heading in the direction of Holland. The captain of the Viking Saga saw this situation and headed off after him. The Marine Offences Act meant that the Saga could hover close to us but wasn't allowed any contact, so hauling him back on board the Mi Amigo wasn't an option. Therefore, they threw him a line and towed him back to the ship. The only problem was that the force of the current had removed his shorts! We took great pleasure in dangling him out of the water on the rope so that he was mooning to those on board the anoraks' boat. I remember some mothers shielding their children's eyes from this alternative version of Frinton Flashing.

Other DJs who joined us included Andy Archer, who had been On Radio City for a short time, and Stevie Merike from Radio Scotland.

I think we had a really strong team of great personalities. Many of those who went left because they couldn't take to the strange offshore life. One whose name I can't remember used to get high on LSD. We found him on deck when he was just about to go over the side, saying he was going to walk to Frinton. For his own safety, we locked him in his cabin and sent him off on the next tender.

I first remember meeting Andy Archer, or Agatha as I called him, on the tender boat from Ijmuiden. He was very shy and reserved. He would later become a wonderful broadcaster and one of Radio Caroline's most loyal servants. Andy is a friend to this day. He was very popular with the ladies, who loved him playing Ray Conniff, even though he loved Country Joe and the "F...ing Fish" as he used to call them. He had a wicked sense of humour. Of course, we were always trying to play jokes on each other, particularly when we had to read the news. My best wind up with Andy was saying, "Here is the news with Aida Camp." He really struggled to read the news straight-faced. I would go on to work with Andy on other occasions later, as you will discover.

To relieve the boredom on board, we were always playing pranks. Trying to put the news reader off was a regular jape. I remember one day I was reading the news and heard the door open so knew something was up. It was one of the Dutch crew, who unzipped his trousers and took out his todger. You will be surprised to know I did keep a straight face and managed to read my bulletin. But afterwards, I chased him round the deck with a fire extinguisher.

The best wind up of all was with Johnnie Walker. He hated anyone being in the studio during his show and usually locked the door. So we devised a wicked plan. During the day, we set up the vacuum cleaner so that the hose was hidden out of site but near the microphone. We traced the lead under the carpet to the dining area next door, connected to the vacuum cleaner, which we had filled with cooking flower. It was one of those machines that could suck as well as blow. We waited till Johnnie got to the part of his show where he said goodnight to one of his many female listeners, got very passionate, and then began to introduce his usual - Percy Sledge Warm and Tender Love. At that point, we turned the vacuum cleaner on. All you could hear was JW coughing and spluttering and the record starting suddenly. The door flew open, and Johnnie was standing there looking like the silent movies when Oliver Hardy gets covered in something. I wish we had recorded it.

I always thought Stevie 'Marjorie' Merike wanted to be a singer rather than a DJ, but that didn't mean he wasn't a good broadcaster. I shared a cabin with him Carl Mitchell was a really good friend with a wicked laugh and sense of humour. I probably saw less of him than anyone on board as his show was after midnight, so we had different sleep patterns. He was so lucky because he didn't have to play the dreadful plug records.

Bud Ballou was the DJ with the most experience, having worked on radio in the USA. He was a very slick operator. All but Carl Mitchell, Spangles Muldoon, and

Robbie Dale are still with us, and we all keep in touch.

As the end of September approached, we were getting ready for the launch by the BBC of Radio One and trying to work out how it would affect us. We knew they had a great line up of DJs but had no idea how it would impact what we did. Caroline head office decided that Johnnie Walker was a bigger name than me and would provide stronger opposition to Tony Blackburn's Radio One breakfast show. I was moved off the slot. There was only one problem. JW loved doing that wonderful late-night show, and when he moved to breakfast, he found it difficult to get up early and sound awake. He did actually oversleep a couple of times. So after a few days, the message came out - get Twiggy back on breakfast, and there I stayed to take on TB for listeners.

Radio One started on a Saturday, and as luck would have it, our generator decided to pack up the day before, so on that most important of days, we weren't on air. Morale hit rock bottom as we listened to the opening of the station designed to replace the pirates. But when we listened to their shows, we just looked at each other and said in unison, "No problem there, boys!" Even with the crap plug records, we knew we could give them a good run for their money.

I bent the rules a little in the battle for listeners. Knowing that Tony started his show at 7 am, I crammed the worst of the plug records before that hour. I made sure I had the best songs between 7 am and 9 am. I guess I've been breaking the management rules ever since. I never got criticised from head office, though. I must admit, I loved the challenge of fighting Tony for listeners as I am a huge fan of Blackburn. I used to listen to him and dreamed of working with him.

We got letters from listeners saying they tried radio One but thought we were better. We even had letters from people containing money to the equivalent of the BBC licence fee. They said as they don't listen to the BBC; they would rather we had it! Even though we had the sometimes really bad plug records, our listeners were very loyal. I think they were also angry that the government wanted to close us down, so were determined to support us.

On shore leave in October, I met up with my fiancé, Anne, who had been responsible for starting me on my journey to Caroline. She journeyed across by ferry from Dover to Ostend, where I met her. I think deep down we both had a feeling that things were at a difficult stage, and it ended with her giving me an ultimatum. It was either her or the job. Well, there was no way anything was going to get in the way of my dream, and we decided to end it. I gather she married and has been happy ever since, which is great. I shall always be grateful to her for getting me started.

Of course, after the British Government passed the MOA (Marine Offences Act), we were based in Holland. We shared a house in Amsterdam, and whoever was on shore leave used it. You can imagine the state of the place with all of us single guys there. Sometimes, it was like a night out with Keith Moon of The Who, and there was even one occasion when a bathtub was thrown out of the window. It was a great city for a young man, and having been stranded on a boat for weeks with nowhere to go and no women, we made the most of the clubs and bars there. You could always find somewhere to get a drink. And before you ask, I never tried the Red Light District.

As much as I loved it in Holland, I missed England, and on my first shore leave in November, I decided to fly home. I didn't tell anybody because none of us had done it since the MOA and I thought management might try to stop me. When I flew into Heathrow, I was pretty damn worried, although my real name on the passport is not the name you know me by. Unfortunately, the customs guy asked me to open my case. Inside, I had brought a lot of my fan letters home to show mum and dad how popular their son was. Out of my case fell the letters addressed to Roger Twiggy Day, Singel 160 Amsterdam.

The customs officer picked up a bunch of letters and said, "What's all this, then?"

I replied, "Oh, letters from friends.

His response was, "I wish I had as many friends as you," and shut the case.

"Aren't you going to arrest me," I asked.

"We've got better things to do than arrest DJ's, and we all think it's a stupid law. Play me a record when you go back on." So, I was the first to test the law, and after I told the rest of the guys, they all flew back on shore leave.

About this time, I set up a fan club, which I told listeners was run by Doris Day. It was actually my dad. We had pens, badges, pictures, and newsletters.

I continued on this level until March 1966 when on my 21st Birthday I met Dave Cash of Big L fame, who put me on to two chaps who were starting a new offshore station called Radio England. After a successful audition I was hired by them, in fact I was the first English D.J. they hired. I couldn't wait to get to work on the Monday morning and gave my notice in and despite a lot of doom talk from workmates I left the following Friday.

After weeks of waiting and learning all about studio equipment in May 1966 I went on the air for the first time, once again nervous but very happy to be a disc jockey on the Radio, and the first record I played was Neil Christian's "That's Nice".

I spent seven very happy months on Radio England. I learnt a lot and gained some very good friends, and during that time I compered a nationwide tour starring the Small Faces which I enjoyed tremendously. Then on the 14th November came one of the saddest days of my life. Radio England closed down due to many things but mainly lack of Publicity and bad management.

I was the last D.J. to be heard on the air as I was the only one left of the original D.J.s who had started that day in May. Disillusioned with the scene I toured around the dance halls again for some months, until I was successfully auditioned for Radio Caroline and on July 21st/22nd at Midnight Roger Day was back on the Air Waves, the first record I played being the last one I played on Radio England, The Beach Boys "Your so good to me".

Now to the nickname of "Twiggy" and how I got it. One day I was walking around in my swimming trunks when one of the Dutch crew said "Oh look, he is as thin as Twiggy". So from that day it stuck, and then followed the Thinner Record Spinner tag. Well, that's the story up to now. I'll keep you up to date in the following newsletters with what's happening to me, so next time you see the name Day be warned. Beware, but most of all be there.

### hi, hello, how are you

This is your Thinner Record Spinner Roger (Twiggy) Day welcoming you to the Daydreamers Club and I hope you will have satisfaction from it.

For some time now my weekly mail has been building up until now it is too much for me to answer personally as I would like to.

So I have formed this club so that you can find out all about me, and just what I am getting up to.

If there is anything that you would like to know about me that isn't in the club literature, and I hope I have put most of it down, don't hesitate to write to G.P.O. Box 1, Margate, but please send an S.A.E. as without it I can't promise a reply.

Right, now that's done with I would like to say thanks very much for the support that you have given me in the past. It really has been appreciated.

**roger day**

*I sent cards to all members*

*Mum and Dad(Doris), who ran the Fan Club*

Christmas 1967 on board the Mi Amigo was different to any other Christmas I'd had. I'd never spent a Christmas away from home before. Our Christmas bonus from Radio Caroline director and owner of the Major Minor record label, Philip Solomon, was white pullovers. We didn't want to be ungrateful, but it did not go down well. We took a picture of us throwing the jumpers over the side of the ship.

On Christmas Eve, the captain got out the Geneva gin. It's a very powerful Dutch drink, about 50% alcohol by volume, and as a result, on Christmas Day, I had to do Stevie Merike's show because he wasn't in a fit state.

I was quite merry but the most sober of the team. On the breakfast show, I got all the Dutch crew to say hi to their families. That was ok until Harry the Mouse, as he was known, used the opportunity to say some Dutch words roughly translated as making love to a chicken! I did get a lot of letters from Dutch listeners saying it was the funniest thing they had ever heard. The cook put on a really great Christmas dinner, and I can honestly say it was one of the most unusual yet enjoyable festive days I'd ever had.

About this time, Gerry Burke returned to the station to be Head of News, as he had been prior to the MOA. It was a great relief to us all. He used the name Henry Morgan. Johnnie used his voice on air as Bill the Boiler Man.

January was a very stormy month, and the weather loosened the massive mast aerial on the deck. Thankfully, a welder got to us before it fell down. During storms, I used to sit on the bridge and watch the huge waves roll over the ship. For some reason, I never felt scared, although it was always nice when the gales subsided. During the bad weather, our supply tender vessel, Offshore 1, had to journey round to the Isle of Man to Radio Caroline North to get diesel and water to them, as their normal and much smaller tender vessel couldn't operate in rough seas. It meant we in the south didn't get a supply of anything for two weeks, and as a result, water was rationed. Luckily, there was no shortage of beer aboard. It was a good job we had no visitors during that period. The worst shortage of all though was record player styli. We got to the point where we were about to run out of them.

People often ask how we stopped the record arms from skipping during heavy weather. The answer was quite simple – placing a coin on the turntable arm. The rougher the weather, the heavier the coin. In a really bad storm, a half a crown did the trick.

By now, we had settled into a routine and thought we were doing ok. Listeners loved us, and there were enough plug records to pay the bills, or so we thought. But it wasn't so, and it came to an abrupt and shocking end on March 3rd 1968.

I got up, as usual, at 5 am and headed for the shower just as a Dutch tug, the Titan, was pulling up alongside the Mi Amigo. There was nothing unusual about that, as the crews worked for the Weissmuller company, who supplied the Caroline crew and would drop by if they were passing for a chat and coffee or beer. Some of the tug crew had worked on the Mi Amigo, and I asked them where they were going. The reply was they were towing us to Japan. That's a funny joke, I thought, and continued getting ready, then headed to the studio. I was sitting in the air chair, ready to play my theme tune, when the captain of the Mi Amigo and the tug boat captain came and said, "Turn the music off!" They then turned to the engineer and said to him, "Turn the transmitter off." I asked them what I should say on air, and they indicated very forcibly that I wasn't to say anything. They added that I had one hour to clear the studio. I have often thought I should have just opened the mike and said,

"Help, we are in trouble!" That moment has troubled me quite often over the years. They wouldn't even let us contact our man onshore at Frinton-on-Sea.

The transmitter was turned off, and I threw a lot of paperwork over the side that the authorities would like to have seen no doubt. If only I'd had the sense to remove some of the equipment, but at that moment, I thought we would return.

The captain asked those of us who were awake to get all those on board into the mess room. Once they were assembled, he informed us that the ship was being towed to Amsterdam but wouldn't tell us why. The anchor chain was cut, and the slow journey across the North Sea began. The chain being cut was an indication to me that we weren't coming back. If we were going to return, they would have put it on a buoy. Many tears were shed as most of us realised that this might be the end. It was a terrible atmosphere.

We arrived at Amsterdam the next evening, where DJ Robbie Dale was waiting on the dockside with George O'Hare, the guy who paid us. Robbie also had no idea what was happening. We were given the wages we were owed, tickets to England, and told to wait for news. I packed all my belongings as I had a feeling I wouldn't be coming back. I do regret not staying in Holland for a few days to await for the Radio Caroline north ship to get there, as I had never seen it.

I returned to the UK and rented a bed sit in Archway near Finsbury Park in London. I wanted to be ready, waiting for any news of the station returning.

When I discovered the Mi Amigo had been towed in because of unpaid bills, I got very angry. I'm sure if they'd allowed me to announce on air that we needed money, listeners would have helped us to stay broadcasting. It was all very avoidable. I know most of our listeners were as upset as we were. We really felt we were more than a radio station - we were part of a family.

After a few weeks, there was an attempt to get back off the coast on the Radio 270 ship, but somebody with a loose tongue leaked it to the papers and the authorities impounded the ship. I never did find out who betrayed us. And that was that. After plans to use the Radio 270 ship were scuppered, I knew it was the end. Next to my parents dying, it was the worst day of my life.

I often get asked what would I have done if Radio Caroline had continued. The answer is easy. I would still be there. It was the happiest time of my life, and I never wanted to leave. We were paid very well – about £30 a week – which meant, with two weeks on board and one week off, it was £90 to spend ashore in Amsterdam.

### My Caroline Timeline

Friday July 21st– First Day. 3 hours on air First Sureshot Spencer Davis Time Seller
July 30th- Shore leave
August 7th- Back on board
Aug 14th– 3 hours on air then off to Harwich
Shore leave

Aug 21st- Tender from Holland Ijmuiden. Monday was always from there.

September 13th- 6 hours on air then the tender to Holland Schevenigen.

Holiday in Spain

Sept 27th– Tender to ship

Sept 28th–On air

October 10th- Tender to Holland

Oct 16th- Tender to Ship

Oct 17th- On air

Oct 31st- Tender to Holland. Flew to the UK

November 6th- Tender to ship

Nov 7th- On air

December 1st- Off on Tender. Had been longer on board as Offshore had to go to Caroline North to top up water and oil as the northern tender from Ireland had smaller tanks. Flew to England.

Dec 11th- Tender back

Dec 12th- On air

Dec 27th - Tender off. Flew to the UK

January 3rd1968- Tender to Holland

Jan 4th- On air

Jan 22nd- Off. Flew to England

Jan 29th- Tender to ship

Jan 30th- On air

February 13th- Off. Flew To England

On what was to be my last shore leave, I had been to Margate to see my parents. I was returning to Heathrow Airport to fly back to Holland, and with me was my good friend Davey, lead singer of Davey Sands and The Essex, when his car broke down, causing me to miss my flight to Holland. Also in the car was his fiancé, and once the car was fixed he said after he'd taken her home to Elstree, he'd take me to his flat, where I could spend the night. It was at his fiancé's house that I met her sister, Jenny. I was attracted to her immediately and asked her for a date the next time I was in England. She agreed.

Feb 19th- Tender to ship

March 2nd- Last breakfast show, although didn't know at the time. Just said we would be off air Monday as the generator needed maintenance.

Last song: Beach Boys, 'You're So Good To Me'. As The Listeners had been.

# Radio Caroline put off DJ 'test' plan

RADIO Caroline, only pirate station to defy the Marine Offences Act which silenced all other pirates at midnight on August 14, have not received any complaint or communication from British Government sources since that date.

But because of continual Press publicity, Caroline have called off "for the time being" a plan to put one of their deejays ashore in England to test the prosecution threats outlined in the Bill.

"We are waiting until things have quietened down completely and then we will do this," Caroline spokesman Pinky Siedenburg told Disc on Tuesday.

Together with her secretary Raymonde Bloemkolk, Dutch girl Pinky is running Caroline's Amsterdam office alone. "Ronan O'Rahilly is forever moving around the Continent, collecting advertising which is mostly French and German," added Pinky. "Tell Disc readers that morale on both the South and North ships is very good and we are getting a lot of letters, not only from Britain, but all over Europe."

# TV SHIP STAYS BY RADIO CAROLINE

RADIO CAROLINE

**Evening Standard Reporter**

A seven-man team from Granada Television were back alongside the pirate radio ship Caroline South off Harwich today—less than 24 hours after being warned that they could be arrested if they boarded the station.

The camera team, from the World in Action programme, are now awaiting legal advice as to whether they can or cannot film material about Caroline's founder Ronan O'Rahilly aboard the pirate ship.

The team were banned from landing at Felixstowe last night—because the dock company "might well be contravening the law of the land by allowing the vessel in."

Said Mr. O'Rahilly in London today: "I really can't believe what I'm reading. I think the Government must be going quackers. When will it reach an people just how far this man Wilson will go?"

'Last freedom'

"The question of the Press is the one last freedom we have in this country, and now it looks as if journalists are going to be arrested. We had a warning about it with the "D" notice row. Soon we'll be saying "Help Ronan it is in Czechoslovakia."

"I hope Heywoon goes ahead and makes this stand. Radio Caroline is totally legal—Radio

# RIDDLE OF RADIO CAROLINE SHIPS

**By SALLY MOORE**

MYSTERY surrounded Radio Caroline, the outlawed pop pirate station, last night when both its ships vanished from their moorings.

The two stations, last of the ten which once broadcast off Britain's coast, had been off the air during the day.

Then came a dramatic report from coastguards at Walton-on-the-

## Last of the pop pirates vanish

Naze, Essex, that the Caroline South ship, Mi Amigo, moored four miles out to sea, had sailed off.

"She's gone from the area and we don't know where to," said one coastguard.

And just before dusk Caroline North, moored off the Isle of Man, was mysteriously towed south out of Ramsey Bay by the ocean-going Dutch tug Utrecht.

A boatman who visited the Utrecht yesterday said: "The cap-

tain has been told to steam south and await further instructions.

"The disc jockeys didn't seem to know what was going on or why they were moving. But they seemed pretty pessimistic about the future."

A GPO spokesman in London said: "We shall be investigating the possibility that the stations have closed down for good."

Caroline North went off the air on Saturday night, followed by the Southern station at 6 a.m. yesterday.

One of the Southern disc jockeys announced last week that the station might be undergoing repairs to a generator.

But last night there was no reply from the Amsterdam offices where Caroline moved when Parliament outlawed the pirates last August.

### Fans

Last night, scores of Radio Caroline fans phoned the Free Radio Association at Rayleigh, Essex.

One of the association's officers, 19-year-old Jonathan Northam, said: "We sincerely hope that isn't the end of Radio Caroline —but at this moment it looks like it is."

Caroline North and South, the first of the pirates, began broadcasting in March, 1964.

---

# CAROLINE: the sounds of silence . . .

ON GOOD FRIDAY this year Radio Caroline would have celebrated her fourth anniversary. Four years of free radio broadcasting, during which time dozens of new household names were created.

Simon Dee, Tony Blackburn, Johnnie Walker, Keith Skues, Norman St. John, Wayne Furbish, Peter Taylor, Stuart Quo and many, many others all openly admit that Caroline contributed greatly to their success.

Today the dial is silent on 259 metres, and the chances of Caroline's music ever reaching your transistor again grow slimmer by the day.

Her disc-jockeys are sad, disillusioned men, yet only a month ago they were talking excitedly of passing new landmarks and being entirely confident.

"Caroline will never die," Robbie Dale told me brightly just three days before she so mysteriously went off the air.

Those boats are as solid as rocks and nothing and nobody can stop us now." Sad words these — and ironic too, for Robbie was in Spain on Sunday morning, March 3, 1968, when at 5.20 am Caroline was heard, probably for the very last time.

The commentators surrounding the silencing of both North and South boats are still not fully explained—a hazy story is all that can be pieced together from all the 'phone calls and rumours.

When the two Dutch tugs arrived, unheralded and unnoticed, and proceeded to tow the ships slowly into Amsterdam harbour, not one disc-jockey on board knew what

ROGER DAY    JOHNNIE WALKER

was going on—and now, even a week later, they are still very much in the dark.

"I really wish I knew what was happening and what I'm supposed to do now," says Andy Archer.

"You probably know more than I do," says Roger Day.

"I've got the feeling I won't be heard on that boat again," says "Daffy" Don Allen.

"I don't know anything until I get back from Spain next week," says Johnnie Walker.

Even Caroline's main spokesman, founder Ronan O'Reilly, has lost his usual bubbling optimism which has kept the station alive through many previous storms.

When I asked him what message he could pass on to Caroline's faithful listeners, he said: "I can only say that I'm very sorry I could not give them further reassurance for ever —but there's a man by the name of Wilson who has now succeeded in messing up every sort of pleasure the teenage public could ever have. That is really where it's at.

"The two boats are currently being inspected by assessors for the insurance company, and

their decision will decide the future of the station. I fully and completely unable to say when Caroline will resume broadcasting, or whether it ever will."

Ronan sounded a tired, disappointed man.

Most of the Caroline DJs are now back in England, in sombre mood until such time as they know they can either go back to the ship, or come out into the open and look for other jobs.

They all feel a deep sense of failure towards Caroline's millions of faithful listeners—listeners who had loyally the idea of which I had never seen before. Pop stars have fans, film stars are jobless, but this fervour is negligible compared with the Caroline following.

For nearly six months Disc readers' mailbag has been filled with letters about the station. These doubled when I wrote the first article on Johnnie Walker, and the continued popularity of the station was further reflected in the results of our Valentine Awards Poll.

There is a small consolation for the Caroline boys. The GPO has indicated that it does not intend to prosecute them, but is content to require us for knowledge that in Marine Offences Bill is now fully effective.

I would guess that the GPO are the only ones rejoicing at this news, though British people are famous for their sympathy with the underdog, and Caroline's spirit to the fore of such enormous obstacles created a feeling in young and old listeners alike which can only be compared with the feeling of Londoners in the blitz.

And Ronan O'Reilly, the man who started it all in my opinion he will not give up. Ronan fought almost to his last penny to keep the principle of Caroline alive, and I doubt if he's finished yet.

But Caroline as we know her, unless a miracle can save her, is dead. And pop music will never be quite the same again.

---

## DAVID HUGHES joins in the mourning at the death of '259'

---

DISC AND MUSIC ECHO
VALENTINE NIGHT BALL
1968
PRESENTATION OF
DISC AND MUSIC ECHO
POP POLL AWARDS

Ray Coleman cordially invites

*The 10th Top Jock in England*
*Roger "Twiggy" Day*

to attend a reception at the Disc and Music Echo Valentine Night Ball for the presentation of the 1968 Pop Poll Awards at the Empire Rooms 161, Tottenham Court Road, London, W.1. on Wednesday February 14th, between 7.30 p.m. and 11.30 p.m.

R.S.V.P. to Disc and Music Echo 161/166, Fleet Street, London, E.C.4.

*My first award. But I couldn't attend as I was on the ship. Just as well, as I might have been arrested.*

AS TOP POPS goes to press the future of the sole pirate radio ship on the air since the Marine Offences Bill remains shrouded in mystery.

Has Caroline's fight to remain on the high seas failed?

Or have the ships, as was claimed, merely returned to port for re-fitting?

Whatever the answer, one thing is sure—the Caroline disc jockeys have developed into folk heroes for their thousands of listeners.

While TOP POPS was on the Continent recently we visited Amsterdam to meet two of the D.J.s spending their one-week-in-three ashore.

They were Andy Archer left, and Roger Day, right.

## CAROLINE CRISIS

ROGER DAY, being so deeply involved, has some strong personal feelings regarding the whole Caroline situation and comments: "Despite everything that's happened we still have a massive listening audience, strongly enough, we still broadcast to more people in England than on the Continent...

# Caroline silenced for ever say GPO

### By PHILIP PHILLIPS

RADIO CAROLINE, the last of the pop pirates, may never be heard again. Post Office experts monitoring the programme have told the Government that advertising is not covering the estimated running costs of £1,000 a week.

The station's two ships, Caroline South and Caroline North, went off the air on Sunday.

Caroline's owner, Mr. Ronan O'Rahilly, said then that both ships were being towed to Holland for dry-dock examination.

Yesterday, Caroline South berthed at Amsterdam. A crew member said that both ships were to return to their positions after an overhaul.

#### Cloak-and-dagger

At Mr. O'Rahilly's home in Bayswater, London, there was something of a cloak-and-dagger atmosphere.

When I called there, a man shouted from behind a locked door that 28-year-old Mr. O'Rahilly was in Holland.

Some time after, a woman let herself in and later said that Mr. O'Rahilly was in London.

At Mr. O'Rahilly's Bond Street offices, his secretary said: "Officially I know nothing about Radio Caroline but I suppose it is right to say that they will be broadcasting again."

In Holland, an insurance agent said the ships had been ordered to come to Amsterdam for a check on seaworthiness.

# WHY CAROLINE SWITCHED OFF

RONAN O'RAHILLY

A SLIP of paper may finally silence Radio Caroline, the pirate station which survived the Government's Marine Broadcasting (Offences) Act.

The paper is an insurance cover note which the two Caroline ships will get only if they are seaworthy.

This is the real reason for the abrupt disappearance of Caroline from the air two weeks ago.

# Radio Caroline mystery—pirate chief speaks

Pirate radio chief Ronan O'Rahilly today scotched rumours that he had given up the fight to keep Radio Caroline on the air.

TREVOR DANKER

# THE TRAGEDY OF CAROLINE

The pirates in harbour; Mi Amigo (Caroline South) and Frederika (North).

*In the Singel 160 Amsterdam Office*

*On a return visit to Holland*

*Outside the Dutch Office Singel 160*
*with Morris Brown. On a later visit.*

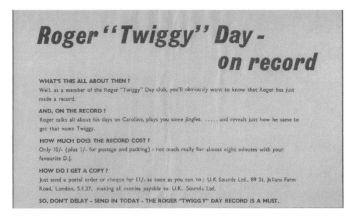

# Roger "Twiggy" Day -
## on record

**WHAT'S THIS ALL ABOUT THEN ?**
Well, as a member of the Roger "Twiggy" Day club, you'll obviously want to know that Roger has just made a record.

**AND, ON THE RECORD ?**
Roger talks all about his days on Caroline, plays you some jingles. ...... and reveals just how he came to get that name Twiggy.

**HOW MUCH DOES THE RECORD COST ?**
Only 10/- (plus 1/- for postage and packing) - not much really for almost eight minutes with your favourite D.J.

**HOW DO I GET A COPY ?**
Just send a postal order or cheque for 11/- as soon as you can to : U.K. Sounds Ltd., 89 St. Julians Farm Road, London, S.E.27, making all monies payable to U.K. Sounds Ltd.

**SO, DON'T DELAY - SEND IN TODAY - THE ROGER "TWIGGY" DAY RECORD IS A MUST.**

*My one and only record*

# CHAPTER 9

# RADIO LUXEMBOURG

When it became obvious that Radio Caroline wasn't coming back, I arranged an audition with the great Radio Luxembourg 208. It was on Monday 6th May at 3.30 pm. I had to introduce 10 records.

That week, I also had three discos – at Felixstowe on Thursday May 9th, on Saturday at The Cavalier Club in Golders Green, and on Tuesday 14th in Henlow in Bedfordshire.

A few weeks later, much to my surprise, I was invited to meet the managing director of Radio Luxembourg, Geoffrey Everett. Nervously, I sat down in the front of this radio big wig, who looked like the Harris Tweed comic character. Anyway, he offered me the job, and on Thursday 30th May, I was on a flight to the Grand Duchy.

As usual, my local paper, the Isle of Thanet Gazette, supported me with the headline, 'Margate's Top DJ Moves to 208'.

# MARGATE'S TOP D.J. MOVES TO '208'

AFTER TWO YEARS in the record business, 'Margate's own' disc jockey, Roger Day, has reached the top. This week he starts working for Radio Luxembourg.

Roger Day, of Canterbury Road, Margate, is 21 years old. He attended Chatham House Grammar School and has always had a great interest in records.

Two years ago he started as a disc jockey touring round dance halls, and this built up until he was working almost every night of the week.

His first big break came when, in March 1966, on his 21st birthday, he met Dave Cash, who arranged for Roger to take a job as a d.j. with Radio England.

Roger said : "After many weeks of waiting and learning, I first went on the air in May, and I remember that the first record I

ever played on Radio England was Neil Christian's 'That's Nice.'

"When Radio England closed down, I again started touring around the dance halls as a disc jockey, and then I was offered an audition for Radio Caroline. I started in July and I had my programme at midnight. My first disc this time was the Beach Boys' 'You're So Good To Me.' "

## OUTLAWED

When the pirate radio stations were outlawed, Roger decided he would stay on with Radio Caroline and he lived in Holland.

Last week the big break which every disc jockey must long for came to Roger. His agent, Roger Squires, arranged an audition with Radio Luxembourg.

On Thursday he flew out to Luxembourg, where he was shown round round the station.

Radio Luxembourg, or, as it is commonly known, '208. The Station of the Stars,' broadcasts popular music over most of the Continent. The station features such disc spinners as Jimmy Saville, Mike Raven and David Jacobs.

Roger, who, because he is 6ft. tall and rather lean, has the nickname of Roger "Twiggy" Day, will be broadcasting from 1.40 a.m. until 3 a.m. each day.

His programme has been estimated to have the largest audience and he will be playing the quieter beat records.

His parents, Mr. and Mrs. B. Day, said this week they were extremely pleased at the opportunity which Roger now has.

"This is a great step up for him and now he is with the top disc jockeys in the country. Although he will be living in

### ANDREW CLYMER WRITES ON TOPICS FOR TEENS AND TWENTIES

*Margate's Top DJ. Well, I was the only one!*

---

# 'TWIGGY' DAY JOINS 208 TEAM

ROGER "Twiggy" Day has been "legalised." He has been signed to join the Radio Luxembourg resident team of deejays and thus becomes the first of the Radio Caroline "rebels" to get a deejaying job ashore.

Twenty-three-year-old "Twiggy," who stayed aboard the defiant Caroline South ship until the station went off the air on March 3 this year, replaces Tony Murphy at 208, flying out to the Grand Duchy today (Thursday) where he will host the late night show between 12.40-3 a.m.

Luxembourg spokesman Don Wardell told Disc : "We do not visualise any trouble over signing Roger. If the British Government had wanted to do anything about the deejays who carried on with Caroline after August 14 last year (when the Marine Offences Bill became law) they would have done so long ago.

"Roger, incidentally, wrote to us for an audition—I make the point because we would be more than welcome to audition the other Caroline favourite, Johnnie Walker. It's up to him to approach us."

Roger told Disc before leaving for Luxembourg : "I wanted to work on land for a change! Seriously, I hung on in the hope that Caroline might come back, but things are so indefinite and I needed a job. Also, I've wanted to be a 208 deejay for as long as I can remember.

"Of course I'll still be isolated to some extent by being in Luxembourg, but the difference from Caroline will be that I shall be meeting people every day — instead of the same 10 old faces!"

## All ex-pirates

Signing of "Twiggy" means that Luxembourg will now have a complete ex-pirate resident line-up. The rest of the team are; Don Nichol (Caroline), Tony Price (Caroline), Paul Burnett (270 and Manx) and newscaster Paul Kay (London).

Coinciding with his arrival in the Grand Duchy, Roger also has a special record released through his fan club this week. In an eight-minute track, Roger talks about his days on Caroline, plays jingles and reveals how he came to collect his nickname. The disc is available only by post (11s) from UK Sounds, 89 St. Julians Farm Road, London. SE27.

---

OUR latest signing, Roger Day, has only been out in the Grand Duchy for a few weeks, but already the mail asking for lots of info on him is pouring into our office. One of the questions that seems to crop up quite often is "How did Roger Day get that nickname 'Twiggy'?"—so I put it to the man in question.

"Well, the name comes from when I was working with Caroline," said Roger. "It all happened on a super

*Roger Day*

hot day last summer. I was strolling around the decks just wearing a pair of bathing trunks and I noticed that one or two of the crew were having a bit of a giggle.

"Apparently, my ribs tend to show themselves quite a bit—so what with that and the fact that I'm fairly tall (5' 11") and slim, they decided that 'Twiggy' was an ideal nickname. Tell you the truth, I quite like it!"

And, so do we, mate.

*208 Publicity photo in Hyde Park*

Once, in Luxembourg, I was met by Colin Nicol, who I had worked with on Swinging Radio England, and he took me to the radio station situated in the middle of a lovely park right in the centre of the city. The other DJs were in the main office. There was Paul Burnet and Tony Prince. Tony had been hired like me because he was from Caroline and 208 wanted to adapt to the pirate style. Tony and I rented rooms at a house nearby. Also, there was the legendary news man from Big L, Radio London's Paul Kaye.

Colin was very kind and showed me around the city. At one stage while walking across a bridge, he told me it was one of the highest in Europe. As I am scared of heights, I virtually crawled along it.

The big-name DJs recorded their shows at 38, Hertford Street in London. So although I never met them, I worked with Pete Murray, David Jacobs, and Alan Freeman, and most of the other star DJs. Who would have thought that 50 years later, I would be on the same station as Pete?

I was expected to go to the office every afternoon to prepare my evening programme. I shall always remember my first visit to the record library. They had kept just about every single ever released. Being a record collector, I was in heaven and used to spend hours there preparing my shows. You could literally think of a record I hadn't heard for ages and it would be there. I had mostly free choice on the late-night programme but had to play certain records that the London office wanted. I discovered later on that the reason they got airtime was Luxembourg owned the publishing rights via a company called Villa Louvigny Music. One that springs to mind is Little Arrows by Leapy Lee. It was the equivalent of the plug records we had on Caroline.

My first programme was Saturday 1st June 1968 between 1.15 am and 3 pm. It was rather hair raising, as on the offshore stations, we operated our own desk, turntables, cart machines, and tapes. Here, I was in a huge room, which was far too big, and all I had was a microphone, headphones, and intercom to speak to the engineer in another room behind a large glass window and a speaker to hear him back. There was one other technical device – a button to press to play the famous Luxembourg chime. It was a thrill to play that for the first time. The engineer next door had my list of records I wanted to play, and I used hand signals to him as to when to fade the record and start the next one. It was very difficult to present a fast, seamless show, particularly as the engineer didn't speak any English. To this day, I never understood why they didn't only employ English-speaking technicians. The reason we couldn't self op. was because the unions had a stranglehold on the company. I did suggest that the DJ could operate the equipment and the engineer could just sit there and still get paid. But that didn't happen in my time. I always prided myself on being a real tight slick operator thanks to the training given to me by Ron O'Quinn. I started getting letters from listeners saying I didn't sound as good as I did on Caroline, which concerned me.

My great friend, Carl 'Weird Beard' Mitchell, came to visit me in Luxembourg from Holland. He liked his drink. I remember we were in a bar and suddenly Carl got up and spoke to a group of Germans who had been sitting near us. He spoke fluent German. It got rather heated, and they left. When I asked what had happened, he said they were taking the mickey out of my long hair and he'd said if they continued, he would take them outside and sort them out. Sadly, Carl is no longer with us. I did track him down in the 1990s and got a letter from his partner, who said he had died the previous year. He was such a lovely man and great company.

I didn't settle into living in Luxembourg. It is a beautiful country with many fine places to visit, but I soon got homesick and lonely. I guess Jenny being back in the UK didn't help. I was living in a rented room, where

The entrance to the station

The view from the studio. Bit different from the North Sea.

Paul Kaye and me(suited)

The engineer, Norbert, who fell asleep on me. How insulting.

Tony Prince, who had joined us, was also staying. I shall always remember June 6th 1968. I got back to the digs, and the landlady who couldn't speak English said, "Mr Kennedy Boom Boom!" pointing a finger like a gun to her head. What a silly woman I thought, and replied, "Oh that was years ago," but she repeated what she said. So I went to my room and turned on AFN to hear the awful news about Robert Kennedy. I thought, like everybody, "Those crazy idiots have done it again". I don't know how I managed to present the radio programme that night.

Before I went to Luxembourg, I didn't realise how expensive it was to live there. Although I was paid £40 a week, which was more than on Caroline, I had to be very careful with my spending.

Phone calls home were difficult. Thankfully, a fan of mine worked at a UK telephone exchange and used to get me free calls. I decided to propose to Jenny, and she accepted. We were married in Elstree on August 3rd 1968. It was just a small affair, with family and a few friends. My best man was Davey Sands, who I first met at Dreamland Ballroom in Margate when he played there with his group, The Essex. They played The Beach Boys type stuff and included Len 'Chip' Hawkes, who would go on to join The Tremeloes.

On the second day of our honeymoon, I thought the car had broken down as there was an awful smell. I looked under the bonnet to see one of my friends had put a fish on top of the engine.

I shall always remember the drive back to

It's your 'thinner record spinner' Roger Twiggy Day who's supplying all the answers this week. Twiggy hasn't been out in the Grand Duchy all that long, but he's already made loads of fans among you 208 listeners. So, here goes with the info . . .

Real name: Roger Malcolm Thomas.
Birthday: March 29th, 1945.
Birthplace: Cheltenham.
Colour of hair/eyes: Brown hair, hazel eyes.
Height: 5' 11".
Weight: 9½st.
Collar size: 14¼.
Shoe size: 9½.
Educated: Chatham House Grammar School. (Ted Heath went there, too!)
Previous jobs: Trainee Accountant.
Likes: Friendly people and country pubs.
Dislikes: Big heads.
Hobbies: Driving and swimming.
Fave colour: Blue.
Fave food: Curry.
Fave Dj: Kenny Everett.
Fave sport: Tiddlywinks.
Styles in clothes: Anything mod.
Tastes in music: Strictly pop. West coast in particular.
Car: Nothing at present.
Pets: I'm not giving her name away!
Toothpaste: Macleans.
Shampoo: Sunsilk for normal hair.
Ambition: To become a personal friend of my bank manager.

# WEDDING (TWIGGY) DAY

**R**OGER 'TWIGGY' DAY came in to see us at FAB-208 on the very eve of his recent wedding to Jenny Brown. I got quite worried before his arrival, expecting a nervous, twitching wreck and wondering whether I ought to arrange some medicinal brandy from the FAB nurse.

There was no cause for concern, however. Roger walked in dead on time and cool as a cucumber, looking very sharp in his trendy suit and modestly ruffled shirt. The only sign of inward disturbance he displayed was a mild complaint about how difficult it was to get a taxi during the London rush hour.

Roger is twenty-three, and was born in Margate. He's been engaged in broadcasting for over two and a half years now, starting as one of those naughty pirates with Radio Britannia and then Radio Caroline. Now he's an eminently respectable and respected Grand Duchy staff member of Radio Luxembourg.

I don't consider he really deserves that 'Twiggy' nickname, either. He got it during his time with Radio Caroline when he was rash enough to appear on deck in his swimming trunks to do some sun-bathing. This caused great hilarity amongst the Dutch crew members, one of whom christened him Twiggy on the spot, and the name has stuck ever since. Actually Roger isn't nearly so emaciated as Britain's famous model, and is considerably broader than our Cliff.

Not only was he not nervous about his impending nuptials, but also quite willing to talk about the momentous event.

"I'm marrying my best friend's fiancée's sister," he declared in complicated fashion, "and I'm very pleased about it. Her name's Jennifer, and she's coming back with me to Luxembourg at the end of my leave."

Roger had a comfortable apartment there ready for their return. It has a bedroom, lounge with balcony, kitchen and bathroom, and is "a very nice pad" according to its tenant. He's been living there during his bachelor days in the Grand Duchy.

"It'll be great with Jenny there," he prophesied. "I like messing about by myself and cooking things, but I wasn't very successful."

Roger doesn't mind living in Luxembourg, although he finds it different and quieter compared with England.

He reckoned Jenny's mini skirts would be a sensation there, and he's got used to people staring in the street at his long (by Grand Duchy standards) hair and coloured shirts.

**NIGEL HUNTER**

# IT'S LIKE LIVING IN THE 18th. CENTURY!

ROGER "TWIGGY" DAY met his wife over tea when he was on leave from Radio Caroline.

"My best friend, Davy Sands, a singer with a group took me to tea with his fiancee and her sister."

The sister was Jenny, a receptionist with a clothing firm. They started talking, and, for the first time in his life, Roger was able to relax talking to a girl.

"It sounds silly for a disc jockey to say this, but usually I get embarrassed trying to make conversation.

"With Jenny I didn't feel I had to put on an act to be interesting. She was the first girl I'd really been able to talk to.

"I had to go back on the ship, so the next time I was on shore I took her out to dinner. That fortnight, while I was on the ship, I found myself thinking about her a lot.

"She's fabulous. Long blonde hair and a very fair skin, about 5 ft 6in. tall and wears mod dresses and clothes.

"She's like me, really—basically shy—although that sounds ridiculous for a disc jockey, too. She's very hard to get to know, reserved."

For their first dinner date, they went to an Angus Steak House, near the London Hilton. Soon after that, they were able to see more of each other than they expected because pirate radio was stopped and Roger was grounded.

"I was doing the breakfast programme on Caroline, and she used to listen to me every morning. When Caroline was towed away no one knew what had happened. She couldn't pick anything up on her radio and she was worried.

"I flew back to England and the first thing I did when I got to Heathrow airport was ring her. I said, 'Hello' and she said, 'Who's that? . . . 'Me' . . . 'Who's you?' When she realised who it was, she collapsed laughing. She was very relieved.

"After that I waited around for Caroline to come back and when it didn't, I applied to Luxembourg for a job."

In the meantime, Roger went out with Jenny. Neither of them are violently social. They like to go to quiet country clubs, pubs and the cinema.

Roger likes driving and Jenny likes being driven, so they go out into the countryside on Sundays.

"My home is in Margate and we used to eat cockles and whelks. It was fun. Neither of us are ravers and we didn't go to clubs because they're noisy. We prefer a quiet restaurant."

Roger knew almost from the first time he met her that Jenny was the girl he would marry.

"I had a strange feeling on the first date about her, but I think three weeks after I'd met her I knew definitely.

"We talked it over and she accepted straight away. We were married five months later."

Now, they live in a flat in Luxembourg just ten minutes away from the studios. They have no home in England although Roger says he doesn't want to spend the rest of his life abroad. He would like to come home if he could work in this country.

"The locals here don't take to us very much," he said. "Jenny wears short dresses. She stops the traffic and so does my longish hair.

"It's a bit like the 18th century here, particularly the clothes shops. We wait until we're in England to buy a lot of our clothes.

"We write every week to our parents and phone now and then. Over here we don't mix much, only with the other dee-jays. We keep to ourselves.

"We go out shopping or go for a walk in the little square and have a drink at a cafe.

"Jenny does the housework and looks after me. I'm an unbearable character and selfish to match! She's very good at looking after me which she needs to be because I'm an untidy swine. If I drop something, I just leave it there.

"But she's always happy, which is what I need.

"I don't like to go home and find someone miserable. I get depressed sometimes. I often do a programme and feel nobody wants to know, nobody is listening.

"She says, 'Well—I was listening. Just that makes me feel better. She's my cheer leader.

"She's a fabulous cook and that's one of the wonderful things about coming home when I've been working late, particularly Jenny's Hot Pot which is a very special dish. I don't know what's in it. I daren't ask but my middle name won't apply much longer if I don't watch it."

Sometimes, they cross the border into Germany to go out for a meal. There are several Chinese restaurants a discotheque and cinemas across the German border.

"We were sitting in the pictures once and I said to Jenny, 'One of these days we'll slip up and the sound will be in German.' The picture started and it was in German. They'd dubbed German voices on to 'Divorce American Style.'

"In Luxembourg, it's completely dead. There's nowhere to go at all and it makes us very homesick for England.

"I think Jenny must miss it even more than I do because I've lived abroad before, in Holland and on the ship, but she's come straight from home to here, and it must have been quite a break. But this is where my work is, and we like to be together so that's it."

Luxembourg. My parents had given me their Triumph Herald as they had no need for it. So we loaded it up with a few possessions, including an ironing board on the roof rack, and headed back to a rather nice, rented apartment.

The only disadvantage of where we lived was it was in the same area as Paul Kaye. He was a lovely man but did like a drink. After work, we would sometimes walk home together. The trouble was that meant calling in at every cafe on the way for a glass of Reisling-Sylvaner, the local wine. He was clearly a regular, as they all knew his name. As I staggered through the door, Jenny would say, "Ah, walked home with Paul, did you?" One particular night, he had quite a few and was slurring and stumbling over the news. Afterwards, he said, "Those sods in London really don't know how to write decent scripts." I didn't have the guts to contradict him.

I often used to follow the great Alan 'Fluff' Freeman, whose show was recorded in the London Studios. He was meant to end at 12.40, a strange time to finish, but he was notorious for not finishing on time. Usually, my programme ended at 3 am. But one particular night, it was going off at 1 am and Alan ended at 12.53. So I went on and said, "Thanks, Alan, this is going to be the shortest programme in the history of Luxembourg" and just played Hey Jude by the Beatles. For that, I got a good telling off the next day.

The Luxembourg studios were where Lord Haw Haw, whose real name was William Joyce, broadcast anti-UK propaganda on behalf of the Nazis during the Second

World War. While wandering around the technical area, I saw some amplifiers that had valves with Swastikas on them. Hitler certainly lost the war, but those Germans knew how to make long-lasting valves!

The local cinema used to show English films with foreign subtitles, but on a couple of occasions, we struck unlucky as they had dubbed German on it. On our first trip, everyone left the cinema at the intermission, and we followed. We realised they'd all gone out to smoke, so us being non-smokers, we returned.

During the autumn of 1968, a new programme controller joined 208 from Australia to revamp the station. His name was Tony Macarthur, and I knew instantly he didn't like me. He said that pirate DJs never grew up and that they had long hair and no education. So when I was offered the chance to compere The Beach Boys 1968 tour of the UK, I asked for the time off. Unbelievably, he wouldn't grant me absence. I wasn't going to miss that opportunity, so I resigned. Apparently, I was only the second DJ to resign from Luxembourg. All the others who'd left were sacked. So while serving my notice, what came next was no surprise.

I went in the office one afternoon and the PC 'prize clown' met me and said, "Did you enjoy last night's show?" My reply was, "Yes of course," and his response was, "Good. It was your last." My last show was Thursday 17th October. I packed my stuff and left. We headed back to the UK. I wasn't pleased that I wasn't allowed to say my farewells on air.

Here's how I got the chance to compere The Beach Boys 1968 UK tour. FAB 208 magazine had printed a story that said my ambition was to compere a Beach Boys' concert. As a result, I received a phone call from someone saying they were from Arthur Howe's office, one of the largest talent agencies, and asking if I would like to compere The Beach Boys UK tour. I thought it was a friend of mine winding me up, so was rather off hand. When I realised it was a genuine call, I of course accepted. I guess the fact that I had played a Beach Boys record on every radio show helped. In fact, no other DJ in the world has played them more than me.

It's good to have worked on 208, but I can't say I enjoyed working there. After the freedom and rebellion of the ships, it was like the BBC with adverts. The strangest thing I did was the Bingo show, which was broadcast to bingo clubs around the UK. Still, at least I can say I worked with Horace Batchelor, that's Keynsham spelt K-E-Y-N-S-H-A-M.

Tony Prince said that I had actually told Radio Luxembourg's managing director, Geoffrey Everett, what was wrong with his station. I don't remember doing that, but I guess that didn't help my cause. Might have been a big mistake as the next step from 208 was Radio One. But that would have meant a lot of other things wouldn't have happened, and I don't think I would have been happy working for such a big organisation.

# BEACH BOYS: LIVE U.K. ALBUM

## PALLADIUM CONCERT TO BE RECORDED

THE Beach Boys are to record their entire performance on the first night of their nationwide tour at the London Palladium on December 1, and will release 12 numbers as a live LP at a later date.

The complete line-up for the package is the Beach Boys, Barry Ryan, Bruce Channel, Vanity Fare, Eclection, Sharon Tandy and compere Roger 'Twiggy' Day.

### Orchestra

At the Palladium, the Beach Boys will be accompanied by a 30-piece orchestra, and by a 12-piece on the rest of the tour.

This will be the first time the group have used other musicians on live appearances.

### Venues

Venues so far arranged after the Palladium are Colston Hall Bristol (2), City Hall Sheffield (4), Odeon Manchester (5), Odeon Birmingham (6), Capitol Cardiff (7), Finsbury Park Astoria (8), and Odeon Glasgow (10).

### Continent

Agent Arthur Howes, who represents the Beach Boys all over the world with the exception of America, has fixed a continental tour for the group immediately following the British tour.

They will visit Paris, Milan, Stockholm, Copenhagen, and

Roger "Twiggy" Day, the Margate disc jockey who graduated from the turntables in local dance halls to his own Radio Luxemburg show, will compere the Beach Boys for their London Palladium Show on 1 December.

The Beach Boys, one of America's top pop groups, will tour British dance halls with the Vanity Fair and Barry Ryan. Roger, whose home is at Canterbury Road, Margate, will be the compere and dee-jay at each engagement.

Roger will resume his Sunday Show and Late Night Final on Radio Luxemburg when the tour is finished.

# TICKET REQUESTS POUR IN FOR BEACH BOYS SHOW

LONDON PALLADIUM has already been inundated for tickets for the opening date of the Beach Boys tour on Sunday, December 1.

Beach Boys play two concerts at the world-famous London venue and will make a "live" recording with a 30-piece orchestra during the show for issue on the Capitol label. Also on the bill: Barry Ryan, Bruce Channel, Vanity Fare, Eclection, Sharon Tandy, Fleur de Lys.

Same Beach Boys bill follows on the Palladium date with two concerts at each of the following venues:

Colston Hall, Bristol (December 2); City Hall, Sheffield (4); Odeon, Manchester (5); Odeon, Birmingham (6); Capitol, Cardiff (7); Finsbury Park Astoria, London 18); and Odeon, Glasgow (9).

This time, a 12-piece band will accompany the Beach Boys to enable them to "recreate" their recorded sound," according to impresario Arthur Howes, who

BEACH BOYS: will make 'live' recording

# CHAPTER 10

# TOURING WITH THE BEACH BOYS

first met The Beach Boys at a reception in London's Hilton Hotel. I was very glad the hotel didn't remember that I'd worked for Radio England, who never paid for the party they'd had there.

Also at the reception was Tony Rivers of the wonderful Castaways and Harmony Grass, who became a good friend, even though he forgot to mention me in his book.

The tour started at the London Palladium, and to say I was nervous would be an understatement. I was looking at the people arriving at the theatre and saw some of The Beatles, The Who, and basically pop royalty. That didn't calm my anticipation. Bob Farmer of Disc & Music Echo was very unkind about me in his review of the show. I did get a big cheer when I mentioned Radio Caroline, which helped me relax. I didn't give a plug to Radio Luxembourg after the way they'd treated me. My relatives and friends were in the royal box.

The entire day was magic. I sat in the stalls

listening to the group practise with their English backing musicians, and I was in heaven. Also in the backing band was Daryl Dragon, who, thanks to Mike Love, was given the name Captain. Tony Tenille was also involved.

The Beach Boys' set list:

Darlin

Wouldn't It Be Nice

Sloop John B

California Girls

Do It Again

Wake the World

Aren't You Glad

Bluebirds Over The Mountain

God Only Knows

Encore

Good Vibrations

Barbara Ann

Young Man In Spring

They recorded a live album from their London gigs. It's the Live in London LP that says 1969, but it was actually 1968, and little old me is on it introducing my heroes.

The tour was a great success. My big one regret is that I never had a photo taken with The Beach Boys.

The group were friendly towards me, particularly Carl, who was a lovely, quiet man, and Bruce. But my favourite was Dennis. They say all drummers are mad, and he certainly lived up to that reputation. Every night, I would hear the tour manager shouting at him to put on his stage suit, which he wasn't keen on wearing.

The funniest moment was in Cardiff. Vanity Fare, my chums from Kent, were unloading their equipment and putting it on stage when Dennis appeared, obviously having been to the pub, and was helping Dick Alix the drummer carry his drums. I remarked that he was the most expensive roadie they would ever have.

After the Birmingham show, Andy Archer took me to the Lafayette Club in Wolverhampton, and who should be performing but Harmony Grass!

For the tour I wore clothes I had bought in Carnaby Street, the home of fashion. They included a blue velvet Regency suit, a white and red shirt with ruffles, and white flared trousers. When I met Bruce many years later, he actually remembered what I was wearing.

I do remember Gordon Coxhill from the Top Pops newspaper, who slagged everybody off except The Beach Boys. He saved his worst words for me, claiming I was unbelievably bad as compere: "His jokes were terrible and his introductions weren't much better." What a charming man.

When the tour was over, Jenny and I moved to our newly furnished flat in Surbiton, and I started trying to get some work.

ARTHUR HOWES LIMITED
EROS HOUSE,
29/31 REGENT STREET,
PICCADILLY CIRCUS,
LONDON, S.W.1.

TO REMIND YOU! PLEASE ACKNOWLEDGE RECEIPT

Artiste booked........ ROGER TWIGGY DAY

Date ........ Sun. Dec. 1st - 10th inc.

Theatre........ BEACH BOYS TOUR

Rehearsal time........ 3.0 p.m. Sun. Dec. 1st - Palladium
2.0

OWING TO THE BEACH BOYS RECORDING AN ALBUM
AT THE LONDON PALLADIUM ON SUND.DEC. 1st
THE RUNNING TIME FOR THE SUPPORTING PRO-
GRAMME IS TO BE CUT FOR BOTH SHOWS AND THE
TIMES ALLOTTED STRICTLY ADHERED TO.

BEACH BOYS TOUR 1968.
RUNNING ORDER & TIMING.
LONDON PALLADIUM ONLY.

| | | |
|---|---|---|
| 1. | SHARON TANDY WITH THE FLEUR DE LYS | 8 mins. |
| 2. | ROGER TWIGGY DAY | 3 mins. |
| 3. | VANITY FARE | 10 mins. |
| 4. | ROGER TWIGGY DAY | 3 mins. |
| 5. | BRUCE CHANNEL | 12 mins. |
| | INTERVAL | 10 mins. |
| 6. | ECLECTION | 10 mins. |
| 7. | ROGER TWIGGY DAY | 4 mins. |
| 8. | BARRY RYAN | 12 mins. |
| 9. | ROGER TWIGGY DAY | 3 mins. |
| 10. | BEACH BOYS | 45 mins. |
| | | 118 mins. |

# Programme

## 1 SHARON TANDY with The Fleur de Lys

## 2 VANITY FARE

## 3 BRUCE CHANNEL

*interval*

## 4 ECLECTION

## 5 BARRY RYAN

## 6 THE BEACH BOYS

Compere:
ROGER "TWIGGY" DAY
☆

*The management reserve the right to alter
this programme at their discretion*

In accordance with the requirements of local authority and watch committees —
1 The public may leave at the end of the performance by all exits and entrances
and the doors of such exits and entrances shall at that time be open. 2 All gang-
ways, passages and staircases shall be kept entirely free from chairs or any other
obstruction. 3 No smoking is permitted to take place on the stage, except as part
of a performance as entertainment. 4 The fireproof safety curtain (where applicable) shall be lowered and raised during each performance to ensure its being kept
in proper working order.

BEACH BOYS TOUR 1968

RUNNING ORDER & TIMING

LONDON PALLADIUM ONLY SUNDAY DEC 1st

| | | | |
|---|---|---|---|
| 1. | SHARON TANDY with THE FLEUR DE LYS | 8 | mins. |
| 2. | ROGER TWIGGY DAY | 3 | mins. |
| 3. | VANITY FARE | 10 | mins. |
| 4. | ROGER TWIGGY DAY | 3 | mins. |
| 5. | BRUCE CHANNEL | 12 | mins. |
| 6. | ROGER TWIGGY DAY | 3 | mins. |
| 7. | ECLECTION | 10 | mins. |
| 8. | ROGER TWIGGY DAY | 2 | mins. |
| 9. | BARRY RYAN | 12 | mins. |
| | INTERVAL | 10 | mins. |
| 10. | BEACH BOYS | 45 | mins. |
| | | 118 | mins. |

NOTE :  FOR THE REMAINDER OF THE TOUR,
THE INTERVAL WILL BE AFTER  BRUCE CHANNEL

*Barry Ryan was backed by some more of
my old friends from Kent, Candy Choir.*

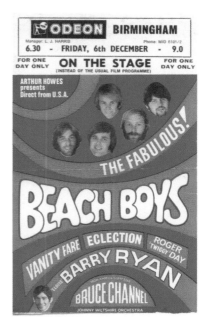

BEACH BOYS TOUR          DECEMBER 1968

ITINERY

| | | | | |
|---|---|---|---|---|
| SUN | DEC | 1 | LONDON PALLADIUM | STAY LONDON |
| MON | DEC | 2 | BRISTOL COLSTON HALL | RETURN LONDON |
| TUE | DEC | 3 | NO SHOW | |
| WED | DEC | 4 | SHEFFIELD CITY HALL | STAY SHEFFIELD |
| THU | DEC | 5 | MANCHESTER ODEON | STAY MANCHESTER |
| FRI | DEC | 6 | BIRMINGHAM ODEON | STAY BIRMINGHAM |
| SAT | DEC | 7 | CARDIFF CAPITOL THEATRE | STAY CARDIFF |
| SUN | DEC | 8 | BRIGHTON DE MONTFORT HALL | STAY LEICESTER |
| MON | DEC | 9 | TRAVEL TO GLASGOW | STAY GLASGOW |
| TUE | DEC | 10 | GLASGOW ODEON | STAY GLASGOW |
| WED | DEC | 11 | RETURN LONDON | |

*Never met Brian Wilson until many
years later at the Albert Hall*

# CHAPTER 11

# ON THE ROAD AGAIN

Friday December 20<sup>th</sup> – First disco gig at Bromley

Saturday January 18<sup>th</sup> – Canterbury University

Monday 20<sup>th</sup> – Bromley Youth Club

Saturday February 8<sup>th</sup> – Hermitage Ballroom

Saturday 22<sup>nd</sup> – Nonington College

**March**

All Month Circle Club in Copenhagen (long hours 21.00–02.00)

It wasn't a happy time for me. I wasn't getting enough DJ work and the bills were piling up, so I had to accept the Danish gig. I had to sleep above the club in a dingy room, but the kitchen staff took pity on me and kept me fed. When my contract ended, I was glad to return to the UK. The disco work improved, and I hired equipment from Newham Audio in Forest Gate in East London. Then I bought my own set up.

## April

Friday 11th –The White Hart, Tottenham.

Sunday 13th – White Hart Hotel

Saturday 19th– Red Cross Hall, East Grinstead

Friday 25th – Scene Club, Hitchen

Saturday 26th – Youth Club, Didcot

## May

Friday 2nd – Sgts Mess, Deepcut, Surrey

Friday 9th – RAOC, Deepcut

Friday 16th – Canterbury Youth Club

Saturday 17th – Blighs Hotel, Sevenoaks

Sunday 25th– Bridge Country Club

Monday 26th – East Grinstead

## June

Monday 2nd – Lady Fatima Hall, Harlow

Tuesday 3rd – Truemans Haystack, Canvey Isle

Thursday 5th – Kings Arms, Berhampstead

Sunday 8th – Shoreditch College, Egham

Tuesday 10th – HMS Mercury, Petersfield

Thursday 12th – The Kings Arms, Berhampstead

Friday 13th– Windmill Pub, Wallington

Saturday 14th – Chequers Hotel,Horley

Tuesday 17th – Langley Green Youth Club

Thursday 19th – Judging Carnival Queen Beauty Contest

Friday 20th – Didcot Youth Centre

Saturday 21st – Bridge Country Club

Sunday 22nd – Charity Cricket Match Farnborough Hants

Monday 23<sup>rd</sup> – White Hart, Frimley
Thursday 26<sup>th</sup> – Park Centre, Burgess Hill
Friday 27<sup>th</sup> – Farnborough, Hants
Saturday 28<sup>th</sup> – Martello Beach Caravan Park, Pevensey Bay

**July**

Thursday 3<sup>rd</sup> – Berkhampstead
Kings Arms (and then every
Thursday)
Saturday5<sup>th</sup> – Martello Beach
Caravan Park
Friday July 4<sup>th</sup> – Beaconsfield
Youth Club
Friday 11<sup>th</sup> – Edmonton Youth Club
Friday 18<sup>th</sup> – Battle Hospital
Saturday 19<sup>th</sup> – Bridge Country
Club
Friday 25<sup>th</sup> – Beaconsfield Youth
Club

**DJ Roger was rally speaker**

AN appeal to bring back "free" radio has been made by Margate disc jockey Roger Day.

**Andrew Clymer** WRITES ON TOPICS FOR TEENS AND TWENTIES

**August**

Saturday 2<sup>nd</sup> – All Saints Hall, Belvedere
Saturday 9<sup>th</sup> – Taboo Dance Club, Hastings
Saturday 30<sup>th</sup> – St Laurence Hospital Club, Caterham
Sunday 31<sup>st</sup> – Lenham Hotel, Streatham

**September**

Monday 1<sup>st</sup> – Bridge Country Club
Saturday 6<sup>th</sup> – Teen & Twenty Club, Tonbridge
Saturday 13<sup>th</sup> & Friday 19<sup>th</sup> – Beaconsfield Youth Club

Saturday 20th – Sundowners, Eastbourne

Friday 26th – Youth Club, Bromley

Saturday 27th – Chelsea College, Eastbourne

## October

Saturday 1st Sloopys, Brighton

Friday 3rd – Chilham Village Hall

Saturday 4th – Hastings Pier

Friday 10th – Queens Hotel, Margate

Friday 17th – Didcot Youth Club Saturday

18th – Hermitage Ballroom, Hitchin

Sunday 19th – Howard Mallet Youth Club, Cambridge

Friday 24th – Beaconsfield Youth Club

Saturday 25th – Bridge Country Club

Friday 31st – RAOC Army Club, Deepcut

## November

Saturday 1st – Gillette Social Club, Isleworth

Wednesday 5th – High Wycombe Youth Club

Friday 7th – Goudhurst PTA

Friday 15th – Beaconsfield YC

Wednesday 26th – Dorothy Ballroom, Cambridge

Friday 28th – Beaconsfield YC

Saturday 29th – Nonington College

## December

Wednesday 3rd – Elstree & Borehamwood Youth Club

Friday 5th – Chequers Hotel, Horley

Sunday 7th – Howard Mallet Club, Cambridge

Friday 12th – Beaconsfield YC
Sunday 14th – Private Party Oakington
Monday 15th – Winter Gardens, Margate
Thursday 18th – Army Club, Mythcett
Friday 19th – Sgts Mess Deepcut Saturday 20th – Private
Party Alloy Metals London
Tuesday 23rd – Beaconsfied YC
Wednesday 24th – Trumans Brewery London in Morning
Hermitage, Hitchin in the Evening
Saturday 27th – Bridge Country Club
Sunday 28th – St Albans YC
Wednesday 31st – Red Cross Hall, East Grinstead

## 1970
### January

Friday 2nd – Beaconsfield YC
Bridge Country Club Saturday Jan 3rd –
Sunday 4th – Red Lion, Barnet (and then every Sunday)
Saturday 10th – Hermitage, Hitchin
Friday 16th – Beaconsfield YC
Saturday 17th – Tonbridge Ten& Twenty Club
Tuesday 27th – The Pilgrim, Haywards Heath
Friday 30th – Bridge Country Club
Saturday 31st – Tunbridge Wells Rugby Club

### February

Friday 6th – Beaconsfield YC
Saturday 7th – Hermitage Ballroom, Hitchin
Friday 13th – Moulscombe YC Brighton
Saturday 14th – Chatham Town Hall

SITUATIONS VACANT

6/12/69

# URGENT

International organisation is looking for young English-speaking Top Disc Jockeys, likely with radio experience. Ex-Pirate DJs particularly welcome. Applicants must be prepared to work on the Continent. First class salary.

Please introduce yourself with a taped application, including some minutes of a programme as you would like to do it as a disc jockey.

Applications to:
Radio Nordsee International,
P.O. Box 1136,
CH-8047 Zurich/Switzerland

## CHAPTER 12

# RADIO NORTHSEA INTERNATIONAL

I t was at the end of 1969 that I saw an ad in Record Mirror for Disc Jockeys to join a European radio station. I sent a letter and a tape off to a PO box in Switzerland, not having the faintest idea what it was all about.

On December 5th, I received a letter from an Erwin Meister saying they were very interested in employing me and would be in touch. Their plan then was to record programmes in Zurich. I found out they had tried to launch the previous year from the MV Galaxy ship, the former home of Radio London Big L.

A month later, I got a phone call from an Edwin

MEBO LTD.
Albisriederstr. 315
8047 Zürich

Telephon 54 24 47
Telex 55503 mebo

Roger "Twiggy" Day,
21, Lovelace Road,
Surbiton,
Surrey,
Great Britain.

Ihr Zeichen          Unser Zeichen me/es 8047 Zürich  December 16th, 1969.

Dear Sir,

With reference to your letter dated December 9th for which we thank you we herewith inform you that the response on our advertise was so large, that we were not able yet to make any final decision. According to these circumstances we also had to change our plans of interviewing the candidates in Rotterdam as it is not possible to have all these people come over to Holland at one time.

Therefore we thought of coming over to London for a few days beginning of January; there is no way of doing it during the Christmas holidays. During these days we shall have all our time at the Disc-Jockeys disposal whereas in Rotterdam would not have been too much time.

As soon as we know the exact date we shall let you know and we once more should like to express our interest in employing you as a disc-jockey for Radio Nordsee International.

Meanwhile have our best wishes for Christmas and a happy New Year and accept our sincere regrets for the delay of our decision. However we thank you for your understanding and looking forward to our meeting in London, we remain,

Yours faithfully,
MEBO LTD SWITZERLAND

Erwin W. Meister

---

MEBO LTD.
Albisriederstr. 315
8047 Zürich

Telephon 54 24 47
Telex 55503 mebo

INTERNATIONAL
TELECOMMUNICATION

Zürich – Portugal – Sierra Leone

Roger "Twiggy" Day,
21, Lovelace Road,
Surbiton,
Surrey,
Great Britain.

Ihr Zeichen          Unser Zeichen me/ej 8047 Zürich  December 5th, 1969.

Dear Sir,

We thank you for your kind letter dated December 4th of which we learned with great pleasure that you would be interested to work for our new radio-station.

According to your request we gladly give you some clother information about the project. As you assume, it is going to be an off-shore station, called "RADIO NORDSEE INTERNATIONAL". We are going to operate off a ship which is now still placed on the dock-yard near Rotterdam. We have planed of going on the air near the middle of this month.

To come back to your request, we are glad to inform you that we would be interested to employ you as a disc-jockey for our English program and we thought of having you work in our studio in Zurich.

As we are going to be in Rotterdam the coming week and most probable the week after and since we should like to show you our ship we think it would be best for either of us to have you come to Rotterdam. Would you therefore let us know if you are still interested at all and what day would be convenient for you to see us in Rotterdam.

Looking forward to hearing from you at your earliest convenience, we remain,

Yours faithfully,
MEBO LTD SWITZERLAND

Erwin W. Meister

Bollier, who said he knew all about me and asked if I'd be interested in helping him set up an off shore station broadcasting off Holland. Now, you have to realise I had received a lot of similar calls since the demise of Radio Caroline in March 1968, so I was rather offhand with him. "Basically," I said, "if you send me a return air ticket, I'll come and meet you."

A few days later, the ticket arrived, and I set off for Schiphol Airport in Amsterdam, a route I was very familiar with, of course. I thought it was another wild goose chase, but at least I would have a meal and a few beers in one of my favourite places.

I met both Edwin and Erwin at the Grand Hotel in Scheveningen. Over dinner, they outlined their plans for an international station in German and English. They wanted me to be the programme controller and hire all the DJs, except the two Germans they had already hired, and to programme the music. Although I was very interested, I was still to be convinced they were genuine. I thanked them for a lovely meal and interesting proposal and told them to please get in touch when they had a ship. They looked rather shocked and said, "We already have a ship. It's ready to broadcast and we'll take you to see it tomorrow."

Nearly 2 years after my last tender trip to a radio ship, I was once again sailing into the North Sea from Holland. To be honest, I still thought it was a Candid Camera wind up. It was a very foggy day, but I could still see the REM Island, then Radio Veronica, which was a thrill because I'd never seen its broadcasting ship, the MV Nordeney. Looming out of the mist was a multi-coloured ship with a huge aerial. My first impression was, *My God, these silly sods have only actually gone and done it!*

Once aboard, I had a look around and discovered a hive of activity, with engineers and crew members hard at work. The studios were ready to go, and I recorded a couple of promos to run during the test transmissions. While heading back to shore, I firmed up a deal and said I'd be back next week to start work. By the time I got back to England, the test transmissions had started. It was 11thFebruary 1970. Immediately, my phone was ringing constantly, with friends calling to say they had heard me on this station called Radio North Sea International. I just said it wasn't me but agreed that the voice did sound familiar. I assured them that my pirate days were over.

Jenny of course needed some convincing, as I was making a very decent living out of the club circuit. But I think she realised that radio was what I badly missed and this was an opportunity I couldn't turn down.

Back in London, I contacted all the record companies and told them about the new project. Needless to say, they were all very keen to supply us with records, despite denying it publicly.

The next day, I phoned all my disco contacts to explain the situation and started making plans. First, I needed a DJ crew. Fortunately, there were a lot of former offshore DJs who didn't have radio gigs. The hardest part was who to choose for a line up. I guess it would have been

## A new Broadcasting Station for Europe

Radio Nordsee International transmits for Europe. For Europe's young. Music—popular in all languages; music—understood everywhere. Ninety percent of all broadcasts is music: A young, international programme for young Europeans.

All disk jockeys of Radio Nordsee International comment in several languages. All short news is given in several languages. Radio Nordsee International also transmits commercials. Commercials that reach many millions of young Europeans.

Get additional details on the following pages.

## 52° 5' 2" Northern Latitude 3° 55' 9" Eastern Longitude

This is the nautical position—because Radio Nordsee International is a ship. A ship by the name of "MS Mebo 2". 180 ft long, 30 ft wide, 670 tons, 2 powerful Diesel engines, 15 knots.

But Radio Nordsee International lies at anchor and transmits for Europe with a heavy-duty medium wave transmitter (105 kW), two short wave transmitters (European band) and a VHF-FM-transmitter (regional). With a 140 ft aerial tower as a medium-wave vertical-emitter. With two ten-channel sound studios aboard and four just-as-powerful studios in Zurich.

## A Programme for young Europeans

Radio Nordsee International transmits young music exclusively. Music that is being greatly neglected by other stations. Music of today, not of the day before yesterday: Pop, Beat, Soul, Hot, Cool, Hits. And new, very different music. The music Radio Nordsee International plays today will enchant all Europe to-morrow. At all events, this is what this young European station wants to do.

**Wave-lengths and frequencies**

**Radio Nordsee International**
transmits on medium wave 186 m
with a frequency of 1605 kc
on short wave 49.30 m (= 49 m European band)
with a frequency of 6210 mc
on short wave 30.16 m (religious programmes)
with a frequency of 9940 mc
and on ultra-short wave
with a frequency of 102 mc

## Commercial for young Europeans

Radio Nordsee International transmits commercials in many languages. And yet: all commercials speak the same language. The common language of the young. Of young Europeans. Radio Nordsee International reaches Warsaw, Naples and Madrid with its commercials. It covers Switzerland, Austria, Italy and Spain.

The following pages give the exact listings of transmitting hours and ranges.

### Short wave
(the year round)

### Medium wave
(October–March)

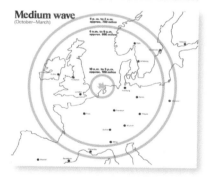

### Ultra-short wave
(the year round)

Advertising rates

**Tariff**

| | |
|---|---|
| 30 seconds | $ 200.– |
| 60 seconds | $ 380.– |

Rates for sponsored broadcasts to be negotiated.

**Discounts**

| Agency discount (commission) | 15% |
|---|---|

Quantity discount per year on sales from

| | |
|---|---|
| $ 12,500 | 5% |
| $ 25,000 | 10% |
| $ 50,000 | 15% |

Further informations will be supplied by:

**RNI RADIO NORDSEE INTERNATIONAL**
**Advertising Dept.**
**CH-8030 Zurich**
**P.O.Box 182**
**Telephone 091 32 27 42**

easy to just take the old Radio Caroline crew. But Johnnie Walker was now at the BBC, Bud Ballou had a gig in the United States, and Robbie Dale was on Radio Veronica.

On Tuesday February 17th, I went to get the tender out to the ship, but it was too rough to get alongside, so I returned to shore and spent the night in the Grand Hotel. The next day, I did get aboard and met two German DJs - Hannibal and Horst Reiner. They'd never broadcast on radio, so I had to teach them how to drive a studio desk. There was also a Scottish lad called Johnny Scott. Apparently, the two owners had met him working at a local disco in Scheveningen. I was not best pleased. So much for me hiring all the staff! It wouldn't be the last time they would interfere. The four of us shared the test transmissions until the others came out. Johnny only lasted two weeks when even the owners realised he wasn't up to it. It was very weird operating with half the output in German. I did think there might be problems as we would struggle to get heard in Germany.

The ship was well fitted out. We all had individual cabins, a large shower room, a large dining room, and a TV lounge.

*The tender in port. It was going to be the radio ship at first. It was bigger than the Mi Amigo.*

Left: My cabin. Middle: The Dining Room. Note the belts for tying to the table in rough weather. Right: The generator

Engineers

Johnny Scott

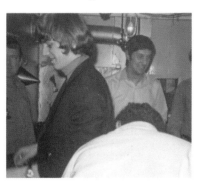

Mebo Crew

Alan West, Andy Archer, Carl Mitchell

Peter Murtha (Chicago), Hannibal, Duncan Johnson, and me.

*On deck with Andy Archer and Hannibal*

*Andy, Lee Groen ('of course' man), a Caroline Crew man*

*My dad on a trip to the Dutch Office. Bringing Bacon and tea.*

*The big studio*

*Horst Reiner, Andy, Carl, RTD, Alan*

*When RNI was going to be on the Galaxy.*

*Me in the small studio, which we preferred.*

*The shower room*

*Transmitter room*

Duncan, Carl, Larry Tremaine, Hannibal, Mark Wesley. Alan West at front.

The Record Library. Most of it my records.

On shore with Edwin Bollier

POP CHART FOR WEEK ENDING 14th.MARCH

1. BRIDGE OVER TROUBLED WATER.............SIMON & GARFUNKEL. (3)
2. THAT SAME OLD FEELING.................PICKETTYWITCH. (5)
3. LET IT BE.............................BEATLES.(1)
4. DON'T CRY DADDY......................ELVIS PRESLEY.(7)
5. MY BABY LOVES LOVING.................WHITE PLAINS.(8)
6. EVERYBODY GET TOGETHER...............DAVE CLARK FIVE (13)
7. YOUNG GIFTED & BLACK.................BOB & MARCIA (25)
8. FAREWELL IS A LONELY SOUND...........JIMMY RUFFIN (26)
9. SOMETHING'S BURNING..................KENNY ROGERS (4)
10. CAN'T HELP FALLING IN LOVE..........ANDY WILLIAMS (28)
11. BRIDESMAIDED REGGAE.................BORIS GARDINER (21)
12. GOMHILL.............................KENNY GRASS (29)
...

RADIO NORDSEE INTERNATIONAL   186 Meters Medium Wave
Top Forty

1. Instant Karma. Plastic Ono Band
2. Let's Work Together. Canned Heat
3. Don't you Jackson Five
...

# NORTH SEA PIRATES ON THE AIR TODAY
## by RODNEY COLLINS

PIRATE RADIO IS BACK IN BRITAIN TODAY! After almost two years of silence a new offshore radio station is scheduled to begin broadcasting to Britain on 186 metres medium wave. It's called Radio North Sea International. And the line-up of disc jockeys is headed by Roger "Twiggy" Day, former Caroline and Luxembourg staff man. The transmissions are expected to start at 5 p.m. today (Friday) and the broadcasts WILL reach England, and it is possible that RNI will pick a better spot on the medium wave for English transmissions later this month. The station's disc jockeys will have a "fairly free choice of the discs they play." Alan Clark reports from England. "The station has been broadcasting regularly in German on the FM band for three weeks now. The broadcasts have included a few English announcements but no direct transmissions. "It is likely that Roger Day will have his own show late afternoon or in the evening. Nordsee, as it is known in Europe, will broadcast in English from 5 p.m. until 7 a.m. each day.

# STAY TUNED FOR RADIO SILVETTA!

While politicians chewed the fat only a few miles away at The Hague over how to unite Europe, two young Swiss businessmen were doing something practical about it in Rotterdam harbour.

They were completing all over the disunited continent.

The two promoters, Erwin Meister, 31, and Edwin Bollier, 32, say: "We'll stand the pop music scene on its ear. This'll be the biggest thing in radio.

## By DAVID HUGHES

RADIO CAROLINE stars Roger "Twiggy" Day, Andy Archer and Carl Mitchell, and Radio 270 man Alan West (also known as Ross Randall) head the DJ team of Radio North Sea, the latest and most reliable "pirate" station to hit the air since the days of Big "L"—Radio London.

# North Sea pop pirates are ready for battle

Radio North Sea can already be heard in London, Essex and North-East England, although no reception is reported to interference from aerial stations.

M/S Mebo II—home of Radio North Sea International

# A LIFE ON THE MEDIUM WAVE

**"I climbed up onto the top deck of the tender .... there was a howling gale ..... the waves were seven feet high ..... I just closed my eyes and jumped"**

*Dinner-time on RNI. "This place is like the Hilton when it comes to meal times", said Roger Day. Pictured are—Roger Day (looking through the porthole), Andy Archer and Carl Mitchell with Alan West (back to photographer).*

*Andy Archer on the air during the first day of full transmissions. Looking on is Radio Nordsee programme director Roger Day, who compares the breakfast show on the station. The picture was taken in the main studio on Mebo 11.*

**Rodney Collins, the first journalist on board Mebo II, reports on Radio Nordsee International**

THE TENDER drew up alongside Mebo 11. "Boy are we glad to see you", shouted Roger Day from the radio ship. "We haven't had a tender for a week the weather has been so bad."

They nearly didn't get one on Saturday, either, the sea had looked calm enough from the lounge of the Grand Hotel, Scheveningen. The weather was overcast and fairly windy. The tender had set off early in the morning in a force seven gale—but was unable to make it out to the ship, so we turned back.

The second attempt at reaching the ship was made in the middle of the afternoon, on the new tide. The captain said we had a "20 per cent chance of getting out to the station. Even then I doubt whether we'll be able to draw up alongside the radio ship", he added.

We reached Radio Nordsee, just before 5 p.m. In one hour the station would begin full broadcasts. It took ten minutes to tie the ships together in very rough seas. Then came the next problem. How to get from the tender onto the radio ship.

It would be stupid to say that I was not frightened—I think most of the people on the tender seriously wondered whether we would ever get onto the ship or not. And there was always the danger that the tender would crash into the station.

The captain, however, had it all worked out. We climbed up onto the top deck of the tender. The waves were seven feet high. "Wait until the waves lift the tender up level with the radio ship and then jump across", he said.

It didn't even look easy. Several of us decided that perhaps we would not try it—everyone else on the tender was used to jumping on and off motor vessels.

I hadn't felt at all sea sick until then. I suppose it was looking at the two ships rolling about in an incredibly cruel sea. I didn't think I'd make it that far. I remembered back only a few years when I had got sea sick on the Catford Boating Pool . . I just closed my eyes and jumped. It took twelve minutes to get everyone to jump onto the radio ship, but we all made it.

The station's directors had arranged for the tender to come back and fetch us in a couple of hours. But now the captain decided that he would not be able to chance another trip out there. We would have to stay on the ship overnight.

My first impression of Mebo 11 was that it resembled a 'floating palace'. It was the right one. The disc jockeys had every comfort. Individual cabins, excellent food and really well-equipped studios. All the disc jockeys were on the top deck to greet us. Roger Day was smiling at the rather pale, sea sick faces.

After a few cracks like "We knew Record Mirror was always first with the news but this is ridiculous", Andy Archer took me on a conducted tour of the ship. I was impressed.

The DJs as well as having their own cabins, have a TV room and lounge all with fitted carpets. The ship Mebo 11 has been repainted and everywhere looked clean and bright. The studios—possibly the best equipped of any of the offshore stations in the past few years—are on a lower deck with the DJs quarters above. The kitchens and dining rooms are on the top deck.

It was decided to open at 6 p.m. with the old Radio London theme. Then Roger Day and Horst Reiner would welcome listeners to the first programme. Apart from a couple of small problems, it all went off well.

The disc jockeys broadcasting are Roger Day, Carl Mitchell, Andy Archer, Alan West, Hanibal and Horst Reiner.

But what makes these people, especially the English ones who live under the constant threat of the Marine Offences Act, work out there, I wondered? Roger Day says: "This is the type of radio I enjoy. I don't go around knocking the BBC but I just don't believe in their way of presenting pop.

I see a future for this station. It is the 'Voice of Europe'. I must admit that I did worry at the beginning though. I wondered what would happen

to me if the station was not successful, things like that. I had a lot of time to think then."

What about Roger's wife? Does she mind him spending three weeks at a time at sea? "She knows that this is what I want to do and she sticks by me. I'm not just sitting on the ship to raise two fingers to the British Government. That doesn't come into it. I believe strongly in commercial radio."

Working for Nordsee means that the English disc jockeys—Roger Day, Andy Archer and Alan West, are unable to come back to Britain.

"Okay that's a problem", said Andy Archer. "But that is outweighed by the wonderful feeling of freedom you get on a pirate station. That may sound odd but this is truly free radio in every sense of the phrase.

"The Marine Offences Act eventually closed down all the pirates. This is not a British station, it is an international one. I'm here because I enjoy it but I suppose I always have been a bit of a rebel. I certainly don't worry about that act. It's just a job, quite frankly. The main thing is that this station is doing absolutely NO harm to anyone.

"Some listeners have asked why we chose 186 metres on the medium wave when some radical cannot pick up the signal. We did it because there was nothing on that wavelength and so nobody would be able to accuse us of interfering with any other stations. Mind you, the complaints still come", smiled Andy.

Personally, I think that most of the disc jockeys on RNI are professionals and they will help the station to get advertising and listeners. Best one on the team in my opinion, is Roger Day, but another, New York-bore Carl Mitchell has improved immeasurably since the old Radio Caroline days. Carl, now 23, spent the months since Caroline's closure working in discotheques.

"This station is really happening. The disc jockeys and crew are really so together. I'm certainly happier here than I have ever been. There were so many hang-ups with Caroline. We don't have them out here."

The disc jockeys believe in commercial radio. The directors do, as well. But they don't make out that it is the only reason for their being in the North sea. Edwin Bollier, one of the two men who brought about RNI will freely admit that they are there to make money. It is so easy to spend half a million dollars. Now the money must start to roll in.

With the same sort of luck RNI has had all the way along the line, the advertising has started rolling in. Rienis Airways are advertising and the station is also carrying commercials for tape recorders and tape systems. It will take a while before the station breaks even though, because of the huge overheads.

The directors have certainly spared no expense to make sure the disc jockeys have decent working conditions. That has not always been the case with the pirates.

When the station is off the air between 1 am and 6 am the ship sleeps. On Saturday night, however, Roger Day was busy listening to the new records and compiling the new RNI chart. He is utterly dedicated to his work. "God I haven't any idea what I would do if the disc jockey thing folded. I don't know what else I could do." For Roger, success has come quickly. To be a programme director at 24 is no mean feat. "I never expected to make this job so soon", he said not sounding in the least big-headed. "I want this station to be ahead of its time and make trends—that's what we're aiming for."

The aims of the station are quite clear. Whatever the listener thinks of the individual DJs, he must admit that they are all competent. The signal to Britain will be improved and RNI will doubtless take over where Caroline and London left off. I'd be prepared to bet they will succeed. Perhaps the best quote comes from one of the Proud Haarem who said over the air on Saturday: "I hope RNI is a success and that this time the British people don't let commercial radio be taken away from them."

# Life aboard the latest pirate radio ship

THE RECORD industry now has another valuable outlet for its material – the new offshore pirate station 'Radio North Sea International'. Broadcasting from the motor vessel Mebo II, anchored five miles off the coast of Holland, North Sea will provide 12 hours of English programmes each day.

English and American disc product will take up 80 per cent of the total of 19 hours of broadcasts daily. The arrival of 'North Sea' means that Europe once again has more than the faithful 'Radio Veronica', which had been beaming programmes to Holland for years now.

I went out to visit the Mebo II to learn about the station format, the announcers and the conditions on board the vessel. I was certainly impressed. The tender drew up alongside the Mebo II: "Boy are we glad to see you," shouted Roger Day from the radio ship. "We haven't had a tender for a week because the weather has been so bad."

They nearly didn't get one that day, either. The sea had looked calm enough from the lounge of the Grand Hotel, Scheveningen. The weather was overcast and fairly windy. The tender had set off early in the morning in a force seven gale – but was unable to make it out to the ship, so turned back.

The second attempt at reaching the ship was successful. One of the crew explained that this was one of the radio ships main problems – communication. At times, the disc jockeys on board Mebo II would go for more than a week without new records and charts for programming.

We reached the radio ship just before 5pm. It took 10 minutes to tie the ships together in very rough seas. Then came the next problem. How to get from the tender to the ship. The supplies were transferred easily enough. The records, sent from most British companies who are obviously ignoring the Marine Offences Act, were parcelled together and thrown onto the ship. Then our party, which included managing director Edwin Bollier and disc jockey Ed Moreno, had to get on board.

The captain had it all worked out. We climbed up onto the top deck of the tender. "Wait until the waves lift the tender up level with the radio ship and then just jump across," he said.....It took 12 minutes to get all of us onto Mebo II. The station's directors had arranged for the tender to come back and fetch us in a couple of hours.

But now the captain decided that he would not be able to change another trip out there and that we would have to stay on the ship overnight.

My first impression of the Mebo II was that it resembled a "floating palace." The disc jockeys have every comfort. Individual cabins, excellent food and really well equipped studios. Andy Archer took me on a conducted tour of the ship.

The DJ's as well as having their own cabins have a TV room and lounge all with fitted carpets. The ship Mebo II has been repainted and looked clean and bright. The studios – possibly the best equipped of any of the offshore stations in the past few years – are on a lower deck with the DJ's rooms above.

About 90 per cent of the

programmes are broadcast 'live'. The only time pre-recorded programmes are used is when disc jockeys are on shore leave. The majority of the programmes are broadcast from studio one which is larger than most Radio One studio and has an extensive record library. Studio two is much smaller and is used for recording promotion tapes, advertisements and jingles.

Walking around, it was almost possible to forget that this was a motor vessel. Only the continual swaying of the ship reminded us of where we were. Certainly it did not give the impression of being a 'pirate' – just a floating radio station.

At any one time, there will be four or five disc jockeys on the ship plus a crew for maintenance. Radio North Sea broadcasts 19 hours each day from 6am–1am. The disc

## RADIO NORDSEE
## AIMS TO LEAD
## THE WAY

jockeys broadcasting are Roger Day, Carl Mitchell, Andy Archer, Hanibal and Irwin Reiner. The German service will broadcast between 6am – 8am and from 8pm – 1am. This means there will now be 12 hours of English language shows between 8am – 8pm.

I wondered exactly what made these disc jockeys, especially the English one who live under the constant threat of prosecution, work out there. Roger Day, formerly with Radio Caroline and Luxembourg and now appointed programme director for RNI said: "This is the type of radio I enjoy. I don't go around knocking the BBC for the sake of it but I just don't believe in their way of presenting pop.

"This station is not for England. As we say it is the 'Voice Of Europe' and as such it has amazing potential. The audience ratings will be very big."

Another announcer Andy Archer said that broadcasting on RNI gave him a wonderful sense of freedom. "That may sound odd but this is truly free radio in every sense of the phrase. The Marine Offences Act eventually closed down all the pirates. This is not a British station, it is an international one. I'm out here because I enjoy it and I suppose I have always been a bit of a rebel."

Some record companies have criticised RNI's decision to use the 186 metre band. Why was this chosen?

"We realise that some radios cannot pick up the signal, but we picked 186 because there was nothing on that wavelength and so nobody would be able to accuse us of interfering with any other stations," said Archer.

One of the best things about RNI is that the disc jockeys have some say in the records they play. Roger Day is responsible for general format and for deciding which discs will get played on the Mebo.

"I want this station to be ahead of its time and make breaks – that's what we're aiming for. We get most of the releases out here and the disc jockeys listen to them as they come in. We play quite a number of LP tracks as well as featuring a lot of material from our own Top 40."

In any one half hour, listeners would be likely to hear three LP tracks, three chart singles, two new releases and one 'flashback'. RNI's directors are aiming to programme more than 16 discs per hour which will mean the disc jockeys will have little time to talk between records – less time than the Radio One DJ's get.

But one of the directors explained that they wanted to cut the chat to the minimum. "Even when we are putting out English programmes they will be aimed at a general European audience, so the less chat the better."

Edwin Bollier, managing director and who, with Erwin Meister, brought about RNI, will freely admit that Mebo is there to make money.

Bollier and Meister are two Swiss businessmen who raised the necessary funds to launch RNI. About half a million dollars has been spent on the station so far." It is so easy to spend the money. Now the money must start to roll in," he said.

No-one is saying how much it costs to run the station, but it is thought that £2,000 a week would cover the cost of the DJ's wages, crew and maintenance of ship. To break even and eventually make a profit, Nordsee needs a sizeable amount of advertising now.

## ADVERTISING
## ROLLS IN

With the same sort of luck RNI has had all the way along the line, the advertising has started rolling in. Swiss Airways are advertising and the station is also carrying commercials for tape recorders and tape systems. No English advertising as yet, though.

RNI hopes to start its own record label and publishing company so naturally the station will plug that product but the directors seem anxious to steer clear of any form of 'payola' – paid record plugs – unless insufficient revenue is forthcoming from advertising.

RNI should succeed because all the disc jockeys are competent, the signal to Britain is strong, but will be further improved. Best announcer on the ship – and the one with peak listening time – in my opinion is Roger Day but whatever the listener's feeling towards the individual disc jockeys, they seem to be responding to requests for reception reports. The industry, too, seems to be supporting the new pirate.

Perhaps the best quote comes from one of the Proool Harum who told listeners over the air: "I hope RNI does well and hope this time that the British people don't let commercial radio be taken away from them."

**RODNEY COLLINS**

The transmitter room on board the Mebo II, anchored five miles off the coast of Scheveningen in Holland. Radio North Sea International will soon be broadcasting on a power of 100 KW to Europe between 6 am–1 am daily.

Oliver sings Jean CBS

The Flying Machine Hanging On The Edge Of Sadness PYE 17414

Bamboos Of Jamaica Reggae Man TN 25016

Tony Hatch And The Cherry Children PYE 17742

Sawinkle And Thunderbopper Your Mother Thinks I'm A Hoodlum PYE 17414

All On Pye

158

ERWIN BOLLIER: No eye patch or cutlass but a pirate nonetheless, with plans to sail the seas with plunder in view.

## Radio Nordsee brings in format plan

*in 14/3/70*

by RODNEY COLLINS

RADIO NORTH SEA INTERNATIONAL introduces its first set of programme schedules tomorrow (Saturday). They feature Roger Day, Andy Archer, Carl Mitchell and Hanibal, all with peak listening shows on Europe's newest pop pirate station.

The station, soon to be broadcasting on full power, will be on the air from 6 am-1 am daily, with English programmes running for 12 hours from 8 am onwards.

Programmes as from tomorrow will be as follows: 6 am Hanibal (German service). 8: Roger Day Breakfast Show. 10: Andy Archer. 12: Carl Mitchell. 3: Afternoon Show. 6: Roger Day. Additionally, the RNI Top 40 will be broadcast at 12 midday on Sunday, to Britain (with Roger Day or Carl Mitchell compering) and repeated at 8 pm the same day with Hanibal for the German service.

The evening shows, from 8-1 am will be entirely in German with some English announcements and commercials. Hanibal will head the German service DJs as Horst Reiner is leaving RNI, RM understands.

The station is still broadcasting on reduced power but reception reports from Britain indicate a favourable signal in the London, South East and Midlands in the mornings and evenings. Once the power is up to almost 100 kw, however, the signal should reach most of the British Isles.

Radio North Sea went off the air for 24 hours over the weekend to make transmitter adjustments as listeners had been complaining of interference on their frequency 186 metres (1605 kcs).

● On the back page of this week's RM is the first colour picture of the Mebo 11, the motor vessel beaming RNI to Europe.

### Nordsee for Britain

RADIO NORDSEE INTERNATIONAL is coming to Britain! The ship will anchor five miles off the coast this weekend, and will broadcast programmes in English. This move, likely to anger the British Government, was decided at a special meeting in Holland on Monday.

RNI will continue to broadcast on 186 metres from the Mebo II and will be serviced by tender Mebo I. Roger Day remains RNI's programme director.

---

**Do you find difficulty in obtaining the latest records from the record companies especially in England?**

No. On the Continent the record companies are quite anxious to have us play their records. As far as English companies are concerned, they practically all have representatives in countries on the Continent so the latest records from England will reach us via them quite quickly.

**Do you consider it possible to have a system of paid plug records?**

Indeed, you may have heard about our so called "pound-sound." However, it won't be possible to get any record plugged through paying for it. We will always make sure that the records are suitable for our programmes. And we won't make a secret out of what records are being paid for.

**Will RNI be starting a music-publishing firm and if so will having the songs of a record in your company affect the frequency of the airplay.**

We will shortly be starting a publishing company in Zurich. It could well be that songs we've the rights to will be plugged more often. In respect to this, I would like to mention that we've made up contracts with Suiza (the copyright control company in Switzerland) and that we will pay all the performing right fees we have to, so that in that subject we won't be a pirate either.

---

## NORTH SEA FEVER ON 186 METRES

# Pirate radio is here ... but record companies refuse to admit it!

by David Hughes
Britain's leading writer on pop-radio

Roger "Twiggy" Day (left) and Andy Archer: 'Morale is high'

RADIO NORTH SEA is go! Despite a two-day silence last Thursday and Friday to try to improve British reception, and despite stern warnings by Postmaster General John Stonehouse, the long-awaited return of the pirate is at fever pitch.

But with all the excitement comes the dilemma for Britain's record companies. Do they send records to North Sea or not?

If they do they'll be giving themselves the most valuable promotion for years. If they do they also officially risk heavy fines or imprisonment for contravening the Marine Offences Bill by aiding an offshore radio station.

Roger "Twiggy" Day, always the biggest threat to Tony Blackburn with his own breakfast show, has been promoted to programme director and chief DJ — a tremendous change of fortune after wrapping a fixing from balloon appearances.

In the hey-day of Caroline's illegal days "Twiggy" was heart-throb number two, surpassed only by now-legitimate star Johnnie Walker.

"Radio North Sea," says Roger, "is the greatest pirate ever. I've never been in a boat where co-operation and morale was so high and where everything was so luxurious. Even Radio London couldn't touch us for comfort.

"When I was first approached by the owners, Edwin, Bollier and Edwin Meister, I was very dubious about the boat on many false claims as the time — but they simply invited me to The Hague to see the ship. They paid for the trip, so I had nothing to lose, and when I got there the boat was already at sea.

"That plan the fact that the owners had worked hard to own their money, so would not want to waste it, convinced me this was the real thing."

"They've both got Rowan O'Rahilly's 'fire.'

"As a guide to the following we've already got, in the first work of transmissions, when we were only writing and not many people knew where we were, I received over 300 letters. In the first days of Caroline, the most I ever received in a week was 400."

Roger and his wife Jennifer plan to move into a flat in Rotterdam (also paid for by the company) and, with DJ colleagues Andy Archer, Carl "Weird Beard" Mitchell, and Alan West, expect a really exciting future.

But what of the problem of stocking the station's record library?

"There's a record going round in the moment by Bob and Marcia. It's called 'Young, Gifted And Black" and Trust Rockinson probably helped it on its way up the chart by playing it every day a couple of weeks back.

But Radio North Sea has mysteriously obtained a copy and who is to say it is not Tony Joe "Twiggy" Day who should chain castle for the hit?

That's the strange thing about North Sea and many of its predecessors — officially it is a palpable offence to support them by supplying them with records.

But somehow records always seem to arrive at the station.

"There is no problem about getting records," says Roger. "Of course our collection is not yet complete, but we are receiving almost all the chart singles and new releases from Britain without having to ask for them and without having to pay for them. They're flooding in by every post.

"At the moment these are no "paid" records on our programmes, although we do intend to help finance the station in this way. But I'm determined to be very selective with singles we are mad to play."

British record companies are being very careful. On the one hand they don't want to miss any opportunity to promote their records; on the other they have to wish to lay themselves open to prosecution.

Of the 14 companies I spoke to this week, only Apple admitted they were supplying the station. Here's what they had to say:

Apple (Derek Taylor): "Yes, of course we're supplying them—on boat. We're not yet sure of the station's selling power, but why turn any good outlet down?"

B & C, including Trojan group (Clive Crawley): "We're not supplying but they're playing our records, especially 'Young, Gifted And Black,' which they've helped considerably. We've not been approached by them for records, but if we are we'll certainly send them. How did they get our records? I suppose they must have bought them."

Island (David Sanctson): There is no official liaison between us and North Sea, but they seem to receive our records. They could be getting them from the Continent."

Liberty/United Artists (Ronnie Bell): "Definitely not. We know the government's legislation and it would obviously be illegal. They do have our records on the station which they must get either from America or Holland or Belgium."

Philips (Roddy Fleming): "We have not yet supplied them and do not intend doing so."

CBS (Bob White): "If we do we're in trouble and it's just not worth our while."

Pye (Peter Prince): "No, simply because it's illegal."

Polydor (Phil Greenop): "We're not going to supply them at this stage. Any Polydor records played on the station must be bought in Holland."

Decca (Chris Denning): "Decca are unable to supply any pirate radio station with records, although though we cannot stop managers, agents, etc., sending Decca records in the ship."

RCA (Ian Gillespie): "We do not intend to do so — RCA's policy is contrary to supplying pirate radio stations."

EMI (Peter Prestige): "We do not supply pirate radio stations and never have done, simply because they are illegal."

Tony Hall (independent record promoter): "I'm in touch with the moment I've not had time to think about it. But I think it's highly unlikely."

David Maud (independent record promoter): "I've not sent them anything so far because I've no idea of their address. When I find that, of course I'll send them. I'm in business to sell records."

Officially these "assurances" by all the major record companies should be enough to virtually stop North Sea's supply. Yet seemingly they can only shake off company's record, but they do so without having to ask for them! Someone, somewhere is defying the British Government!

### 'Just like old days'

● First send on North Sea from Johnnie Walker "Twiggy" Day's very happy that Roger is back on radio once again as we both began our careers in 1967 on Radio England. Recently we've had the government telling us how much we can spend on our foreign holidays, virtually telling us which stations we should tune to, and even to listen to the radio we have to buy a government 'ticket.' So the move proving enterprise the better.

"I'm delighted to hear North Sea — it sounds just like the old days again, and I hope they can increase their power to cover the whole country."

Disc and Music Echo—March 14, 1970    5

BEWARE...THIS...SHIP..
IS...A....PIRATE..

ON THE AIR . . . disc jockeys Duncan Johnson, Roger Day, Andy Archer and Hannibal in the pirate ship's studio.

TIME TO RELAX . . . in front of the skull and crossbones, the disc jockeys (right) take it easy while a crewman keeps the pirate shipshape.

# Drama as I sail to meet

fishing boat.

Soon we were out among the big ships waiting to go into the Thames, and through the channels scoring the Maplins. In the dim and eerie half light, the pirate looked like a ghost ship.

But our journey into the North Sea was about to be dramatically interrupted.

As we neared the ship, the tall transmitting mast glinting 60 feet above the psychedelic paintwork on its side, a high-powered rubber dinghy raced towards us.

Our fisherman skipper, nervous of the law even though we were seven miles out and at least one mile beyond the reach of British justice, pulled away from the pirate.

The small boat zoomed astern of us and I could see the words "Fish Lab" on her

Sorry, I explained, I had been advised to take nothing.

This isolation is the keynote of a pirate's life. One disc jockey said: "It's like living in a monastery."

It was a well chosen description.

The driving force among the disc jockeys — as among monks — is dedication.

It would be absurd to pretend that the owners, two men from Zurich backed by millions of Swiss francs, were broadcasting from a ship in the North Sea to Britain and Germany because they want to strike a blow for freedom of the airwaves.

But the disc jockeys are. They regard Radio One as laughable. They regard the BBC's local stations as useless. And as for the Tories ideas of local radio, they could hardly speak for indignation.

They are certainly not in it for the money, not at £35 a week.

They are certainly not in it for the bright lights. There are eight disc jockeys — four of them Germans for the German language broadcasts — and they are divided into two watches.

Each watch spends a fortnight at sea and a fortnight on shore.

At sea, they get up at 7 a.m., split 20

They are the pirates, the BBC and their unions pretending to be what they're not.

"If you listen to Radio One you hear a disc jockey apparently putting on records and chattering stupidly.

"But the records are all chosen by the producer, and by the nature of things, BBC producers are middle-aged men who have no real part of the modern youth scene. They go on what people are buying.

"So the BBC is only playing records that people were buying a short time ago. The records of people who are already a success. The new groups don't get a look in.

"It's a vicious circle. The old men of the BBC perpetuate the old men of pop and their records are always that bit behind."

Another disc jockey Andy Archer, broke in. "I did some Radio One Club broadcasts for the BBC," he said "See this, this finger pushed a button," they have a man do that. The producer can do it, the disc jockey can do it, but, no, they have a man to do it.

"They give you a pile of records and your script and that would be the programme. They do everything, push the buttons, and I just talk.

"Here we've got spontaneity. If I don't like the records, I don't play them."

DISC jockey Roger Day takes a quick break between programmes in the pirate ship's studio.

What about the finances of the radio? Roger Day wasn't sure. "They've a wad of money behind them," he said. "We're getting more and more advertisements — from Japan, Spain and Switzerland.

"I know that though, we'll soon be breaking even."

In a week at Radio North Sea International they get 600 letters from all over the British Isles.

Radio North Sea International began broadcasting off Staveling in early February.

The ship was named Mebo, which has a dual significance. It is the initial letters of the owners' names. It is also the initial letters of the law which outlawed the pirates, known for short as the Marine etc Broadcasting Offences Act.

Perhaps this is the most subtle of the cheeky pirates' jibes at authority.

# Ministry act to silence pirate radio

Urgent action was promised last night by the Ministry of Posts and Telecommunications to drive a pirate radio station, Radio Nordsee International, off the air. The programme broadcast from the Panamanian ship Mebo II, anchored five miles off Holland, was being picked up strongly last night on medium and short wavebands in Kent, Sussex, and many parts of Europe.

A Ministry official said: "The transmissions on medium wave are interfering with maritime broadcasts right along the coasts and we are getting complaints from ship-to-shore radio. At the present moment the broadcasts are only on test strength, but they have already given rise to complaints from the Norwegians.

"The ship is registered in Panama and we have requested that country for urgent action to stop the transmission by withdrawing the ship's registration. Norway has made similar representations. We are also circulating information to western European countries, urging them to take action against the broadcasts."

No advertising was broadcast from the station last night. People concerned said the programme headquarters in Zurich were waiting until an audience had been built up before seeking commercial support.

# Storm ahead for pop pirates

BRITAIN'S little pop pirate brought closer to ship' radio communications on their first day's broadcasting yesterday.

Transmissions between Coastguards and lightships might be endangered, said Mr John Stonehouse, Minister for Posts and Telecommunications, warned that lifeboats might be endangered.

Trawler skippers off Iceland and in the Eastern Atlantic made dozens of complaints about radio inter-

ference while four disc-jockeys aboard the 670-ton converted coaster pumped non-stop pop music.

Coastguards at Walton-on-the-Naze, Essex, abandoned an attempt to contact eight lightships with weather information. One said: "The interference is very bad. It is causing great danger to shipping but the international distress frequencies are not affected."

The pop pirates, who call their station Radio North Sea International, are anchored ten miles south-east of Clacton, Essex, outside British territorial waters.

Mr Stonehouse, who has already passed information on the station to the Director of Public Prosecutions, said: "This vessel is making illicit broadcasts on a frequency band reserved for radio services between ships, lifeboats, light vessels and the shore."

Earlier Trinity House, the lighthouse authority, said that lightships off Essex and Suffolk had been unable to contact each other or coastal stations. There could be difficulty in alerting a lifeboat or a ship in distress, they said.

Two directors of the station left Britain on Monday after failing to get any British firm to advertise with them.

# The monastic life of pop pirates

Pictures: Jan Turnbull

Story: Peter Blacklock

## Pirate radio is back... and it's a

**21/1/70**

# NORTH SEA GAS!

**DAVID HUGHES aboard Mebo II**

'TWIGGY' DAY: the "thinner record spinner"

---

## Evening News

London Monday March 23, 1970 No. 25,617 6d

### Radio North Sea sails for Britain tonight

# POP PIRATES AHOY! A NEW FIGHT BEGINS

THE BATTLE of the pirates seems about to start all over again. Radio North Sea International, which has been transmitting pop music from the Dutch coast for several weeks, intends to set sail for England this evening.

Sometime during the night the ship will anchor four miles off the Essex coast at Frinton.

### Big audience claimed

---

**Restwell Spring Interior MATTRESSES** £5.10.0 £7.19.6 **The Belfast**

## Evening Star

Ipswich, Tuesday, March 24, 1970 No. 33,022 Price 6d.

Mebo II takes up her post

# Pirate ship anchors near Clacton

● Pictorial on this map is the spot where Mebo II dropped anchor off the Essex coast today.

Audience trebled

"PIRATE" ship Mebo II, operated by Radio North Sea International, dropped anchor off the Essex coast at Clacton today and began pumping non - stop pop into Britain.

But British companies were heeding Government advice and not advertising with the station.

The ship left the Dutch coast yesterday evening.

The Mebo Two's transmitter is twice as strong as Radio Caroline, the former "pirate" station, and broadcasts should be heard throughout Britain.

## On leave

Yesterday two Swiss directors of the pirate ship, Mr. Erwin Meister and Mr. Urs Emmenegger, left Britain after an abortive attempt to secure advertising accounts.

Four of the seven disc jockeys were today aboard the boat. The other three were on shore leave in Holland.

The Campaign for Independent Broadcasting said today it was "delighted" with the news that the pirate ship had anchored just outside territorial waters.

Its only criticism was that Mebo Two was playing a "cat and mouse" game with a nearby wavelength.

A spokesman said "The pirate is on the edge of the medium wavelength. But there is a marine station on a nearby waveband and as the two interfere with each other, both increase the strength of their signal."

## Short break

There was a short break in transmission this morning as the ship manoeuvred and dropped anchor and then disc jockey Andy Archer reopened the station.

"We are 6½ miles off Clacton," he said, "but we can't see the coast because it is so misty. It seems such a pity after coming so far."

Mebo Two is positioned one mile from the Harrow Deep lightship, ten miles S.E. of Clacton, near the spot where pirate Radio Caroline broadcast for nearly three years.

---

● "Evening Star" photographer David Kindred flew in a plane to get this picture of Mebo II arriving off the Essex coast today.

---

8 EVENING STAR, Wednesday, March 25, 1970

## COMMENT

# Piracy problem

THE ARRIVAL of pop pirates on the scene again after the ban imposed in 1967 poses some interesting points. First and foremost it will be very interesting to see what attempts are made to scupper them.

Mr. John Stonehouse, Minister of Posts and Telecommunications, has spoken of "piracy on the high seas" and says the Government intends to stop it. But how will it set about this? Radio North Sea's ship, Mebo II, is anchored outside territorial waters 'o gunboats are surely not on. The musical Captain Morgans and the Black Beards of Beat would seem to be safe from such action.

Something has got to be done if transmissions from the ship are interfering with vital shipping communications. Yesterday Trinity House said that lightships off Essex and Suffolk had been unable to contact each other or coastal stations. "In the event of an emergency," said a spokesman, "there could be difficulty in alerting a lifeboat or a ship in distress."

Last night it was reported that the pop station had closed down temporarily, possibly to change its wavelength. But the medium waveband is already crowded with broadcasts which are legal and the arrival of a pirate only makes matters worse.

We would have thought that if the pirate captains wanted to get off to a good start they would have given a great deal more thought to the question of wavelengths.

## Chance missed

But they are here and cannot easily be brushed off— this was tried once before. The youngsters of today obviously enjoy their style and presentation and the illegal broadcasters could gain a substantial following. When the previous "outbreak" occurred the Government had an ideal opportunity to formulate a new policy on the freedom of choice about broadcasting but instead they stifled all but the BBC.

"Aunty" tried to cater for the pop demand by establishing Radio 1, but in many parts of the country, East Anglia included, reception is difficult. Wouldn't an answer be that attack is better than defence, and set up something so good that no one would want the pirates? It's worth thinking about.

Economics plays a vital role in the launching and maintaining of a pirate ship, and unless they get advertising they are likely to be becalmed—Radio Caroline gave up for this reason. Any association with the pirates carries heavy penalties in this country so we can't help feeling that the lifespan of any "beat brigand" is limited. But each time a new one pops up the same troubles occur.

Far better to settle the matter once and for all and do a big rethink on the question of sound broadcasting in Britain.

---

The spacious studio aboard Mebo II—the ship that seems like a floating hotel.

By PETER COLE

"AS FAR as we are concerned it's visiting a foreign country," said the Customs man. The foreign country in this case, is Radio North Sea International.

The Customs following a Government directive is doing its best to make things awkward for anyone who wants to visit Mebo II, Radio North Sea's pirate ship, anchored off the Essex coast.

Those who want to travel out to see the crew of the pirate ship from Harwich, Felixstowe and Clacton have to pass through a rigorous Customs examination on the way out.

They don't even notify the police of the Marine Offences Act, 1967.

But they did worry about the trip.

The Customs man, I was assured have done away with a ship from the North Sea and actually wanted to go.

## Bearded sea-dog

Together wanting to attend a Government directive is doing his best to make things awkward being taken over and actually decided a trip aboard involved. Boarding an occasional, he must care about another at Customs and was accosting. We could go anywhere.

---

162

FLO PEPE — THE SHERRY

London
Thursday
March 26, 1970
No. 27,410  6d

# Evening News

## PETER COLE meets the DJs who defy Britain

# PIRATES AHOY! I BOARD THE POP PRIVATEER

## PO may scuttle pop pirates

*NEW. 28/1/70*

New plans to scuttle Britain's latest pop pirates—Radio North Sea International—are being considered by the Post Office.

During the past 24 hours engineers successfully jammed the radio's medium wave broadcasts by stepping up maritime radio broadcasts five times their normal power.

## Challenge to Britain as pop pirates set sail

A PIRATE radio ship was early today preparing to anchor off the East Coast and beam pop music to England.

The Swiss owned pirate ship Mebo II—which broadcasts Radio North Sea International—left the Dutch coast yesterday evening, announcing cheekily: "People of England, we're on our way."

It has been broadcasting off the Dutch coast for several months.

The ship will anchor fifteen miles off Frinton, Essex—three miles outside British territorial waters.

The station has three British disc-jockeys on board.

Eighteen companies, in Japan, America, Switzerland, Austria and Holland, have signed advertising contracts with the pirates.

### Boasted

Since the introduction of the Marine Broadcasting (Offences) Act in 1967, it has been an offence to supply, work or advertise on pirate stations.

But 31-year-old Mr. Erwin Meister, of Zurich—one of the station's three directors—has boasted: "The British Government can't touch us as long as we stay outside its territorial waters."

---

We were just getting into the racing boat to go out to Arthur's trawler when she appeared in the form of the Brightlingen Chateau officer.

"You're liable for a £200 fine," he said. "You have to get customs clearance."

So we ended up into the Colchester bureaucratic, doing our best to unravel the red tape which formed a stranglejacket around our every action.

### Any cigarettes or alcohol?

They inquired whether we were carrying cigarettes or alcohol with us.

They read up the Marine Offences Act which seemed frightening, so we didn't know. And eventually they signed papers and we were free to go.

But three hours and around 20 miles from Brightlingsea to Radio North Sea International, the sea was rough and our shirt. Skipper trawler was soaked record like the proverbial cork.

I'm not a good sailor, and I felt far from good.

Going along the deeper water knocks locally as the Swin we sighted her after about two hours.

There's no mistaking her. She's decorated like a piece of R.N. nouveau, the hull covered in red, green and yellow panels and is dominated by her high mast racing into the North Sea horizon.

### Danger on the waves

We drew towards her, the swell tossing us ten feet up and then crashing us down again.

The pirates were cut on deck and I yelled at them.

"Have you got proof?" they shouted, and I produced a Press card.

Then came the most frightening part as we tried to draw alongside. We were inches away when the stern of Mebo II swung round.

I was standing on the rail, board deck of our lowlife Suddenly there was a great crash.

**Continued on Back Page**

Roger Day at the controls and Johnnie Scott, in dark glasses, aboard Mebo II before she moved close to the Essex coast.

## RADIO BLOT-OUT? WE CAN DO WITHOUT IT

RADIO North Sea International is still interfering with the activities of the coastguards and is consequently a danger to shipping.

"We just can't contact the Trinity House lightship, any of the Harwich group, when they are on the air," the Walton-on-the-Naze coastguard said today.

"All we can hear between 6 a.m. and 1 a.m. is pop music."

Although the coastguards say the 183 metre wavelength and Radio North Sea is on 186 (the strength of the pirate's signal is blotting out everything else right down to 180 metres.

So the coastguards can only contact the lightships during the night between 1 a.m. and 6 a.m. when Radio North Sea is off the air.

### MORE POWER

But from this weekend, say the pirates, they will be transmitting pop music 24 hours a day.

"Normally we talk to the lightshipmen about every hour," said the coastguard. "Still there's nothing we can do. We realise it's up to the Post Office."

Apparently there was some interference when Radio North Sea was off Holland. But now, with the increased power and the anchorage only six miles off Clacton, the jamming is in total.

"They don't help any," said the coastguard. "We can do without them."

### SPIRIT OF ADVENTURE

*7/4/70*

SO THERE I WAS standing in the front of Scheveningen looking to board Radio North Sea International's tender for the Mebo II. But Swiss's I been through all this before? No, not quite. You see, last time I broke the law Marine Offences Act 1967) I went out to the Mebo II where it was anchored five miles off the Dutch coast. Now, it had moved to England—and it would take the tender 12 hours to reach the Essex coast of the on-off-minute.

I almost chickened out of the tender trip. I had a much better idea when I went to the hotel for the disc jockeys to move in and I realised that the Mebo II would not operate until the official licence and spirit of adventure? asked Roger Day—and I went. The Mebo Mirror spirit of adventure made up in the North Sea swing with my breakfast and lunch, as clear as that was that the spirit of adventure, DOES more around and it was time for THAT calm back to Holland. We sailed away from the Mebo II in the 9 a.m. daylight. Cast was on the tender which bobbed off for two weeks' shore leave. "You come back in a couple of months and this station will be a big!" he said.

"So via Holland and no one will be any the wiser." Oh no? Then was the man in Scheveningen who sang "Radio North Sea International" to me as I reached the passport. "How long are you staying out there," he asked. "About four days, I think,"

proceeded meekly. "Okay. I listen to them," he added quietly.

Aft those pirates. So why raise the roar? Listen Esther, managing director told me: "We are getting a much better signal now England now and that is important. We will reach our German listeners, too. The new medium wave position will not interfere with anyone and will give us a better signal."

Esther sat genuinely worried about the interference Mebo caused on 186 metre. So much so that he went all the way to the Trinity House to apologise to the lightship authorities. Esten Sellier is now 27 and he is the main man behind RNI. He first attempted to start a pirate station when he bought the Radio London 'Galaxy' last year? It was really for broadcasting, the ship was about the most Hamburg when Germany signed the international agreement stocking the offshore stations. But Esther was safe enough with Radio wouldn't sign the agreement, because of Monaco—and that had been done for years. So now his £400,000 dream has come true and he faces a long way from the tiny first radio station he ran away his college days. He has the DJ's he wants and a new lineup—100 metres and he some full broadcasts again today.

"We are safe now as long as we stay outside territorial waters," Sellier told me confidently. "And our moves to England was good."

What was it like, leaving the radio ship to Britain? "We hardly felt anything at all," said Carl. "We remained broadcasting throughout the night so that the listeners didn't 'cool' with us. The ship hardly moved — even as all art Clacton."

The sooner, however, DOES move around and it was time for THAT calm back to Holland. We sailed away from the Mebo II in the 9 a.m. darkness. Cast was on the tender, too, going off for two weeks' shore leave. "You come back in a couple of months and this station will be a big!" he said.

I believe him. The reason is successful. Its 20,000 letter Market is huge jobs to be Zurich office point this. And it might go back. After 70 hours jumping around beside is the North Sea I'm ready for anything.

Well, almost.

RODNEY COLLINS

# NORDSEE STARTS FM BROADCASTS TO LONDON

LONDON is to have its first FM (VHF) pop station. Radio Northsea International, the pop pirate which moved its base motor vessel Mebo II to the English coast on Tuesday morning, is beginning FM broadcasts to the London area on Channel 50 (102 megs) this weekend.

The station will also continue on 186 metres Medium Wave and 49 metres short wave. Decision to move the ship to Britain was taken by Mebo's director 33-year-old Edwin Bollier. He told RM on Tuesday: "We are increasing our signal to give us better coverage of Europe and we will continue to broadcast in both English and German." RNI will anchor outside British territorial waters to avoid trouble with the British Marine Offences Act.

British disc jockey Mark Wesley told listeners the ship was moving to Britain during transmissions on Monday. "We are coming over. We will stay on the air throughout the night as we prepare to anchor off the Essex coast."

Northsea's directors had originally intended to move the ship to the Belgian coast on Friday and then on to Britain if the signal from Belgium was not strong enough.

# air waves
## RADIO COLUMN
### by Rodney Collins

I'M WRITING this week's radio column from the small fishing port of Scheveningen in Holland, the centre of 'offshore' radio activities in recent weeks. Suddenly this sleepy little town has become famous with the arrival of Radio North Sea International.

It doesn't seem to be quite the place to run 'offshore' radio from. Already tourists are coming down to take pictures of the Mebo 1, RNI's tender which now has to brave an eight hour journey each way out to the Mebo II with DJ's and supplies.

But even though the radio ship is some eight hours away, communication with the station's HQ in Zurich is no longer a problem, as the directors have installed a Telex machine on the ship. It is this machine that has enabled RNI to broadcast up-to-date information about the station's future plans during the past few days.

## MINUTES 14/4/70

When the Zurich office decided to stop medium wave transmissions after confirmed reports of interference with British coastal signals, it took them minutes to inform the ship of their decision. Carl Mitchell was broadcasting at the time.

"It came as a big surprise to all the DJ's out here," Carl told me. "But we read our Telex message to the listeners and we did continue broadcasting on short wave and FM and announced details of the new frequencies as soon as it was possible."

## POTENTIAL

Carl spends up to three weeks at a time aboard the Mebo II. How does he find life out there? "It's great fun and we do have more or less everything we want out here. It's better than Caroline because there aren't too many problems".

This 24-year-old soft spoken American believes that RNI has "amazing potential as a European station". He declines to knock the British Government and takes every opportunity to underline his support of commercial radio . . .

But while the Press spotlight is well and truly fixed upon the Mebo II, let's not forget the other boat in the North Sea — Radio Veronica. Veronica broadcasts on 192 metres for 20 hours each day. Like most of the offshore stations, they compile their own 'hit parade' which takes in Europe's top-selling discs — and they also feature a special Billboard Hot 100 show each Sunday afternoon.

Veronica's sound is professional and I was impressed with what I saw when I visited their offices this week. All their programmes are pre-recorded in their Dutch studios — only the news is broadcast 'live' from the ship each hour.

# Local D. J. hits at Government

MR. WILLIAM REES-DAVIES, Thanet's Tory candidate, laughed this week at the suggestion that he had anything to do with advertisements being broadcast by the pirate radio station Radio North Sea for a Tory political "rave-in" being held in Margate on Monday.

And the father of Roger "Twiggy" Day, the Margate disc jockey who has been plugging the event in his pirate broadcasts, said his son had done it off his own bat as a protest against the Labour Government's opposition to commercial and pirate radios.

Mr. Rees-Davies said he had heard of the pirate radio broadcasts, but they had nothing to do with him.

"I am 100 per cent for commercial radio and this is a well-known fact. I was one of the legal advisers for Radio Caroline and I am a marked man in that respect.

"The radio pirates know me and know my views and they probably picked up the news of my rave-in from the national press. Naturally I am delighted with the publicity for what will be the country's first political rave-in," he added.

Roger Day's father, Mr. B. Thomas, of Canterbury Road, Margate, who is also his manager, told the Gazette, "Roger is doing this off his own bat, without any payment or favour from anybody. The Labour Government is against commercial radio and this is the only way in which the stations can battle against them."

Mr. Douglas Harrison, general manager of Dreamland, where the rave-in is to be held, also denied that his organization had anything to do with the advertisements.

"We fully realise that it is an offence to do so," he added.

The second mystery surrounding the Tory rave-in is "Who is really organising it?"

Mr. Rees-Davies said, "Dreamland are providing the hall and the entertainment. The idea was mine, but I am only providing the political content. Dreamland are charging admission."

Mr. Leslie Whickman, the Tory agent, said it was a normal dance run by Dreamland and they had asked the Tory candidate to appear.

But at Dreamland, ballroom and cinema manager Mr. Derek Wright said Mr. Rees-Davies had approached Dreamland, asking them to organise an event for him at which young people could ask him questions about his policies.

And Mr. Harrison added. "Mr. Rees-Davies is paying a fee for the hire of the ballroom in the normal way. We should be delighted to do the same for any other political party or local organization."

# Nordsee back on 217 metres

RADIO NORTH Sea International engineers worked throughout the weekend preparing for broadcasting on their new frequency, 217 metres.

The station returned to the airways on Wednesday with a clear signal on 217 metres. Broadcasting from the Mebo 11 were Alan West, Carl Mitchell, Mark Wesley, and Axel Nash.

RNI's directors issued a strongly-worded statement when they began new transmissions: "Radio North Sea International on 190 metres was not contravening the Marine Offences Broadcasting Act and the station is located outside British territorial waters . . . therefore the deliberate jamming of RNI's broadcasts by the GPO was illegal.

Orders to stop transmissions on 190 metres were sent out to the Mebo 11 from Zurich after the Ministry of Posts and Telecommunications has successfully blocked RNI's signal.

The station's owner, Mr. Edwin Bollier, told me "We are changing to another frequency. There is no point in continuing broadcasts on 190 metres with the jamming. We will move and re-commence programmes after the weekend."

And on Sunday, RNI's transmitters were switched on to 217 metres, but the ship did NOT broadcast any programmes or test material. The Campaign for Independent Broadcasting issued a statement about the jamming:

"In our view this places Britain in the same category as Communist countries who adopt this most unsavoury practice in order to condition their populations. This has set a precedent which could have far reaching repercussions and must lower the value of British democracy in the eyes of the world."

Free radio supporters gathered outside Broadcasting House over the weekend to protest against the Ministry's jamming of Radio North Sea International, and a new organisation has been formed by a group of RNI supporters to help keep the station on the air.

"If the Ministry block RNI again, then we will take action immediately," their leader told RM this week.

## RNI TO PRESS ON DESPITE JAMMING

by RODNEY COLLINS

RADIO NORTHSEA INTERNATIONAL will continue test broadcasting despite the jamming from the Ministry of Posts and Telecommunications.

"We have no intention whatsoever of stopping transmissions and we will do all we can to maintain normal programmes despite the interference on the frequency," said co-owner Erwin Meister.

Jamming, designed to drive the pop pirates off the air, was resumed last week following the pirate's move to 244 metres — just next to Radio One. Throughout the weekend the Post Office broadcast a signal on top of RNI's wavelength from a naval local near Rochester in Kent. The Post Office signal, which may or may not continue to be broadcast, is 10 kW in strength, about roughly half the pirate's output.

Although effective in South London, parts of the Midlands and East Anglia were hard affected by the Ministry's broadcast. Transmissions were heard normally in Holland and Germany.

But almost as soon as jamming was resumed complaints began rolling in to national newspapers and free radio organisations. In parts of Kent Radio One was unable to be heard said the Campaign For Independent Broadcasting in a statement on Monday.

Although the RNI team is determined to remain on the air — it kept the Ministry on the toes over the weekend as the pirates switched wavelength twice an hour throughout Sunday at Monday — the station cannot make any money from advertising while this situation continues.

RNI began on Saturday by announcing that jamming was "directed by the Labour Government and carried out by the Ministry of Posts and Telecommunications." They later dropped this announcement but still insisted that the Post Office jamming was illegal.

"We will continue I promise that," said Meister "The only station on our wave length is in Czechoslovakia and we have applied to this country for permission to use the wavelength for Western Europe".

# POP PIRATES RAISE A POLITICAL STORM

"And now a special request from Jack, Dennis, Arthur, Jim, Robert and all the lads at the local lifeboat station."

"You realise our last selection jammed the emergency lifeboat reception?"

"We're from the B.B.C. Which eight records do you want to take on your desert Island?"

My RNI timeline on air:

**February**

18th 3pm – 6pm, first live transmission
19th 6am – 9am & 6pm – 8pm
20th 23rd 8am – 10am 2pm – 4pm & 8pm – 10pm
24th 8am – 10 am, 2pm – 4pm
25th –27th 8am – 10am & 8pm – 10pm
28th 8am – 10am, first official broadcast from RNI
after tests.

It was an absolute shambles with me in the main studio and one of the German DJs in the other studio. There was lots of dead air and bad levels.

**March**

1st 12pm – 3pm, station now broadcasting in English 8am – 8 pm, in
German 8pm – 11pm, and in English 11pm – 1am
2nd 8am – 10am
3rd 8am – 10am, then off on tender. ITN News at Ten with Geoffrey Archer on board

Despite our poor first broadcast, the response was incredible. There were sack loads of mail, and reception reports kept arriving. This was despite no publicity. I reckon being so close to Radio Veronica's frequency helped, and word of mouth worked a treat.

**March**

10th, I was back on board with Mark Wesley and David Hughes of Disc & Music Echo.
On air 3pm – 6pm

11th – March 14th 8am – 10 am & 3pm – 6pm
15th 8am – 10 am & 12pm – 3pm, the first chart show
16th – March 19th 8am–10am & 3pm – 6pm
20th – Came ashore. Met old Caroline crew member, Lee Groen, who was famous for saying "Of course man" on my show). Then I caught a plane to London.

On March 24th, the ship moved to an anchorage near where the sixties stations had been. I was totally against this as I thought it might cause problems. How right I was! The owners thought they would get more advertising with a better signal into London. The broadcasts in German had been dropped and it was all English now.

On March 26th, I met Claude, the Swiss engineer, in London, and the next day drove him to Margate, where we met Jimmy Houlihan, who had been involved as Ronan O'Rahilly's fixer on Radio Caroline. The first thing we had to do was get a message to the ship telling them to shut down on 186 metres as it was interfering with the coastguard frequencies. We drove to a deserted area on a one-track road, not far from Birchington-on-Sea in Kent, where we had a clear view if any GPO officials were tracking our signals. We eventually got through to them on the ship to shore communication and told them to get off air. In the distance, we saw a car, so we threw the transmitting equipment into the car boot. We thought it might be the police. A man got out of the car and asked us if we going to be moving soon as he was the local farmer who wanted to bring a lorry load of cattle through. We apologised and said our car had broken down, but it was alright now. We were laughing in the car as we drove off.

The next task was to get Claude on a boat out to the Mebo to change the frequency. So we went to Ramsgate harbour, where Jimmy left us in a pub as I was too well known. He searched for a fishing boat captain who wouldn't mind a bit of spare cash to help us. He wasn't Ronan's fixer for nothing, and of course, he got Claude his lift.

On Saturday 28th March, I went away with Jenny to the Queen's Hotel in Cheltenham, where I was born, to celebrate my birthday. Earlier in the week, I had been interviewed by Clive Cook of the Sunday People. He had somehow got my phone number and address and said if I didn't give him an interview, he would publish my real name and where I lived. I arranged to meet him at the Hilton Hotel in London. Rodney Collins of Record Mirror accompanied me to kick my shin if he asked a question I shouldn't answer. He mainly wanted to know who paid us and who supplied our records. I didn't drop my friends in the record business in it, so said I'd bought the records in HMV and One Stop. With the interview completed, we headed out of the hotel only for a photographer to leap out of the shadows and take a picture of me with the Hilton sign in the background. Also, a waiter chased us and said the bill for the bar hadn't been paid by Clive Cook so we had to cough up. The journalist told us he had been threatened by the Krays. I can understand why.

So there we were coming down to breakfast on

Sunday March 29th, my birthday, at this posh hotel in Cheltenham, with just about everybody reading the People with a huge photo of me on the front page. People kept looking at the picture then me. Fame at last! I phoned my dad, who said Scotland Yard had phoned and they wanted to interview me. We quickly left the hotel and headed back to Surbiton. I certainly didn't contact the police. The trouble was the next tender wasn't until Wednesday, and I was dreading a knock on the door. Thankfully, it never happened.

This is what the Sunday People wrote:

"He should be called Jolly Roger, for he's the most audacious pirate of all. This is swashbuckling Roger 'Twiggy' Day in LONDON LAST WEEK" - *Note the capitals for emphasis.*

"Roger, 25 today, is an 'outlaw'. He's on the Post Office's 'Wanted' list, poor chap. But he actually slips in and out of Britain at will to pick up the records he plays on the newest pop pirate station, Radio North Sea International. Every time he puts a highly polished shoe on his native soil he risks up to two years in jail. How does he do it? Simple. By using the phony name of 'Roger Thomas'"- *So the journalist thought Twiggy Day was my real name! What an idiot!*

"'It's quite true,' he told me over a drink at one of London's most exclusive hotels, "People in the business know I'm here. They send records to my address, and I take them back to the ship." Our Roger is not alone in the cloak-and-dagger game, though. British record companies, recording managers, and publicists are thumbing their noses at government warnings that they're breaking the law by supplying the pirates. Roger said, 'They can send records to their agents in Amsterdam or anywhere else and they just take them to the ship.' - *Of course I never said that at all.*

"Post office boxes and a Dutch Hotel are being used as receiving for the illegal operation. Leading British record companies deny any liaison with the pirates. However, Decca Records said, 'They're certainly not getting any discs from us'." - *Oh yes, we did.*

"And from Phillips, "We are not supplying them at all'."- *Another lie.*

"The 600-ton pop ship anchored six miles off the Essex coast earlier this week. After allegations of interference with lightship communications, it stopped it's medium wave broadcasts two days ago to change wavelengths

There was a lot of interest from not just the press but television. Geoffrey Archer from ITN news paid us a visit. It was great publicity. He asked me if I would ever go back to the UK. I said, "Of course not." He came off on the same tender as I did. I then headed off to the airport to catch a plane to London. Guess who was also on the plane. Yes, Geoffrey Archer. Ho told me not to worry; he wouldn't say anything.

On Tuesday 31st March, I phoned Duncan Johnson to offer him a job and the next day met him at Gatwick, and we flew to Holland. We couldn't get to the ship as

# The People

. 4606      Sunday, March 29, 1970      8d. ★ ★ ⁻ ;

Hotel and car park driveway

**By CLIVE COOKE**

HE should be called Jolly Roger. For he's the most audacious pop pirate of them all.

This is swashbuckling Roger "Twiggy" Day—pictured IN LONDON LAST WEEK.

Roger — 25 today — is an "outlaw." He's on the Post Office's "Wanted" list, poor chap.

But he actually slips in and out of Britain at will to pick up the records he plays on the newest pop pirate station, Radio North Sea International.

And every time he puts a highly polished shoe on to his native soil he risks up to two years in jail.

How does he do it? Simple.

By using the phony name of "Roger Thomas."

"It's quite true," he told me over a drink at one of London's most exclusive hotels.

"People in the business know I'm here. They send records to my address and I take them back to the ship."

Our Roger is not alone in the cloak-and-dagger game, though.

British record companies, recording managers and pop publicists are thumbing their noses at Government warnings that they're breaking the law by supplying the pirates.

## Denied

Roger said: "They can send records to their agents in Amsterdam or anywhere else and he can just take them to the ship."

Post Office boxes and a Dutch hotel are being used as receiving depots abroad for the illegal operation.

Leading British record companies hotly deny any liaison with the pirates, however Decca said: "They're certainly not getting any discs from us." And from Philips "We're not supplying them at all."

The 600-ton pop ship anchored six miles off Essex early last week. After allegations of interference with lightship communications, it stopped its medium-wave broadcasts two days ago to change wavelengths.

it was rough weather, so we stayed at the Grand Hotel. The next day, we managed to get on board and arrived at midnight. As we boarded, the station was off air, having its frequency on the MW wavelength changed. There is no stranger place than being on a radio ship that isn't broadcasting. It was a bit like the lockdown we had during the Covid pandemic. We didn't get back on air until Friday 10th April on 190 metres. I was on 9am – 10 am and again between 3 pm and 6pm. Transmissions were intermittent though. The next day, I was on at 2:30pm – 3pm and 6pm – 8pm. It meant I had a break to watch the FA Cup Final, that famous 2:2 draw between Chelsea and Leeds United.

12th April 8am – 10am & 12pm – 3pm with the Nifty
Fifty Chart Show
13th April 8am – 10am & 3pm – 6pm
14th April & 15th 8am – 10am & 12pm –3pm

After the show on 15th April, I got a call on the link that we had to Percy Scadden in Frinton-on-Sea, the same guy who looked after contacting us on Radio Caroline. He said the British Government was jamming us and we should go off air.

The next day, a fishing boat came out from England with Radio RNI director Urs Emmeneger from Switzerland and American presenter Larry Tremaine on board. I took an instant dislike to Larry.

On Friday 17th, I took the tender to Holland and flew to Heathrow with RNI colleague engineer, Peter Chicago, not knowing what lay ahead.

I was back aboard after my shore leave on Thursday 30th April with Duncan Johnson, Andy Archer, and Hannibal. The next day, I was back on air on another new frequency – 217 metres between 8.15am – 9am. The next couple of weeks, we were on and off on FM until Wednesday 13th May when we started on 244 metres and I was on air 10.15am – 11am.

The idea to constantly change frequencies was to try to stop the jamming for a while. I was amazed how loyal listeners were, following us up and down the dial. We tried a new tactic on Saturday 13th June when we changed our name to Caroline.

That was a wonderful moment. It felt so good to be back on air announcing, "You are listening to Radio Caroline," though sadly not on 259. The reason behind our name change was because there was a general election coming up and eighteen-years-olds had the vote for the first time. We also thought the name change would remind listeners of all ages that it was Harold Wilson's Labour Government who had taken the other offshore stations off air. We made promos which broadcast how wrong it was to jam us, something the British Government hadn't even done during the second world war to Lord Haw Haw as he broadcast his Nazi propaganda. We added that if people wanted commercial radio, they should vote Conservative. One might argue that radio shouldn't get involved in politics, but we had no choice. We also hoped the Conservatives, if elected, would stop the jamming.

The government received thousands of letters of protest about the jamming. I've kept some of the replies, as you can see later.

Rumours about the Mebo being a spy ship were rubbish. It had been spread around that there were areas on board which were no-go areas. It was false news to discredit the company.

On shore, our supporters took to the streets. There was a huge demonstration in London on Sunday June 14th organised by the Free Radio Association. Radio

Caroline founder and owner Ronan O'Rahilly turned up, accompanied by radio and TV presenter Simon Dee. Ronan had organised buses to tour the southeast that week to remind people about what had happened to Radio Caroline and tell them about the jamming attacks. We began playing the record, Who Do You Think You Are Kidding Mr Wilson, and posters were published depicting Harold Wilson as Chairman Mao. One demonstrator even put up a placard outside Downing Street saying 'Roger Day for Prime Minister'.

The election, on Thursday 18th June, was forecast as a Labour win – it didn't look good. I went to bed that night quite depressed. Imagine my surprise when I got up to do the breakfast show to discover Labour had been defeated. Ironically, the new Prime Minister was Edward Heath, the most famous old boy from my old school, Chatham House Grammar School in Ramsgate. I was a very happy bunny. I am convinced it was fans of the offshore radio stations that swung the result as there were so many marginal seats in the areas where offshore radio was popular.

I came off the Mebo on Friday 19th June to take a holiday in Torremolinos in Spain as I needed a break after the traumas of the previous six months. Little did I suspect I wouldn't be going back. After two fabulous weeks, Jenny and I came back to the UK and I phoned Larry Tremaine, by now Programme Director, on Sunday July 12th to ask when the tender was going to the ship. I shall never forget the idiot's reply – "For you, Roger, the tender is never going!" I suppose I should have smelt a rat. He had sold the Swiss owners a story about how he was a big name in US radio and he could run it better than me. The trouble was I knew his story was false and he saw me as a threat. I was heartbroken.

I would make one final visit to the ship, this time from the UK. A friend of mine in Essex, Mike Baker, who would go on to work at Capital Radio and Wolverhampton's Beacon Radio, knew somebody with a small boat in Clacton-on-Sea. I needed to get out there because my record collection was RNI's oldies library. There was no way I was leaving that on board. It was a very scary trip as a rough sea blew up. When we pulled alongside, those on board weren't expecting me, and they weren't pleased to see me, particularly when I said I was taking my records off. Anyway, we managed to get them off, and a rather over-loaded little boat sailed back to Clacton, and surprisingly, we were not met by the police or customs! How the boat didn't sink with the weight of the records is a miracle.

I was proud to have been involved in creating a fantastic, ground-breaking station. Under my programme direction, RNI was the first to have album tracks as part of the normal format, and we had a really good team of DJs. We also built a very large audience despite the jamming. The Swiss owners did make a lot of mistakes, not just hiring Tremaine. Why did they hire German DJs when the station could hardly be heard in Germany? In Holland there was still a lot of anti-German feeling among the Dutch over how the Nazis had treated them.

Moving the mooring from Holland to off the UK was the single biggest mistake. I think if they had remained off Holland, we would have been left alone.

The response from listeners was incredible. We were getting as many letters as Radio Caroline received, and we made Number One hit records with our radio plays. The best example is Spirit in The Sky by Norman Greenbaum.

The Mebo was well fitted out, as you can see from my pictures. We broadcast on short wave, medium wave, and FM. We each had cabins to ourselves, and there was a good Dutch crew. I think the main studio was too big though and the equipment wasn't as good as on Radio Caroline or Radio London.

I must have been a little naive, thinking Edward Heath would stop jamming RNI. The new government continued what the Labour government had done, and a few weeks after the election, they sailed the Mebo back to Holland. The jamming ceased, but it was too late. They soon they went off air.

As for Larry Tremaine, I did manage to get my revenge. My father, who was furious at my treatment, informed the Home Office how Larry Tremaine was involved with the pirate radio station and was living illegally in London when on shore. The Home Office acted on my father's information and Larry Tremaine was deported. Never mess with my family! I did actually meet Larry when I was in LA many years later, and he admitted he was wrong, so I forgave him.

At least the listeners liked me.

# radio nordsee international

the ship broadcasting 6½ miles off Clacton on 244 meters has been "jammed" by the G.P.O. for the past two months.

"Jamming" is a practice only exercised so far by communist government's dictatorships—*and in the case of R.N.I.—By the Labour Government.*

Radio Nordsee International is a *legal* station operating in International waters *and therefore not under British jurisdiction.*

Therefore, the "jamming" of R.N.I. by the G.P.O. is *illegal,* according to the International Radio Regulations signed in Geneva in 1959.

This "jamming" can only be called a **dictatorial** action by the Labour Government.

## if you disagree

With these tactics, if you want to be free to tune into the radio station of your choice, if you agree with us that the "jamming" of R.N.I. could be the beginning of the end of freedom in Britain then you

**Vote** against the illegal "jamming" of R.N.I. by the Labour Government.

*Make sure that the candidate you vote for is willing to bring*

## free radio back to britain!

---

10, Downing Street,
Whitehall.

16 June, 1970

Dear Mr. Colquhoun,

I have been asked to reply to your recent letter to the Prime Minister about the action taken by the Ministry of Posts and Telecommunications to stop broadcasts from the pirate station Radio North Sea International.

This station broadcast in breach of No. 422 of the Radio Regulations annexed to the International Telecommunication Convention, Montreux 1965, which our own and other European countries are under treaty obligations to uphold. Its transmissions caused serious interference to maritime radio services over a wide area when it operated on 186 metres. When forced to change to 190 metres it ceased, because of the strength of its signals, further interference to local maritime communications and to foreign listeners to their own broadcast services in Norway and Italy. Once it was evident that the pirate station had ignored complaints of interference to other radio services, the Ministry arranged in compliance with the International Telecommunication Convention to activate a transmitter and put the pirate station off the air.

The position of Radio Veronica is somewhat different since the transmissions from this pirate station are not aimed at the United Kingdom, and since they do not interfere with our domestic broadcasting or other radio services we are not directly concerned. It would be up to neighbouring countries to protest to the Netherlands if transmissions from Radio Veronica caused harmful interference to their authorised broadcasting services.

I am sorry that you feel so strongly in this matter, but I hope you will agree that we must preserve law and order in the field of broadcasting, in the use of scarce radio frequencies and also, that we must protect the rights of individuals, wherever they may live, to listen to their own authorised broadcasting services. Without this nobody's radio services would remain free from interference for very long. Against this background I hope you will accept that this is not a matter of freedom of choice but of action against people who, for their own gain, cause interference and usurp frequencies assigned by international agreement to others.

Yours sincerely,

David Candler

David Candler
Political Office

*My last shore leave —Tremaine, Alan West, Mark Wesley, Carl Mitchell, and crew.*

**Councillor Dennis Hobden**
Prospective Labour Parliamentary Candidate for Kemp Town

3 Queen's Park Terrace
Brighton BN2 2YA

10th June 1970

Dear Mrs.Turner,

I feel your letter is an example of how
people get their priorities mixed up.

As I stated in my earlier letter candidates
or M.P's give these matters every consideration but they
cannot give in to threats otherwise we would be in
anarchy.

This election will be about whether we
have better education for our children, better housing,
better health services, better roads and the running of
the economy.

In all these things the Conservatives failed
and if you see you duty to persuade people to vote merely
on the issue of pirate radio that is a matter for you to
have on your conscience. Mine will be clear.

As I said before the issue is not about radio
but as to whether a small clique of people can make a
fortune out of advertising.

Support them by all means but don't ask your
friends to come running to me when the election is over
complaining about the effects of Conservative policies.

It will then be too late.

Sincerely,

Dennis Hobden.

A LETTER RECEIVED BY MR DAVID PREWETT OF THE NATIONAL COMMERCIAL
RADIO MOVEMENT DURING AUGUST 1969 PLEDGING FULL CONSERVATIVE
SUPPORT FOR FREE RADIO:

"Thank you for your letter of August 10 and for your courtesy in sending to me
the Petition signed at the Public Meeting which took place earlier that day in
Trafalgar Square.

"In response to the petition, I would like to make it clear that the
Conservative Party is convinced that there is now a wide public demand for
local radio, and that local radio can make a valuable contribution to the
well-being of the community. After examining the experience of our own and
other countries, we have come to the conclusion that local radio can only be
successfully financed from advertising.

"A Conservative Government will therefore encourage the establishment of
local radio stations financed by advertising and responsible to an independent
authority which will, on the analogy of the existing ITA, ensure a high standard
both of programmes and advertising.

"I believe that by this policy we can achieve a position where British Radio,
in the words of your petition, will be 'unique in its range of educational and
entertaining programmes'. "

-EDWARD HEATH

# Bid to scupper pop pirates

THE GOVERNMENT set sail today to scupper the pop pirate ship Mebo II.

It launched an international hunt for the country that registered the vessel, now anchored six miles off Clacton.

And that country will be asked to make the Mebo II an outlaw of the high seas by scrapping its registration.

In this way action can be taken against her by any nation for violating the laws on free passage on the high seas.

## In the clear

Most countries would be likely to heed Britain's request as a member of the International Telecommunications Union.

But, apart from registration, Radio North Sea seems to be in the clear as far as British law is concerned.

The 1967 Marine Broadcasting (Offences) Act that scuppered Radio Caroline and Radio London makes it illegal for anybody in Britain to operate, supply or advertise with a pirate radio ship.

The maximum penalty is two years in prison or a fine or both.

But as long as Mebo II stays outside territorial waters and has no contact with the shore it does not contravene the Act.

POP FANS tuning in to Radio North Sea are risking a £10 fine for listening to a pirate.

# Massive rally for Indie disc stations!

RM 13/6/70

THE GENERAL ELECTION just one week away, the row over pirate radio is hotting up. RNI has announced the closure of the station on June 19 if a Labour government is returned and free radio organisations are busy making last minute attempts to keep Radio North Sea International on the air.

A massive rally is being organised at Speaker's Corner, Marble Arch, on Sunday afternoon and this will be followed by a march to Downing Street.

Martin Rosen of the Campaign for Independent Broadcasting told Record Mirror: "We are hoping for a really large gathering. Announcements about the rally are being given over the air."

The result of next week's election will obviously determine the future of RNI. Mr. Urs Emmenegger, the company's managing director, who was last week refused entry into Britain, has slipped into the country, and had this to say about the election: "It is not a matter of just one party against another. This is freedom. We are fighting for the freedom of the individual and his right to listen to whatever he wants".

Emmenegger intends to remain in Britain until "things are sorted out".

Disc jockeys on board the Mebo II are asking people to attend the rally, planned for 3pm. "Please go along and don't leave it to your friends. Otherwise next week RNI will not be broadcasting", Roger Day told listeners on Tuesday.

Meanwhile normal programmes continue even though the Ministry of Posts and Telecommunications is still jamming all broadcasts. "To give in now would be wrong. We will continue this fight at least till after the election", said Emmenegger who also hinted the station might take "drastic action if necessary" to stay on the air until June 19.

The 1970 Free Radio Rally. On the
left, a placard says RTD for PM

Ronan at the rally

# THE DAY DJ ROGER GOT 'MAROONED'

**Roger "Twiggy" Day**

15/8/70 DISC

AS THE hot air clears from around the BBC over the sacking of dear Kenny Everett, spare a thought for another dearly loved DJ whose fate has almost slipped by unnoticed.

For at almost the same time that Everett received the bad news from Ian Trethowan, Roger "Twiggy" Day was fired from Radio North Sea.

Here the reasons were not quite so obvious, but it seems due to a certain contretemps between

Roger, the first DJ RNI ever hired, and current station manager Larry Tremaine over the way the station should be run.

"I have been very disillusioned by the way things were being run on the ship. They were always changing their minds and never seemed to be able to find the right format. Mind you, I'd still like to have a bash and I'd go back if they asked me, but it's true I haven't been seeing eye to eye with some of the people connected with the boat."

In some ways, Roger's situation is even more lamentable than Kenny's. At least Everett has his own TV show and was a respected and established disc-jockey, Roger has come out of four years' loyalty to free radio with precisely nothing.

"Naturally I do feel a bit cheated and don't seem to have much to show for my DJ career. I've got a job coming up, but

it's not radio and really I'm just back where I started, trying to get into radio from the bottom again."

To refresh those with short memories, Roger's DJ career began in the ballrooms around his Margate home, he joined Radio England in 1966 and then moved to Caroline South where he stayed until the ship's very last day. After a few blank months he joined Luxembourg but there again the strict programme format didn't suit him.

"Now, it's difficult to know what to look forward to," says Roger. "North Sea was a good move. I proved the call for free radio is not dead and I hope it has been a pointer to the type of thing we want to hear from commercial radio when it arrives. But I've got a feeling these stations are going to be quite dreadful—like local BBC stations with ad-

vertising. If only the Government could create just one national commercial station it would be nice."

Roger also wonders where the new stations will get their DJs from. "Look at the BBC—the only new disc-jockey they've had in the last three years is Noel Edmonds. All the others were in business long before that. There are no prospects for new DJs anywhere—either the commercial people will have to try for the established names or gamble on people with no previous experience."

But what of the future for Roger himself?

"I want to get back into radio again just as soon as possible. I'm really encouraged by the amount of letters I've had from people during North Sea and since. In fact I've had more letters a week this year than when I was on Caroline, which really surprised me."

---

# RNI GOES EUROPE — ROGER DAY OUT

8/8/70

**by RODNEY COLLINS**

RADIO NORTH Sea International, the pop pirate ship anchored three-and-a-half miles off Scheveningen, Holland, is axeing its German service, RM understands.

This will be replaced by a second European service — probably Dutch — within the next few weeks.

The new Dutch service will broadcast early mornings and during the evenings on the new medium wave frequency of 217 metres medium wave (1385 kcs).

But the chief Erman disc jockey — Axel Nash (24) is likely to remain with the station . . ."

Since the Mebo 11 moved back to Holland, there has been a very encouraging reaction from European listeners," said Eva Fister, the station's office manager on Wednesday.

"We have received so many letters from people saying that the programmes are better that we want of course carry on. The directors of RNI do not intend to give up now!"

Radio North Sea International is at last making headway into Europe. Audience figures for Germany and Holland are expected later this month, and they are likely to be very encouraging for the pop pirate.

Decision to stop German transmissions will in no way effect the English service which will continue to broadcast between 7 am — 8 pm and 11 pm and 2 am. The Mebo 11 ship is now serviced entirely from Holland.

"I think that this station is really making headway into Europe," said managing director Larry Tremaine. "Our intention now is to serve the European audience — all our advertising is geared to Dutch, English and German listeners."

Roger Day, formerly chief disc jockey of Radio Norther Sea International has confirmed that he has left the station. "My contract with the station expired before I went on holiday and the company has decided not to re-new it," he told RM.

"I have several other offers in hand which I am considering at the moment. I obviously have my eye on the development of commercial radio in Britain," said Roger.

Managing director Larry Tremaine said Roger Day had left the station because of a disagreement over station policy. He has not resigned as such — but I can say at this stage that he will not be returning to the ship."

---

7.  **UK Nationals involved**

    (1)  *Announcers*

    +* Roger Day from: Margate, Kent

    +* Andy Archer from Kings Lynn, Norfolk

    * Alan West (aliss Ross Randall) from Morden, Surrey

    * John Scott (now sacked) from Scotland

    Mark Wesley (alias Barnett) from Hammersmith, London

    * Tape recordings and transcripts available

    + Featured in ITN broadcast

    According to Press reports and the ITN report these announcers were well aware of their liability to prosecution under our Act.

    (2)  *Other persons engaging in broadcasting*

    * Ed Marino (nationality to be determined)

    * Dorothy Squires, entertainer

    John Lennon

    The voices of all three were heard. From press reports and the broadcast itself the interview of Dorothy Squires by Marino was conducted on board and was transmitted live. From a press report Dorothy Squires admitted defying the Act.

    John Lennon's voice was heard by a member of MPT staff in an interview broadcast from the ship. It has been alleged this took place during a visit to the ship by Lennon and about thirty other persons. Evidence to verify this has not yet been obtained.

    (3)  *Other persons involved*

    Mr Day, father of Roger Day, of 27 Canterbury Road, Margate, believed to be engaged in procuring persons for service on the ship. Evidence of this has to be obtained.

8.  **Offences by the Press**

    Copies of articles are enclosed in attached folder (Annex A) in chronological order. The items in which an offence against Clause

    - 3 -

# CHAPTER 13

# ON THE ROAD AGAIN 2

In August I did something I had vowed never to do. On my behalf, one of my loyal listeners applied to the BBC for a job at Radio One. Needless to say, it didn't do the trick.

After that, I had a tricky few months with no income, but a flat to pay for. If it hadn't been for the generosity of my parents, God knows what would have happened to me.

So it was back on the disco circuit:

Thursday 17th–Sittingbourne Town Hall
Saturday 19th–Bury St Edmunds: private party
Sunday 20th–Tudor House, Bearsted
Monday 28th–Didcot Youth Centre

**October**
Friday 2nd–Beaconsfield Youth Club
Wednesday 7th–Hatfield Polytechnic
Thursday 8th–Berkhamsted
Friday 9th–White City Youth Club

B.B.C.

BRITISH BROADCASTING CORPORATION

PO Box 1AA Broadcasting House,
London, W.1.

Telephone 01-580 4468     Telegrams Broadcasts London
                                                    Telex
Cables Broadcasts London W1     Telex 22182

18th August 1970

Dear Dorothy Edwards,

    Thank you very much for your letter of 12th August.  It was good to hear from you again.

    I am glad you are enjoying the Johnnie Walker show.  I agree with you that he has fitted admirably into his early morning spot and, as you will have seen from the press, his "Housewife of the Day" item is now becoming famous.

    We were extremely sorry about his recent accident but we are keeping his spot open for him and I hope he will be returning, fit and well, in about a month.

    I was interested in what you said about Roger Day.  As you know, there are a great number of disc jockeys we are not able to employ at the moment.  However, I promise to keep him in mind if a suitable opportunity arises in the future.

    I am glad you find the programmes on Radio 1 good and I hope you will continue to enjoy many happy hours of listening.

          Yours sincerely,


          (Douglas Muggeridge)
          Controller, Radio 1 and 2

Miss Dorothy Edwards,
1 West Avenue,
Warrington, Lancs.

Tuesday 20th–I was offered to tour as one of The Pipkins of Gimme Dat Ding fame, but I turned it down

Thursday 22nd–Regency Lounge, Herne Bay

Friday 23rd–Beaconsfield Youth Club

Tuesday 27th–Thanet Technical College, Ramsgate

Friday 30th–Maidenhead Youth Centre

## November

Tuesday 3rd–Berkhamsted

Thursday 5th–The Pilgrim, Haywards Heath

Friday 6th–East Grinstead Cricket Club

Saturday 7th– Lakenheath Air Force Base

Wednesday 11th–Bookham Youth Club, Surrey

Friday 13th–Beaconsfield Youth Club
Saturday 21st–Golders Green: private party
Monday 23rd–Tiffany's London
Friday 27th–Beaconsfield Youth Club
Saturday 28th–Balls Park College, Hertford
Monday 30th–Nero's Ramsgate
Tuesday December 1st–Berkhamsted
Saturday 5th–Hermitage Ballroom, Hitchin
Friday 11th–Beaconsfield Youth Club
Saturday 12th–Hermitage Ballroom, Hitchin
Tuesday 15th–Thanet Technical College at Nero's
Saturday 19th–Alloy Metals' Christmas Party, Stratford
Tuesday 22nd–Berkhamsted
Wednesday 23rd–Beaconsfield Youth Club
Monday 28th–Royston Town Hall
Tuesday 29th–Berhamsted
Thursday 31st–The A Train Disco, Guildford

**1971:**

Here's a list of the discos I presented: Beaconsfield YC; USAF
Lakenheath, Guildford; Chatham Town Hall; Richmond
Rugby Club; Balls Park College; University of Reading;
Berkhamsted Kings Arms; Hermitage Ballroom, Hitchen;
Army Pay Corps Worthy Down; Farnborough Cricket
Club; Tilehurst Youth Club; Tech College Colchester;
Workingmen's Club, Kettering; Royston Town Hall; Clouds,
East Grinstead; Youth Centre, Chingford; Thanet Technical
College; Officers' Mess, Liphook; Ealing Village Hall, Bury
St Edmunds; Queens Hotel, Farnborough; Masonic Hall,

Wallingford; White Lion, Barnet; Wanstead Youth Club; Hatfield Polytechnic; Festival Centre, Glossop; Redbourne Youth Club; The Barn, Daventry; Nonington College; Astor Theatre Deal; Social Centre Aylesbury; King George's Hall, Esher; Town Hall, Petersfield; Cricket Club, Charlesworth; Clacton with Uriah Heap; Marston Club, Bedford; Rebecca Club and Flamingo Northampton; Cavendish Memorial Hall; Maidenhead Youth Club; Aylesbury Social Club; St Nicholas Church Hall; Shepperton Youth Club; Laporte Social Cub, Luton; RAF Rissington; Gate Pub, Luton; Grand Ballroom, Broadstairs; Johnfields Club, Guildford; Sanderstead Youth Club; Stanton Village Hall; Sergeants' Mess, Arborfield; Marston Club, Bedford; Liphook Village Hall; Nettleswell Youth Centre, Harlow; Youth Centre, Loughton; Dreamland Ballroom; Saffron Walden Cinema; Pavilion Hemel Hempstead; Town House, Wellington; Broomfield County Secondary School; Manor House Ballroom, Isle Of Wight; Ailwyn School, Ramsey, Cambridgeshire; Baldock Youth Centre; Chiltlee Manor, Liphook; Alloy Metals' Christmas Party in Forest Gate, Northumberland Grand London; Oakley Village Hall.

In September 1971, I ventured out and put on my own disco at the Grand Ballroom, in Broadstairs. It wasn't to play the normal dance music but the heavier, progressive music, which was becoming popular. It was a great success, with a full house, and I planned to repeat it every week. But some of Broadstairs' residents accused the people attending of bad behaviour. It wasn't true, but the owners of the venue got cold feet and cancelled.

# 1972

Hatfield Polytechnic; Dreamland Ballroom; Maidenhead Youth Centre; Army Camp Worthy Down; Marston Social Club; Balls Park College; Anne Brown Youth Club, Watlington; Shepperton Youth Centre; Sandy Youth Club, Bedfordshire; Beaconsfield Youth Club; Tofts Club, Folkestone; Tudor House, Bearsted; Sanderstead Young Conservatives, University of Reading; Horsham Youth Centre; Long Bridge Youth Club, Canterbury; Oxford Polytechnic; Nonington College; Greensward School, Hockley; Officers' Mess, Liphook; Rainsford Youth Club, Chelmsford; Bowaters Social Club, Sittingbourne; Marquee Club London; Connaught Hall, Attleborough, Norfolk; RAF Grafton Club, Swaffham; Royal Marines' Churchill Club, Deal; Saffron Walden Cinema; RAF St Mawgan, Newquay; Honiton Youth Centre; Park Ballroom, Plymouth; Tiverton Youth Centre; YMCA St Austell, Cornwall; Staines Town Hall; AEI FC, Gravesend; Astor Theatre; Deal; RAF Marham, Norfolk; WI Hall Hockwold, Suffolk; Thanet Technical College; Tilehurst YC; Queen's Hall, Watton, Norfolk; Banbury Rugby Club; Police Club; Papworth Everard, Cambrigheshire; Aylesbury Social Club; Staines Town Hall; Athenium, Bury St Edmunds; New Malden Squash Club; RAF Halton; Wendover, Buckinghamshire; Sandy Youth Club; Speakeasy Club, Harlow; Horsham Youth Centre; Winter Gardens, Banbury; Beachcomber Club, Grimsby; Haverhill Youth Centre, Suffolk; Carnegie Rooms, Thetford; Camelot Ballroom, Taunton; Mistrale Club, Beckenham; Gravesend Civic Hall, Greensward School, Hockley; The Belfry,

Great Milton, Oxford; Bletchley Youth Centre; Moreton In The Marsh Youth Centre; Riverside Club, Leatherhead; Colchester Young Conservatives; Lilley Village Hall, Luton; Blighs Hotel, Sevenoaks; RAF Coningsby, Lincolnshire; Laporte Social Cub, Luton; Braintree College; Alloy Metals' Christmas Party, London; Gadebridge Youth Club; Hemel Hempstead; Edgbarrow Youth Club, Crowthorne; The Forum, Kidlington; Officers' Mess, Liphook; Dunstable Youth Club.

It was during 1972 that Ronan O'Rahilly actually managed to get the Mi Amigo back at sea. I did record a few programmes for the re-launch of Radio Caroline. But there were many problems, and the broadcasts were irregular. In an ideal world, I would have loved to go back, but I had to earn money to pay the bills and there wasn't that much around from the station.

I began doing so well I could buy a new car with a trailer to carry the DJ equipment.

*Disco for Thanet Technical College*

**1973:**

Bletchley Youth Club; Henham Village Hall, Essex; Tudor House, Bearsted; Brooklands Youth Centre, Colchester; Horsham Youth Centre; Longbridge Youth Centre, Canterbury; Camelot Club, Taunton; Mistrale Club, Beckenham; Balls Park College, Hertford; Little Easton Village Hall; Town Hall, Sittingbourne; Bushey Mead School, Bushey; Nero's, Southsea; Lady Spencer Churchill College, Oxford; Shepperton Youth Club; Isleworth Village Hall; Guildford Youth Centre; Worth Down Army Pay Corps; Royal Star, Maidstone; AEI Gravesend; Nonington College; Forum Club, Kidlington; Blackheath Rugby Club; Tamworth Youth Centre; Edgebarrow Youth Centre, Crowthorne; Civic Hall Gravesend; Bessingham Village Hall; Wickford Youth Centre; Downham Market Youth Centre; Sandy Youth Centre; Ordnance Survey Club, Southampton; a club in Zurich; Clouds Disco, Canvey Island; Castle Club, Mottingham; Streatham Young Conservatives; George Rowney Social Club, Bracknell; Sultan Club, Gosport; Forum Club, Kidlington; Laporte Sports & Social Club, Luton; Marquee, Papworth Everard; Sele School, Hertford; Gilberd School, Colchester; Robert Brett, Canterbury; Owen Memorial Hall, North Cheam; Elliot's Social Cub, Gillingham; Ratling Club, Aylesham; Sanderstead Young Conservatives; Leatherhead Golf Club, Streatham Young Conservatives; Polar Baths, London; Canterbury Technical College; George Rowney Social Club, Bracknell; Alloy Metals' Christmas Party; Simon Langton School, Canterbury.

# Roger tries to fill a gap in the local scene

Roger "Twiggy" Day, former pirate disc jockey, has an exciting plan for Medway's night life.

AT LAST! Someone is trying to get a regular dance going in the Medway area. Roger "Twiggy" Day, formerly of Radio Caroline Radio Luxembourg and more recently of Radio North Sea fame, is arranging a series of dances at Chatham Town Hall.

Initially, these events are to be held on Thursdays, 14 and 21 January. If they are a success there will be one a week. It is up to the public to show how much the Medway Towns need regular dances by giving its support to this venture.

The first two "happenings" will be run on the lines of a discotheque. If they are well attended, Roger intends to try and book both local and big name acts.

He is very enthusiastic about the project: "I hope they are a success," he said. "I feel that the Medway Towns deserve good dances and I hope that mine will fill that gap."

At the moment Roger is touring the country making personal appearances, building up his following all the time. His life as a disc jockey started five years ago when he began to compere dances at Margate. From then he moved to Radio England. When it folded, he joined Radio Caroline where he really made his name.

After a short time with Radio Luxembourg and then Radio North Sea, he went on the road with his mobile discotheque. Roger, who was voted fifth best D.J. in a national poll, and whose show was twice as many votes as the Tony Blackburn Show, is hoping eventually to return to radio.

But at present he is happy to organise dances. He intends to present a variety of music. Obviously the majority of it will be music with a good beat for dancing.

It will be a pity if the local dances are not well attended. It is Roger's sort of enthusiasm that will give the young people of this area good varied entertainment.

# CHAPTER 14

# RADIO AWARDS

My listeners have always been so lovely, and their support has kept me going all these years. They also voted for me in various popularity polls.

**1968:**

Disc & Music Echo 10th

I was invited to the awards ceremony at the Empire Rooms, Tottenham Court Road, London. But thought I would get arrested, so I didn't go.

Top Pops: 10th Best Radio Show. Also 10th Best DJ

# 1968 ✳ POP

## BRITISH SECTION

| MALE SINGER | GROUP |
|---|---|
| 1. SCOTT WALKER | 1. BEATLES |
| 2. TOM JONES | 2. ROLLING STONES |
| 3. DONOVAN | 3. CREAM |
| 4. Cliff Richard | 4. Small Faces |
| 5. Mick Jagger | 5. Shadows |
| 6. John Mayall | 6. Jimi Hendrix |
| 7. Paul McCartney | 7. Herd |
| 8. John Lennon | 8. Bee Gees |
| 9. Engelbert Humperdinck | 9. Nice |

| GIRL SINGER | MUSICIAN |
|---|---|
| 1. JULIE DRISCOLL | 1. ERIC CLAPTON |
| 2. LULU | 2. JIMI HENDRIX |
| 3. DUSTY SPRINGFIELD | 3. HANK MARVIN |
| 4. Cilla Black | 4. Brian Auger |
| 5. Sandie Shaw | 5. John Mayall |
| 6. Christine Perfect | 6. Don Partridge |
| 7. P. P. Arnold | 7. Paul McCartney |
| 8. Petula Clark | 8. George Harrison |
| | 9. Donovan |

CILLA: second TV artist

### SINGLE DISC

1. JUMPIN' JACK FLASH
   Rolling Stones
2. THIS WHEEL'S ON FIRE
   Julie Driscoll and the Brian Auger Trinity

3. JOANNA
   Scott Walker
4. Lady Madonna
   Beatles
5. America
   Nice
6. Hurdy Gurdy Man
   Donovan
7. Baby Come Back
   Equals
8. I Close My Eyes And Count To Ten
   Dusty Springfield
9. Lazy Sunday
   Small Faces

### DISC JOCKEY
1. JOHN PEEL
2. TONY BLACKBURN
3. JIMMY SAVILE
4. Emperor Rosko
5. Stuart Henry
6. Johnnie Walker
7. Mike Raven
8. Simon Dee
9. Roger Day

## BEST RADIO SHOW

| | |
|---|---|
| 1 TOP GEAR | 21.3 % |
| 2 Tony Blackburn Show | 20.7 % |
| 3 For Everett | 17.2 % |
| 4 Stuart Henry Show | |
| 5 Emperor Rosko Show | |
| 6 Pick Of The Pops | |
| 7 Scene And Heard | |
| 8 Robbie Dale Show | |
| 9 Presenting Elvis Presley | |
| 10 Roger "Twiggy" Day Show | |

## DISC JOCKEY

| | |
|---|---|
| 1 JOHN PEEL | 22.4 % |
| 2 Stuart Henry | 20.9 % |
| 3 Tony Blackburn | 20.6 % |
| 4 Jimmy Savile | |
| 5 Kenny Everett | |
| 6 Johnnie Walker | |
| 7 Emperor Rosko | |
| 8 Robbie Dale | |
| 9 Tony Prince | |
| 10 Roger Day | |

*10th in Melody Maker*

## BEST RADIO/TV SHOW

| | |
|---|---|
| 1 Top of the Pops | 1495 |
| 2 Scene and Heard | 307 |
| 3 Top Gear | 286 |
| 4 Roger Day Breakfast Show (RNI) | 259 |
| 5 Disco 2 | 253 |
| 6 Elvis NBC Special | 228 |
| 7 Pick of the Pops | 187 |
| 8 Kenny Everett | 168 |
| 9 Tony Blackburn | 148 |
| 10 Savile's Travels | 137 |
| 11 'Nifty Fifty' Show (RNI) | 118 |
| 12 John Peel's Sunday Show | 110 |
| 13 Russ Hour | 105 |
| 14 It's Cliff Richard | 92 |
| 15 The Andy Williams Show | 89 |
| 16 Mike Raven's R & B Show | 88 |
| 17 Dave Cash | 73 |
| 18 Emperor Rosko | 65 |
| 19 Sounds of the 70's | 62 |
| 20 This is Tom Jones | 59 |

## BEST DISC JOCKEY

| | |
|---|---|
| 1 (2) Jimmy Savile | 1054 |
| 2 (3) Tony Blackburn | 673 |
| 3 (4) Kenny Everett | 531 |
| 4 (1) John Peel | 465 |
| 5 (13) Roger 'Twiggy' Day | 432 |
| 6 (5) Emperor Rosko | 238 |
| 7 (12) Dave Cash | 215 |
| 8 (19) Tony Prince | 141 |
| 9 (6) Johnnie Walker | 119 |
| 10 (8) Mike Raven | 106 |
| 11 (—) Dave Lee Travis | 102 |
| 12 (10) Alan Freeman | 100 |
| 13 (15) David Symonds | 80 |
| 14 (16) Pete Murray | 71 |
| 15 (—) Alan Clark | 62 |
| 16 (—) Andy Archer | 61 |
| 17 (7) Stuart Henry | 54 |
| 18 (—) Pete Drummond | 51 |
| 19 (—) Tony Brandon | 50 |
| 20 (—) Carl Mitchell | 48 |

Last years positions in brackets

# AIR WAVES

R mirror 6/6/70

THE WEEK OF THE POP POLL and a few surprises on the Radio-TV side. Congratulations must go to Roger Day for securing the third highest placed radio show — his breakfast programme has ended up five places above Tony Blackburn's show.

But this week's radio column is devoted to the complete disc jockey poll. We have listed more than 40 names. Everyone, in fact, that got anything like a sizeable vote scoring.

It's good to see BBC staffmen in the poll. Bruce Wyndham and John Dunn both thoroughly deserve to figure in the ratings. Radio Veronica is represented, as is Radio Nederland, the Dutch World Service, by Alan Clark. All the Radio Nordsee disc jockeys are featured, as are all five of Radio Luxembourg's DJ's.

These results may prove one thing. A disc jockey is unable to get to the top of the section without at least some TV exposure. "Top Of The Pops" for Savile and Blackburn and "Nice Time" for Kenny Everett. Definitely a case for more pop on TV!

| | | |
|---|---|---|
| 1 | JOHN PEEL (6) | 1811 |
| 2 | JIMMY SAVILE (1) | 1294 |
| 3 | TONY BLACKBURN (3) | 1014 |
| 4 | KENNY EVERETT (9) | 897 |
| 5 | ROSKO (—) | 815 |
| 6 | JOHNNY WALKER (5) | 486 |
| 7 | STUART HENRY (—) | 378 |
| 8 | MIKE RAVEN (—) | 271 |
| 9 | TONY PRINCE (—) | 246 |
| 10 | ALAN FREEMAN (4) | 224 |
| 11 | SIMON DEE (2) | 148 |
| 12 | DAVE CASH (—) | 143 |
| 13 | ROGER DAY (—) | 129 |
| 14 | KEITH SKUES (15) | 167 |
| 15 | DAVID SYMONDS (19) | 162 |
| 16 | PETE MURRAY (17) | 90 |
| 17 | DAVE BRISBANE (—) | 87 |
| 18 | ED STEWART (7) | 83 |
| 19 | ROBBIE DALE (12) | 77 |
| 20 | JONATHAN KING (—) | 73 |

## DISC JOCKEY

| | | | |
|---|---|---|---|
| 1 | JIMMY SAVILE | (1) | 1070 |
| 2 | TONY BLACKBURN | (2) | 653 |
| 3 | NOEL EDMUNDS | (5) | 478 |
| 4 | JOHN PEEL | (4) | 403 |
| 5 | DAVE LEE TRAVIS | (3) | 389 |
| 6 | ROGER DAY | (19) | 347 |
| 7 | ROSKO | (8) | 224 |
| 8 | STUART HENRY | — | 200 |
| 9 | JOHNNIE WALKER | (12) | 169 |
| 10 | ALAN FREEMAN | (10) | 162 |
| 11 | KID JENSEN | (20) | 145 |
| 12 | BOB HARRIS | — | 87 |
| 13 | JOHNNY MORAN | (13) | 69 |
| 14 | DAVE ROGERS | — | 65 |
| 15 | MARK WESLEY | — | 64 |
| 16 | TERRY WOGAN | (14) | 61 |
| 17 | ED STEWART | (18) | 58 |
| 18 | PAUL BURNETT | (16) | 49 |
| 19 | DAVE CHRISTIAN | — | 37 |
| 20 | KENNY EVERETT | (7) | 36 |

**1970:**

5th Top Disc Jockey Record Mirror 4th Best Radio Show Only beaten by Jimmy Saville(yuck), Tony Blackburn, Kenny Everett, and John Peel

**1971:**

13th Top DJ Record Mirror

March 1972 of that year, I was voted 6h most popular DJ in the Record Mirror. Not bad considering I hadn't been on the air for two years. I was above Rosko, Johnnie (sorry mate), Alan Freeman, Kid Jenson, Terry Wogan, Ed Stewart, and Kenny Everett. In fact, I was the only one not on the radio.

**1972:**

Second Best Disc DJ, Dee Jay & Radio Monthly. Beaten by Rosko. DJ Awards 20th March 1972. The awards ceremony was at the Inn On The Park, Park Lane, London

# MALE VOCAL GROUP—BRITISH

WHILE the Beatles clearly and beyond dispute nick the honours here again, there's a revival scene going on for the Stones—up from seven to second place. And once again there is activity for the Dave Clark Five whose fans have been energetic following "Red Balloon" and the like.

Though still amazingly consistent, the Tremeloes have slumped a bit, though again seventh place is not half bad. But a sad bit is the departure of Alan Price Set—now fronted by Paul Williams while Alan himself, a magnificent all-round musician, takes a turn as a backroom man of pop.

The Bee Gees and the Moody Blues can be pleased with themselves and so can Amen Corner and the Love Affair. But this is always a topsy-turvey sort of rating . . . no fewer than nine new entries in the top twenty.

Let's look at those who are OUT for this year. They are: Alan Price, as mentioned earlier, Seekers, Manfred Mann (surely only temporary), Procol Harum, Searchers, Bachelors, Move, Herman's Hermits.

And a special word for the ever-consistent Hollies, who are ALWAYS here or thereabouts. But again it's all down to the Beatles who remain stratospherically streets ahead.

| | | |
|---|---|---|
| 1 | BEATLES (1) | 1859 |
| 2 | ROLLING STONES (7) | 725 |
| 3 | DAVE CLARK FIVE (15) | 652 |
| 4 | HOLLIES (4) | 495 |
| 5 | BEE GEES (—) | 341 |
| 6 | MOODY BLUES (—) | 306 |
| 7 | THE TREMELOES (2) | 289 |
| 8 | WHO (12) | 225 |
| 9 | CREAM (9) | 219 |
| 10 | LOVE AFFAIR (—) | 207 |
| 11 | AMEN CORNER (—) | 130 |
| 12 | SMALL FACES (8) | 126 |
| 13 | SHADOWS (5) | 122 |
| 14 | KINKS (10) | 103 |
| 15 | EQUALS (—) | 82 |
| 16 | PINK FLOYD (11) | 79 |
| 17 | TRAFFIC (—) | 75 |
| 18 | NICE (—) | 71 |
| 19 | CASUALS (—) | 67 |
| 20 | FLEETWOOD MAC (—) | 63 |

is on a more even keel . . . though last year's runner-up, your actual Simon Dee, has dropped away a lot—obviously because he doesn't now do much disc-jockeying anyway.

Very good to see Emperor Rosko coming up so fast, as well as Mike Raven, Stuart Henry and Tony Prince. Must here mention Dave Brisbane who got a lot of local support for his efforts in clubs.

But alas, as some come in, some must go out. This includes Tony Hall, now a backroom promotional boy of high success ratio. David Jacobs, Jack Jackson, Tom Lodge, Tommy Vance, Sam Costa, Mike Ahern, Chuck Blair.

D'ye ken John Peel? His really is THE big success story. And he's done it with a most rigid set of personal standards in pop music. Good luck to both John and the ever-present Jimmy Savile.

| | | |
|---|---|---|
| 1 | JOHN PEEL (6) | 1811 |
| 2 | JIMMY SAVILE (1) | 1294 |
| 3 | TONY BLACKBURN (3) | 1014 |
| 4 | KENNY EVERETT (9) | 897 |
| 5 | ROSKO (—) | 815 |
| 6 | JOHNNY WALKER (5) | 486 |
| 7 | STUART HENRY (—) | 378 |
| 8 | MIKE RAVEN (—) | 271 |
| 9 | TONY PRINCE (—) | 246 |
| 10 | ALAN FREEMAN (4) | 224 |
| 11 | SIMON DEE (2) | 148 |
| 12 | DAVE CASH (—) | 143 |
| 13 | ROGER DAY (—) | 129 |
| 14 | KEITH SKUES (15) | 117 |
| 15 | DAVID SYMONDS (19) | 162 |
| 16 | PETE MURRAY (17) | 90 |
| 17 | DAVE BRISBANE (—) | 87 |
| 18 | ED STEWART (7) | 83 |
| 19 | ROBBIE DALE (12) | 77 |
| 20 | JONATHAN KING (—) | 73 |

# TOP OF THE POLLS

What a fantastic response! Literally thousands of votes were received for our first "DEE JAY AND RADIO MONTHLY" poll – in fact at one stage they were arriving by the sackload, much to the annoyance of our local postman. So to all of you who voted a very sincere thank you – let's make sure that the "DEE JAY AND RADIO MONTHLY" poll becomes recognised as THE definitive radio poll.

As for the results – no real major upsets we feel, and so we offer our congratulations to messrs Blackburn, Walker, Rosko, Wogan, Wesley and Ross plus messrs Glitter and Stewart for two excellent records.

Special "DEE JAY AND RADIO MONTHLY" trophies are now being prepared and will be presented to the winners at a special party to be held on March 20. Pictures and news of this event will be included in our next issue.

# POLL SUCCESS FOR THANET PIRATE 16/6/70.

### Andrew Clymer

WRITES ON TOPICS FOR TEENS AND TWENTIES

## TOP RADIO DJ

1. **TONY BLACKBURN** (BBC Radio 1)
2. **NOEL EDMUNDS** (BBC Radio 1)
3. **DAVE LEE TRAVIS** (BBC Radio 1)
4. JOHNNIE WALKER (BBC Radio 1)
5. MARK WESLEY (208)
6. BRIAN McKENZIE (RNI)
7. KID JENSEN (208)
8. ROSKO (BBC Radio 1)
9. JIMMY SAVILE (BBC Radio 1)
10. TONY BRANDON (BBC Radio 2)
11. ROGER 'TWIGGY' DAY (—, soon BBC Radio 1)
12. KENNY EVERETT (BBC Radio 1)
13. ED STEWART (BBC Radio 1 & 2)
14. PAUL BURNETT (208)
15. MIKE ROSS (RNI)

**TONY BLACKBURN**

## TOP RADIO ONE DJ

1. **JOHNNIE WALKER**
2. **NOEL EDMUNDS**
3. **TONY BLACKBURN**
4. DAVE LEE TRAVIS
5. ROSKO
6. ALAN FREEMAN
7. ED STEWART
8. JOHN PEEL
9. JIMMY SAVILE
10. JIMMY YOUNG
11. STUART HENRY
12. STEVE JONES
13. BOB HARRIS
14. ANNE NIGHTINGALE
15. ALAN BLACK

**JOHNNIE WALKER**

*Left To Right: Me, DLT, JW, Lynsey De Paul, Gary Glitter, Tony Brandon, Terry Wogan. Front: Mark Wesley, Brian McKenzie, Mike Ross, Rosco.*

*Here I am getting my award. The room was full of BBC producers. In my speech, I said, "I doubt anybody in this room voted for me."*

# CHAPTER 15

# UNITED BISCUITS NETWORK

I had heard about a radio station in Harlesden in northwest London that was run like a professional station broadcasting to the workers of McFarlane Lang's biscuit factories over in the UK.

Neil Spence, the former Double D Dave Dennis of Radio London, was in charge, so I contacted him in early 1972. He invited me over. UBN had great studios, good jingles, and a decent record library. I was signed up, and at first, I filled in for sickness and holiday relief. My first show was on January 30th. Then, on September 10th 1973, I started presenting the daily 6am – 10am show and remained with UBN until I left to join Piccadilly Radio in Manchester the following year.

I kept the discos going and found myself very busy. Quite often I would travel back from a disco a long way away and either grab about two hours sleep or even go straight to the studio, present the show, and catch up on sleep later in the day.

It was useful for me to keep my hand in working in a radio studio just as independent local radio was about to take off.

There were many presenters who started at United Biscuits Network and later went on to top jobs in radio. Graham Dene, Peter Young, Roger Scott, and Adrian Love went on to make up the backbone daily line up on Capital Radio. It was a great team. If UBN had been on medium wave, it would have got a big audience.

There was a young man there called Giles Squire who was barely 20, and it was his first DJ gig. I decided to play a joke on him. I sent his details to a dating agency and was in the office when the postman delivered a bumper bundle of letters from females who wanted to meet him. "Who the hell has done this?" Giles exploded, and I just burst out laughing, so instantly he knew it was me. I am well-known for my practical jokes.

As soon Capital Radio, the winner of the licence to broadcast pop music to London was announced in February 1973, I sent a job application to them. In July, I had an interview with Michael Bukht, the Programme Director. It went well enough, and I was asked back for an audition on 17th July. I felt confident I would get the job. So you can imagine how I felt when they told me I hadn't been chosen to join them. To be honest, I was ruddy angry, as without me and my other DJ friends broadcasting offshore, there wouldn't have been a Capital Radio.

The irony was that after I left RNI, I was approached in August 1970 by a couple of young men who said they

The UBN Studio with my leaving present, engraved 'The UBN Drinking Team'.

were going to apply for the licence to broadcast to London and wanted me to be the Programme Director. They didn't impress me, so I didn't follow it up. Imagine my horror when years later I came across the letter they had written me. It was from the sons of one of the founder directors at Capital. I came across the contract they offered when researching this book. Oh well!

**1974 Discos:**

Tudor House Bearsted; Bell Records Party at the Grosvenor Hotel with the Radio One & Two Producers; Horsham Youth Club; Balls Park College; Civic Hall Gravesend; Reading University

# TWIGGY'S TALE

Roger "Twiggy" Day is without doubt pretty unique in the world of the disc jockey. Reference to almost any Radio DJ poll (and the recent "Dee Jay and Radio Monthly" poll was no exception) will doubtless find his name among those listed – AND YET ROGER HAS NOT BEEN "ON THE AIR" FOR OVER 18 MONTHS!

His previous radio experience, however, includes such names as Radio England, Radio Caroline, Radio Luxembourg and Radio Northsea. When I met him in London, recently, I asked him what prompted this interest in radio?

"Well really listening to Radio Luxembourg. Things like Jack Jackson's 'Wow It's Saturday' or whatever he used to say on those D-E-C-C-A programmes. I think people of my age either wanted to be pop singers or disc jockeys. I couldn't sing – so it was disc jockeying for me! Well, there was a fella who left the office where I worked to become manager of a local ballroom, and as a joke I said 'Don't forget if you ever need a disc jockey just call on me.'.

"I didn't expect to hear anything more, and then some of my friends who knew I was mad on pop music entered me for a Southern tv quiz programme 'Pop The Question'. This guy saw me on the programme, liked what he saw and offered me the job as DJ at Dreamland, Margate."

And so Roger became, like so many radio DJs, a part-time ballroom DJ, working days as an accountant, and nights as a DJ. It was at Dreamland that he met Dave Cash, who was just on the point of leaving Radio London, and asked him what the chances were of a job on

"Big L" – and although Dave was not very hopeful he did put Roger on to the bosses of a new project – Radio England.

"I went round to see these guys at the Hilton – they'd only flown in that morning. I was the first DJ they saw – they didn't hear a tape or anything – they just liked my 'cute little English voice' and so that was it. I was hired."

So Roger went to sea, and joined Radio England, aboard the MV Laissez Faire. How did he find life afloat?

"It was a new experience. I'd never even lived away from home. It was a bit frightening, but it was very exciting working with a lot of Americans who had a lot of radio experience. These people who had worked in Top 40 radio in the States did me a lot of good. The only disadvantage was that they wanted us to sound American – we didn't and started pulling much more mail, which, of course, used to annoy them considerably. It was probably the most Americanised station this

country has ever known, and I think if they'd left it a little longer it would have caught on. It was probably a bit too early for the British public to take at that stage. But it was really a fantastic station – very underestimated."

In November 1966 Radio England closed down, and Roger returned to disco work, working for, of all people, boxer Billy Walker at a new club he'd opened at Forest Gate. Then one day he dropped into the Radio Caroline offices and asked them for a job.

"They were really a bit short of people, because it was coming up to the Marine Offences Bill, and most of their big name people were leaving to try and get themselves in with the BBC. So there I was, and I joined Caroline South about a month before the Bill came in."

On board at that time were DJs Robbie Dale, Johnnie Walker, Steve Young, Keith Hampshire and Mike Ahern. When the

Bill came along Roger, along with Robbie and Johnnie decided to stay put.

"We had a choice – we could have left. They said we can't guarantee anything, but if you stay on we would appreciate it. I felt very strongly on the subject – and still do. It was suppression of freedom and so I thought you've got to take a risk now and then, and they might clap us in jail – but it's something I believe in so it's worth taking a risk. Besides I thought someone's got to do it, or the listeners will be without a station that they love, and they did love Caroline – more so after we carried on. So I stayed and it proved to be the best thing I ever did because we all got on well together and had a really fantastic time."

Fantastic or not, the story of the final demise of the two Caroline ships was to come. Roger was on board at the time. What were his recollections of that fateful morning?

"It was sad – oh so sad. It's very hard to explain the feeling. But the tug came alongside and I was up to do my breakfast show – I started at 5.30 am. It was a Sunday morning and I heard this boat alongside. I was worried because we had heard a rumour that students from the University of Essex were going to capture a DJ for a Rag Week stunt – so we were on our guard. So I went up on deck and there was this big Tug from Wijsmullers which was the company that tendered us. I saw one of the Dutch crew and asked what they were doing here because they often called in for a chat if they were passing, and he said 'They have come to tow you off to Japan'. So I just laughed and went off to the washroom, then went and collected my records and went to the studio. The

---

## Part one of a two part feature on one of free radio's most popular D.J.s—Roger Day

Captain then came in and said 'Off with the transmitter'. I hadn't actually started broadcasting yet – we played continuous music for half an hour to warm up the transmitter. So I was waiting to go on, and I said 'Well, can I say anything?' and 'Why are we going off?' To this he replied that we were going to Amsterdam for repairs, and that I had two hours to clear all my stuff out of the studio. So then we realised that we were going in – and so we threw masses of documents over the side in case the wrong people got them. These were documents referring to 'paid' records – because we had been existing on 'paid plays', and we felt that it would be wrong if people

knew which companies had been supporting us illegally – so we got rid of all the stuff and threw it over the side.

"I woke Johnnie up to tell him that we were being towed in. At first he thought I was joking, but when we passed one of the lightships he knew I wasn't. We just mooched around all day – we didn't know what to do. There was a depressed feeling about the whole thing, because although they told us we would be back in three weeks – we all knew that it was the end. And that was before we knew that the Caroline North ship had been seized as well."

What made Roger and the other DJs have this feeling?

"It was literally just a feeling, because we knew

that once we were in port there would be lots of hassles – you know like the British Government could have put pressure on the Dutch Government to stop us going out again – that sort of thing. We all had these feelings and it was very sad – a few tears were wept I don't mind admitting. The thing that annoyed me most was that we weren't allowed to say anything to the listeners. I thought that for the tremendous loyalty they'd shown us, we weren't allowed to give something back – and I mean they wouldn't know that it wasn't our fault."

This is true as I'm sure most people can well remember the many rumours and counter-rumours that

swept the radio world following the closure of the two stations.

"Well we got them as well, you know. We were told to stand by our phones and we almost made it once. We were on the old Radio 270 ship – but someone blabbed to the authorities and they stopped it going out – otherwise we would have been back in three weeks."

So Roger was back on land – and back, once again to the odd disco booking . . and to waiting.

Next month: Roger joins Radio Luxembourg, and tells his story of RNI.

**Ben Cre**

Telephone: 01-452 8977

Please reply to:-
26 PASSMORE GARDENS,
BOUNDS GREEN
N.11.

7th August, 1970.

R. DAY, Esq.,
21 Lovelace Road,
SURBITON, Surrey.

Dear Mr. Day,

Subject to our conversation on the 5th August, we have enclosed an Agreement for your approval. Owing to possible delay between obtaining a licence and actual commencement of broadcasting, we have made a provision that you should enter into our employ one calendar month before operation commences, and not at the time of the licence being granted. There is also a clause that releases you from the Agreement if we have not obtained a licence within 18 months from when the Agreement and counterpart are signed

Also enclosed is a brief expansion of the format you suggested, and we will be grateful if you will incorporate more material.

Yours sincerely,

David Maule-Ffinch.

---

RADIO CAPITAL LIMITED

and

MR. ROGER DAY

DRAFT

SERVICE AGREEMENT

Freke Palmer, Romain & Gassman,
120 & 122 Seymour Place,
LONDON, W1H 5LJ.

6th August, 1970
RAP/DGS

THIS AGREEMENT made this       day of
1970 between RADIO CAPITAL LIMITED whose registered
office is at
(hereinafter called 'The Company') of the one part
and ROGER DAY of
(hereinafter called 'Mr. Day') of the other part
WHEREAS the Company is shortly to make application
for a licence to operate a commercial radio transmitting
station and WHEREAS the parties hereto have agreed that
in the event that such licence is obtained the Company
shall employ Mr. Day
IT IS HEREBY AGREED:-

1.   The Company will use its best
endeavours to obtain a licence
to operate a commercial radio
station

2.   Upon the date that such licence
is obtained and provided that
such date be within 18 months
of the date hereof the Company
will employ Mr. Day and Mr. Day
will accept employment by the
Company as a Disc Jockey and
Programme Producer upon the
following terms:-

(i)  The employment shall continue
until determined by either part
giving six months written notice
to the other party provided that
(subject to the provisions of

Clause 5 hereof) no such notice shall
be effective if given to take effect
before the expiry of one year from
the date of commencement

(ii) Mr. Day while so employed shall act
as Disc Jockey and Programme Producer
shall be responsible for all 'needle-time'
and shall carry out such further duties
as the Company may reasonably require

3.   Mr. Day shall receive a salary at the
rate of three thousand five hundred pounds
per annum and shall devote his whole time
and attention to his employment and to the
affairs of the Company

4.   Mr. Day shall be entitled to        weeks
holiday in each year

5.   In the event that either party shall be in
breach of any of the terms or conditions
of this Agreement the other party may
determine this Agreement forthwith and
Mr. Day's employment shall then cease but
without prejudice to the rights of either
party hereunder

IN WITNESS ETC.

Capital Radio Limited

49 Park Lane London W1Y 3LB Telephone 01-491 7356

MFF/LV.                                    February, 1973.

96, PICCADILLY.
409-2155

Dear Sir,

With reference to your recent application for a post with
our company, I would like to inform you that the various
particulars you have submitted are being noted and will be
put before our Programme Director for consideration, as
soon as he joins the company. He will thereafter be in
touch with you. No decisions can be taken or interviews
take place until that time, which is unlikely to be before
the end of March.

Thank you for your interest.

Yours faithfully,

CAPITAL RADIO LIMITED.

2 WBS

Richard Attenborough CBE (Chairman)  B Barclay-White  A F Bartlett  W H Beets
Graham Binns  R M Denny  Bryan Forbes  J C Littlejohns  R A Stiby
Reg Office: 1 Aldersgate Street London EC1A 4ES  Registered in England No 923454

---

Capital Radio Limited

96 Piccadilly London W1V 0QU  Telephone 01-409 2155  Telex No 28351

Mr R Day
27 Dulverton Court
Adelaide Road
SURBITON
Surrey                        13th August 1973

Dear Mr Day,

Thank you for coming to audition for a broadcasting
job with Capital Radio.

Auditions are always a bit of an ordeal, but I do
think that your performance was well worth
listening to. However, I am afraid that at this
time I am not able to offer you one of the posts.
As I am sure you will realise, there are only a
limited number of openings available and the
quality of completition has been extremely high.

I am sorry to disappoint you. We will, of course,
keep your correspondence on our files and if the
situation changes we will get back in touch with
you.

Thank you once again for your interest.

Yours sincerely,

MICHAEL BUKHT

Richard Attenborough CBE (Chairman)  John Whitney (Managing Director)  B Barclay-White  A F Bartlett
W H Beets  Graham Binns  R M Denny  Bryan Forbes  J C Littlejohns  B Nicholson  R A Stiby  Lord Willis
Reg Office: 1 Aldersgate Street London EC1A 4ES Registered in England No 923454

Mr.Michael Bukht,
Capital Radio Ltd,
96, Piccadilly,London W1V 0QU.          15.8.73

Dear Mr.Bukht,
        Replying to yours of the 13th August, whilst
thanking you for the consideration shown, I must express
bitter disappointment with your news.

        I feel that I must have something to offer
as I have always attracted a large audience - as recently as
April I was voted second in a Poll organised by D.J & Radio
Monthly; last year I was also voted top in the Record Mirror
poll and this seems quite remarkable considering my absence
from the air for sometime.

        Once again - your letter was a bitter blow,
but I still hope to be able to plan my Career with Commercial
Radio. Perhaps before long you will have the opportunity to
offer for which I have been waiting,should things not work
out with your present Team.

                        Yours sincerely,

# CHAPTER 16

# PICCADILLY RADIO

D espite doing discos and presenting the breakfast show at UBN, I wasn't happy with my life at the beginning of 1974. The rejection by Capital Radio had hit me hard. I started to make enquiries about radio work in the USA and Canada, deciding it was time to emigrate.

Then, out of the blue, I got a call from Pete Reeves, who had also been at UBN. He had been hired by the new independent pop music station in Manchester, Piccadilly Radio. When I told him of my plans to leave Britain, he told me that Philip Birch was the Managing Director of the station and that they wanted to talk to me. I had been disappointed with the sound of Capital Radio and thought the man who made Big L so successful might have better ideas.

I sent an audition tape to Programme Controller Colin Walters, and pretty quickly his secretary called to ask me up for an interview. On Wednesday January 23rd, I took the train to Manchester. I had only been there twice before, for The Small Faces and The Beach

Boys tour. We had a very productive meeting about what both of us wanted, and I returned to Surbiton. When I got home, Jenny told me that Colin had phoned to offer me the job of Breakfast DJ. Apparently, what impressed him was the fact that I was still getting voted in the top ten DJs despite not having been on air for four years. Once again, my lovely fans had continued supporting me.

*A letter I received from EMI before I got the Piccadilly job. Bet Terry regretted that when I became head of music!*

I did my last disco at The Mistrale in Beckenham, Kent. I then sold my disco gear. That was a mistake. I should have kept it.

On March 1st, Jenny and I drove to Manchester to start my new career with legal, land-based, commercial radio. Sorry, I mean independent local radio, as the Independent Broadcasting Authority insisted we call it, funded by advertising. I did eventually get into trouble with the IBA later on for calling the station 'commercial radio'.

We stayed in a hotel while looking for a house to rent. I spent every weekday at the studios, which were still being built. It was touch and go whether they would be ready for the planned launch date of April 2nd. It was the time of the three-day week, brought on by the miners' strike. While looking for places to rent, I got back to the offices, looking a bit downcast. I was asked what was up and I said the place we'd looked at was rather rough. Bearing in mind I was what locals called a Southern Jessie and didn't know anything about Manchester, they asked where it was. When I replied Moss Side, they all burst out laughing. Apparently, it was the roughest part of Manchester. Thankfully, I was told where I should look in future. It was good advice, and we ended up in a rather nice place in Heaton Mersey near Stockport. Once we'd found it, it was back to Surbiton to pack up our furniture and arrange for Salford Van Hire to transport it up north.

It was an exciting time knowing I was going to be the first voice on the fifth legal local commercial, sorry independent, station in the UK. LBC was first, followed by Capital Radio, Radio Clyde, and BRMB. I began to get to know the other members of the launch team, the DJs, news team, engineers, sales team, and office staff. There was such a buzz about the place. A week before the on-air date, we started dry runs.

I thought the studios, which had been designed by a TV engineer, were too big, but the equipment was very good. The test transmissions featured only classical music, which I couldn't understand as we were to be a pop music station. The name 'Piccadilly Radio' came from where we were situated. The offices were just below the Piccadilly Hotel, overlooking Piccadilly Gardens.

# A PIN UP PROFILE
# OF PICCADILLY RADIO

**Broadcasting 21 hours a day on 261 metres Medium wave and 97.0 VHF - in STEREO**

### PICCADILLY RADIO

PHILIP T. BIRCH
Managing Director

### ENGINEERING INFORMATION

G. P. J. White
CHIEF ENGINEER

### PROGRAMME SCHEDULES

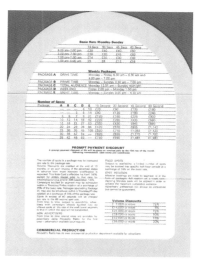

Eventually, the great day arrived and the great and good of Manchester arrived for the launch, where we popped the champagne. I had decided to play a little prank on everybody, making them think I'd overslept. I had been in the previous evening to prepare everything, and I had of course arrived in good time for the 5.30am start. I was sitting in the Piccadilly Plaza with a good view of the reception area. Colin Walters started pacing up and down the area from about five o'clock. At about 5.20, I walked into reception to a very frosty greeting and a few rude words. I said, "What's the problem? It's no big deal. I'm sure it's going to be alright."

Off I went to do my usual routine, to clean my teeth and head for the studio, to find Martin, an old pirate radio engineer, still under the mixing desk, making some final adjustments.

At 5.30, I played the first jingle, welcomed listeners to the new radio station for Manchester, and played The Beach Boys' 'Good Vibrations'. The trouble was the EMT, so called instant start turntables, let me down and the record wowed in. What made it worse was my start was rebroadcast over the entire network. To this day, I am constantly reminded of that moment. I guess it was God paying me back for my little prank.

Apart from that wobble, the first show went very well, like clockwork, and the reaction was terrific. That's not to say I wasn't nervous. One thing I didn't know was that my parents had come to Manchester without telling me. They were staying in a hotel so that they could hear my first legal show. I should have known my biggest fans wouldn't have missed that moment. I am so lucky to have had such a great mother and father.

During those first few weeks, we had a cleaner who was deaf. He used to come in the studio while I was on air and vacuum the studio, regardless of if I was on air. So he didn't last. I used to park at the Piccadilly hotel and drive up the same ramp that Simon Dee used to open his 1960s Deetime TV show with an E Type Jag with dolly birds on the bonnet. I didn't have the dolly birds or the Jaguar, but I used to tell myself that I was doing better than him now.

I settled down to hosting the breakfast show, Monday to Friday 5.30am to 9am, and the chart show on Sunday. It was a good line up. Dave Eastwood followed me at 9.00. He was from BBC local radio and had also been on Radio One. Steve Merike was on next, then briefly it was Bob Schneider from Radio 270, soon replaced by Pete Reeves. Evenings were with Andy Peebles, who had worked at the Hard Rock, and Tony Emerson from UBN on late nights.

Locals will remember that the windows of the office looking out over Portland Street used to have large pictures of the DJs there. Sometimes, during my show, while a record was playing, I used to go and stand by mine. It nearly caused a few cars to crash.

One of the reasons I was so pleased to move to Manchester was my love for Manchester United. I had been a fan of the Busby Babes before the Munich air crash, in which so many of a promising team lost their lives. I had never seen a live game until my move up north. The first game I saw was not what I had dreamed of. It was a Manchester derby. Yes, the atmosphere was electric, but United were on their way down from the first division. Former United forward, Denis Law, scored for Manchester City, and their fans would gloat that they sent us down, even though we were already relegated before that match.

Over the next six seasons, I wouldn't miss many home games and travelled to quite a few away fixtures.

It didn't take me long to discover a good local pub. The Crown served a fine pint of Robinsons Bitter, which was brewed in Stockport. I shall always remember my initiation by the landlord.

The second night we went in, Alec said, "Not you again. I thought we'd got rid of you last night." I was a bit shocked at that, but he was smiling, and I realised this was northern humour.

I replied, "It was so bad last night I had to see if it had improved."

He and the others in the bar burst out laughing, and he said, "You'll do, you Southern Jessie." He became such a good friend, I was best man at his wedding.

One weekend, I was in the pub, and as closing time approached, I became one of the chosen ones and was asked to stay behind for a lock-in. We had to pretend we were leaving and then wait by the back door until the bar was clear. We all trooped in, and the beer flowed until a couple of policemen came in. I quickly hid my pint, and Alec said, "What are you doing? They've come in for a drink as well!"

At the end of 1974, fellow presenter and head of music, Stevie Merike, left to join the new radio station in Bradford, and I replaced him as head of music. It gave me more work, as before I headed straight back home after the breakfast show. Now, I stayed in the office to listen to the new records and meet the record company promotion reps. I loved creating the playlist and spotting potential new hits, which I was very good at. Unlike today, we had playlist meetings once a week and we listened to the best of the many we received. Each DJ had his suggestions. It was a system that worked very well. I'm not a great fan of the way music is chosen for radio now. DJs have no say and no freedom to play their choice. Although we had a playlist that worked on a four-hour rotation, there were lots of opportunities for the DJs to play their own choices too and choose their own oldies. I trusted them as they all loved and knew music.

The record companies had lots of money to spend on promotion, and I could get copies of any record I wanted. It also meant a lot of wining and dining at the expense of the record men and women. One week, I was taken to four lunches and five dinners at the best restaurants. It was a good job I played a lot of sport as I would have got very fat and couldn't have called myself 'twiggy' anymore! Also, I had to be careful during the week, as I had to get up early for the breakfast show. The pluggers were only too aware and tried to get me merry and would set their alarm clocks to see if I made it. I was never late.

When the station went 24 hours, the late-night show at Piccadilly Radio was presented by James Stannage. It was a very controversial programme, and everyone was talking about how rude he was to listeners. I had actually never heard him as I went to bed early to be up for the breakfast show. One night, I was out later so tuned in. A lady came on and was really having a go at him. He wasn't answering her criticisms, so I thought, where is the rudeness I was told about? After a long rant, he said to the lady, "Is that all you have to say?" "Yes," she replied. "Well in that case, you can sod off you stupid old cow," James said. I almost crashed the car. Jasper Carrot used to talk about him in his stage act. James Stannage was

the first shock jock. People used to come to Manchester just to listen to him.

His show helped Piccadilly get publicity. The Daily Telegraph did a feature on us, describing me as having a facetious style based on the Eric Idle character in Monty Python. They meant it as an insult. I took it as a compliment.

*The On-Air Studio*

Lots of big stars came into the station. They would come to Manchester to appear on Granada TV, so obviously we also wanted to get them on air.

I also started getting regular requests for people who were attending St. Luke's. I assumed it was a church, but one night in the pub, I was asked why I was mentioning the place so often. I found out it was the local sexual disease clinic! Callers were obviously making a joke of it. Pronouncing local place names correctly is important for us radio presenters, particularly when we're broadcasting in an area we're only just getting used to. I mentioned a place spelled PeeOver in Cheshire, only to pick up the phone to hear a rather posh gentleman informing me it was pronounced Peever.

As the station became more popular, we started getting requests for disco appearances. The first were at Copperfields in Bolton, Playground Manchester, and the Nevada Bolton. Charities also requested our appearances. We even formed our own football team, the 'Piccadilly Attackers', playing for charity. It was a mixture of DJs and retired footballers. I got to play with many of my Manchester United heroes, such as Paddy Crerand and 1966 England World Cup winners Nobby Stiles, and Bobby Charlton. Paddy passed an inch perfect ball to me, I didn't trap it, and it went out for a throw in. He gave me a real telling off. We played at all the grounds in the area but never at Old Trafford, much to my regret. I remember playing at Edgeley Park, Stockport County's ground, and it was packed. Stockport County never used to get huge attendances. I used to go on Fridays to watch them, and if I missed a game, they'd ask where I'd been. The chairman even approached me and asked, "Could you play here every week?"

I had joined Davenport Tennis Club but wanted a game I could play in winter. There weren't many facilities to play tennis indoors. A friend suggested I try squash. I had always taken the mickey out of squash players, saying there was no skill and all they did was get sweaty. I gave it a try, and guess what? I was hooked and played about five times a week.

In October, I did more disco gigs in Blackburn, Sergeant Pepper's in Stockport, Warmingham Grange Cricket Club, Tiffany's in Ashton-under-Lyne, and Copperfields in Bolton. Piccadilly Radio charged £75 for our appearances, but we only received £20, and the DJs were unhappy about it. At one of our monthly meetings with Colin Walters and Philip Birch, we decided to bring up the subject. As I was the senior DJ, it was up to me to ask whether there could be an improvement in our fees. It didn't go down very well, and nobody backed me up. In fact, it was quite the reverse when I said it wasn't just me, we all feel like that. Not one of them spoke up. It looked like I was the troublemaker. I learned my lesson. I'd fight my own battles in future.

My November gigs were at Placemate Seven, Manchester, Warmingham Grange, Warrington, Stockport, and Didsbury College. In December, there were no gigs, but I got to see in concert Guys and Dolls, Pink Floyd, and Neil

Sedaka. It was great to be able to get tickets for any concert I fancied. In January 1975, Warner Brothers invited me to some of their two-night promotion gigs at Manchester's Free Trade Hall. I got to see Little Feat and The Doobie Brothers. My favourite gig a little later in 1975 was the wonderful David Gates, formerly of Bread. There was just one disco in January at the Hard Rock.

It was around this time that I became friendly with Manchester City player Dennis Tueart and his lovely wife, Joan. My support of rivals United wasn't discussed until there was a Derby game at Maine Road in the league cup. Joan said to my wife that "Roger knows an awful lot about the United players". In fact, a lot of City players became my friends. As United were in Division Two, I did attend some City games because I wanted to see Division One games.

In February, I hosted discos at Hard Rock, Stockport, and Parr Hall in Warrington.

Piccadilly Radio's promotion man, Tony Ingham, came up with the idea that I should do a marathon radio broadcast for publicity. I foolishly agreed and started at 10am on Monday March 3rd. By coincidence, it was the anniversary of Radio Caroline being towed away. Lots of VIP guests dropped in to support me, including Slade and Labi Siffre. One of the other highlights was food served to me by Playboy bunnies from the Playboy Club. Shortly afterwards, a listener joined me to try to beat the Guinness world record for tea drinking. He didn't manage it, throwing up in the waste bin in the studio.

Four days later, I was still going, but I was almost hallucinating. That became obvious when our newsman, Bob Kilby, came in to read the news early in the morning. He had a very strange way of reading the news, and when he finished, I tried to imitate his delivery before I read the weather. The studio was rather full, and everyone erupted into laughter, including me. I never did finish reading that weather forecast.

By midday, it was decided I was in no state to continue, though I did complete 74 hours, but sadly it never made the Guinness Book of Records.

I was rewarded with a night at The Last Drop Inn in Bolton and a week in Torremolinos. That gave me a good tan, which looked strange back in Manchester in February.

*The end of the marathon. Colin Walters giving me champagne.*

I also started doing voice pieces for Granada TV. If ever they wanted a scene with a radio on, it was little old me. So I can say I've been in Elsie Tanner's kitchen in Coronation Street. I've also been in The Cuckoo Waltz and Send in the Girls.

The weirdest and most scary thing I did while at Piccadilly Radio was take part in a celebrity car race at Oulton Park. Anyone who knows me will tell you I don't like going fast in cars. Before we were allowed to drive the circuit, we had to be taken around the course for a practise session with a professional racer. On the first lap, the driver said, "I'll take it quite slow, then speed up for the second lap." After the first lap, I needed a new pair of underpants, and I said to the driver, "If that was slow, can we not bother with the faster lap?" The race started, and my plan was to stay at the back and keep the car in front just in my sight. That didn't work because everybody lapped me. I thought, never again.

In June, I made my one and only TV appearance in the pop show Rock on With 45. I was sitting in for Kid Jenson, who, I think, was on honeymoon. The show was for Granada TV, and the stars were Marc Bolan, Chip

Hawkes, and Johnny Nash. TV never really appealed to me as I prefer the intimacy of radio broadcasting, but I was paid the princely sum of £15.

In July, I took part in a charity walk with some Manchester United players from Lytham St Annes to Manchester. I was proud that I kept up with the football stars. I remember Jim Holton said that I was a fit f****r.

Over the next few months, I was lucky enough to see Barclay James Harvest, Thin Lizzy, Mud, Fox and The Four Tops, and in March 1976, Diana Ross. Looking at my diary, I was on Granada reports but can't remember why.

As a laugh, I sent a copy of Des O'Connor's new record to Eric Morecambe. I got a lovely reply from him, saying, "Thanks for that. I actually enjoy him singing!"

April: Four Seasons at Free Trade Hall
June: Doctor Hook Concert

I appeared in July 1976 in what is probably the most unusual concert I've ever experienced. The world-famous Halle Orchestra had come to Manchester, and local celebrities were invited to take part, playing kitchen utensils. I was chosen to play a vacuum cleaner.

In August, we did a broadcast exchange with CHQT radio station in Edmonton, Canada. I flew out there, and as well as broadcasting their breakfast show, was taken on sightseeing trips and put up in a top hotel. I was treated like royalty, visiting the Commonwealth Games venues and taking in a Canadian football match. The people were very hospitable, and they gave me a pair of

## International touch

It isn't very often that a radio station gets involved in an international exhange program, but CHQT is giving it a try.

They're sending morning man Bob Bradburn to Manchester, England, where he'll do a week-long stint for that city's Piccadilly radio station. In return, Roger Day, of Manchester, will be taking Bradburn's 6 to 9 a.m. spot for one week, starting Wednesday.

"A director from Piccadilly station visited Edmonton on a promotional tour last year," Larry Ross of CHQT promotions says. "It grew out of that."

Who knows? Maybe other radio station will catch on to the exchange gimmick. Think of the possibilities. We could have Howard Cosell sitting in for Bryan Hall.

**The Briton is coming!**

WIN A TRIP!

CHQT RADIO 1110

genuine cowboy boots as a souvenir to take home. I was embarrassed because I knew DJ Bob Bradbourn, who had swapped with me at Piccadilly, probably wasn't getting the same five-star treatment.

In the autumn of 1976, there was a change in the schedule. I came off the breakfast show and went to the other end of the day, 10pm till 1am, Monday to Friday. It was a welcome break as getting up so early disrupts your social life. The only downside was the new hours. I had to leave concerts early, and there were no nights in the pub.

However, I was given freedom to play what I liked and invite who I liked onto the show. I was also working with Pat Broome, who was taking the phone calls. I did wind her up, poor girl, but we did have a laugh. She was a great giggler, and I often played The Goons' 'Raspberry Song' and The Goodies' 'Blowing Off', which always made her laugh.

Among the great guests who came in was Graham Nash. I had just played The Hollies' record 'Sorry Suzanne' and Pat said, "Graham Nash has phoned to say, 'Why don't you play a track that he was on?'" He'd left the group before that record was made.

I thought it was one of our listeners who'd had a bit too much to drink and was pretending to be him, so I dismissed it and said, "Tell him I'm the Archbishop of Canterbury!"

She did and returned saying, "He insists he is who he says he is and can you call him back?"

I did so, and it turned out he was staying at the Midland Hotel, one of the best and most expensive in Manchester. I thought, well if he is a drunk, he is a wealthy one. When he answered the phone, there was no mistaking who he was. He said he enjoyed the show. I said, "Thanks, I'll play a Hollies track you're on and something from Crosby, Stills, and Nash, providing you come on the programme."

He agreed, and the very next day, he joined me for the entire show. It was probably my favourite interview. He talked about the early days and what was happening with Crosby, Stills, and Nash. The most magical moment was when he said he had written a song on the plane over to the UK and asked if I would like to hear it. We had a piano in the big studio used for live sessions, and he got up and walked over to it, and for the first time anywhere in the world, he played, 'Just A Song Before I Go'.

After the show, I took him to the Cellar Vie Wine Bar, a regular watering hole for me after my late show. His presence caused quite a commotion as he was one of the area's most famous sons.

The next day, I was in the office, and I took a call from Atlantic records. They said, "We have heard from

Radio One that you had Graham Nash on last night, and they are very peed off. But that can't be true as he doesn't do interviews."

I confirmed he had been on and actually he enjoyed it so much he was coming back next week!

Elton John also came in for an interview. He had a reputation for swearing, so I told him I don't allow that on my programme. His assistant almost passed out as apparently nobody had ever talked to him like that before. But to be fair, he was a good boy. Not long before, I had been to the midsummer's day concert at Wembley Stadium, where he was top of the bill with The Beach Boys. Also appearing were The Eagles and Joe Walsh, before he joined them. I actually sat in the Royal Box. It was a hot summer's day, and The Beach Boys were on great form, getting the huge crowd rocking to their greatest hits. Then on came Elton, who said, "I'm not going to play the hits, but all of my new album, Blue Moves." You could hear the groan of the audience, and about two songs in, they started to leave.

So when Elton came in for his interview, my first question was, "Hi Elton, I was at Wembley."

But before I could finish, he said, "I know what you're going to say. It was a mistake. I won't do that again!"

He also wanted to read the news. I declined that offer but allowed him to read the weather, which he did, and at the end, he gave the temperature as Sharon Fart. It was hilarious. Elton John sent me a letter thanking me for the interview.

# THE ROCKET RECORD COMPANY LTD

Four Audley Square. London W1Y 5DR Tel: 01-499 9714

9th June, 1977

Mr. Roger Day,
Piccadilly Radio,
127-131 The Piazza,
Piccadilly Plaza,
Manchester,
M1 4AW.

Dear Roger,

When we first discussed bringing our two current records around
the country, I must admit I was in some doubt as to how the idea
would be received at the stations.

However, the trip that Arthur and I undertook last week was so
enjoyable and informative that I wanted to thank you for the
hospitality you showed us, it was really heartening to be given
such treatment and to be able to discuss our records and the
company frankly. Please pass on my thanks to Colin and Andy,
we really had a great evening.

Lastly, I look forward to seeing you again in the autumn.

Yours sincerely,

Elton

Directors Elton John John Reid David Croker
Registered Office 995 High Road London N12 8QX England Registration No 1078650

---

**ERIC MORECAMBE**

7th. March, 1976

Dear Roger,

I don't know whether to thank you or not for
the record!

What can I say other than that I actually enjoy
his singing, dammit!

All the best.

Yours sincerely,

*I had sent a copy of a Des O'Connor record to Eric, and this was his reply.*

223

I also had fun with Hank Marvin and Bruce Welch of The Shadows, as they set about promoting their Best Of album. They did their famous Shadows walk in the studio. After they'd finished their interview and were back in their hotel, Bruce called the studio, and I put him on air.

"I've got a complaint about the Manchester Underground," he said.

"We haven't got an underground in Manchester," I replied.

"That's my complaint," he said.

Another of my favourite guests were Ray Sawyer and Dennis Locorriere from Dr Hook. They came for what was scheduled to be a thirty minute interview and ended up taking over the show. Like Elton John, they wanted to read the news too, but I wasn't going to let that happen.

My saddest night on air at Piccadilly Radio was August 16th 1977. The newsman came in the studio and told me that Elvis Presley had died. I told him to check it was true. Sadly, it was, and the show became an Elvis memorial show with wall-to-wall classics from the King and memories of him from my listeners.

Independent local radio was well-known for its creative listener competitions. The one I remember on my show was trying to find the sexiest voice in Manchester. The prize was a set of black satin sheets.

1977 was a good year for concerts. In January, I got to see Chicago, followed by Abba in February. I compered shows for Bob Williamson and Jan Akkerman, formerly of Focus, in March, and in April, I managed to see Graham

Parker, Fleetwood Mac, Roy Harper, and Harry Chapin. In May, I compered The Four Seasons and George Benson and drove to Glasgow to see The Eagles. In June, I was lucky enough to see 10cc.

My time on the late show came to an end in October, when I was asked to take over afternoons, 3pm till 6pm, Monday to Friday. It was the perfect show as I had all morning to work on the playlist, listen to the new music, and meet the record promotion people, plus I could go out socialising and not have to rush off early to the studio. Oh, and it meant I could have a drink. Because I was wined and dined by the record company executives, I'd become quite well-known in the Manchester restaurants. Money was no object for the record companies, so I ordered the most expensive food and wines. My favourite was Mario and Franco's, where the maître d' would embarrass me by saying, "The usual, Mister Day?" I shall always remember going in there with Dave Clark of the Dave Clark Five. He was a very handsome man and was wearing a white fur coat. To say his entrance caused a sensation is an understatement. Just about every woman in the restaurant couldn't stop looking at him, much to the annoyance of their partners.

In early 1978, I splashed out on what would become my favourite car ever – a metallic blue Toyota Celica. It was like a Jaguar E type in design. One of the up-and-coming groups in 1978 were Sad Café, and they were from Manchester. I compered their concert in March, and in May, I compered Jethro Tull. I was invited to the premieres of what would turn out to be two of the biggest films ever made – Star Wars and Saturday Night Fever, and I also took on a new venture – judging Miss Stockport. You might think I enjoyed an evening with the area's most beautiful ladies, but I vowed never to do it again after getting so much stick from the relatives of the losing finalists.

**January:**

Concerts–Barron Knights at the Golden Garter

**April:**

Disco Carriages, Droylsden, Fagins, CIS disco, Wigan, Disco CIS New Century Hall. This was a Piccadilly promotion

Discos: Stockade Walkden. Bees Knees Bolton, Park Hall, Compere Randy Newman Concert,

**June**

DiscoBees Knees, Checkmates Stretford, Bovis Hall Prestbury, Placemate.

**July:**

Placemate, New Century Hall.

1978, as disco music really took off, I did gigs in Wigan, the home of northern soul, at Rats in Stockport, Carriages in Doylsden, and discos promoted by the radio station.

It was about this time that I was injured while playing in a charity football match and had to have a knee operation. Years later, here in Spain, I was doing a disco and this chap came up to me and said he had played in a football match against me. It turned out he was the bloke who had injured me. What a small world!

## Guests on the Afternoon Show

*Abe Ginsbourg arm wrestling Demiss Rousos, a regular guest who insisted we always had food in the studio for him. My favourite story about him is when I did the late show he was coming in for an interview but we had forgotten to put his name on the guest list for the security people in the Sunley building who controlled the building at night. When he arrived they asked who he was and when he told them there reply was your name isn't on the list you can't come in.*

*Kenny Jones of The Faces*

*Labi Siffre*

It was the summer of 1978, July 9th to be exact, and it was one of the saddest days of my life. That day, I'd presented the morning show and had just got in the door at home when Jenny said, "You'd better sit down." She told me my dad had gone out for a walk in Margate, collapsed in the street, and died on the spot. It was a complete shock. We packed a few things, and Jenny drove us to Margate. She had just passed her driving test, but I was in no state to drive. I know most people think their father is the best, but mine was my best friend as well. He was so supportive of my career and used to arrive at most of my gigs and even came out to the pirate ships on the tenders. He used to get me disco bookings and always got top money for me. God help anyone who queried the price. He even managed to get into the Beach Boys' dressing room. Many DJs and some top pop stars used to say they wished their fathers supported them as much as my dad supported me. People I still meet mention him. It was even sadder because a few days earlier, I had told him the news that we were expecting our first child. It was a definite case of one in, one out.

The following month, I was tempted to apply for the programme controller's job at Radio Clyde in Glasgow. I didn't tell anyone at Piccadilly, but when I got back to Manchester, I bumped into the chief executive, Philip Birch, who said, "How did the interview go?" Crafty old fox he was.

In September 1978, I made another TV appearance, this time on BBC TVs Omnibus programme, hosted by Paul Gambaccini. They were doing a programme about how radio stations choose music. I was asked what my job was, and I answered, "I have to keep the people listening between the commercials." It was true, and I saw nothing wrong in what I'd said. But once the programme was aired, the Independent Broadcasting Authority was less than pleased, and although Philip Birch agreed with me, he had to issue a severe rebuke.

## More gigs in November:

CIS Disco, Bowden Hotel Altrincham, Civic Hall Oldham, Disco Walkden, Leeds University.

## December:

Walkden Disco, CIS, Bolton CIS, Set Club Stoke, Rivington Barn.

## 1979

## January:

Walkden Disco.

**February:**

Olivers Disco Leigh, Orell Rugby Club, Walkden, Civic Hall Oldham, Lion Hotel Warrington, Winsford, Albert Inn Whitefield, Rotters Disco.

On March 1st1979, our daughter Michelle was born. The previous evening with Jenny, we had been at Old Trafford watching a very boring game against QPR. Our guest was songwriter Bill Martin, who had co-penned such classics as 'Congratulations'. During the game, Jenny started getting a few twinges, which concerned Bill, who had two children, so knew the signs. Jenny insisted she was ok and we went out for dinner after the game. As usual, much red wine was drunk, not by Jenny of course, and we got home, where I went into a deep sleep.

The next thing I knew, the light was on and Jenny said we had better go. I drove very carefully in the snow to Queen Mary's Hospital. It was 4am. Eight hours later, Michelle Caroline (wonder why that name?) was born. I often think how near we were to having the baby at Old Trafford. That would have been incredible. I think it's no coincidence that she was born on St David's Day as my dad was Welsh. In the lead up to the birth, the date of delivery wasn't really known. I had warned Piccadilly Radio's Colin Walters to have somebody on standby to do my show, but I couldn't let him know an exact date. His reaction was, "That's a bit f***ing inconsiderate," and he wasn't joking. His man management skills left much to be desired!

That night, I left the car at home and went to my favourite pub in Wilmslow. They lined up several tots of whisky, and the instruction was that I wasn't leaving until I'd drunk them, which of course I did. After closing time, I went to sands Disco in Stretford, where more drink was consumed. Eventually, I was poured into a taxi and arrived home, where I threw up on the porch. Too drunk to do anything about it, I went to bed. Come the morning, I had the awful task of clearing up the mess as Jenny's mother was arriving soon. Then that day, I was back on my afternoon show.

Despite being a new dad, I kept up my disco work at Orell rugby club, Swinton rugby club, Rotters in in Walkden, Romeo and Juliet's in Winsford, and lots of others.

**April Discos:**

Rotters Disco, Walkden, Oldham, Wildespool, Romeo and Juliet's, Winsford. Concert–Elton John

**May Discos:**

Walkden, Compere Mike Oldfield, Discos Oldham, Winsford

**June Discos:**

Quaffers Stockport, Wilmslow, Oldham

**July Discos:**

Fagins, Oldham, Quaffers, Walkden

**August Discos:**

Oldham, Quaffers, Boogeys Stretford

**September Discos:**

Oldham, Fagins, The Village, Wigan Casino

Cliff Richard was the big guest on my afternoon show, as he was enjoying another renaissance, having topped the charts with 'We Don't Talk Anymore'.

*Always a pleasure to interview Cliff*

*Graham Nash*

*Elton John*

*Beach Boy Bruce Johnston*

*Kiki Dee*

RECORD BUSINES[S]

7/2/79

## Edited by Brian Harrigan

THE OSMONDS, recent visitors to the UK, called in on Piccadilly where they [d]id an on-air interview with Roger Day. Pictured (l to r) are Roger Finnegan and [R]oger Day (Piccadilly presenters) Alan and Merrill Osmond.

*Free Trade Hall, with Colin Crompton, Dennis Tueart, and Joe Corrigan*

*The Piccadilly Attackers, our charity team, with a few decent footballers.*

*Football in Warrington with Granada TVs Tony Wilson*

At Old Trafford

At the end of September 1979, I was told I was to come off the afternoon show and was going to be offered the overnight shift. In radio, this is a shift for those who are either starting out or who aren't good enough for daytime. I guess their move could be classed as constructive dismissal. I resigned.

My final show was on Friday 28th September. It was an emotional last show, playing all my favourites and talking about all the great things that had happened during my time in Manchester. I was ok until I said my farewells. I would have got through it, but most of the staff came in and sang 'For He's a Jolly Good Fellow'. I just burst into tears.

When I left the studio, all the staff had gathered in reception to give me a leaving present. It was a squash racket and was presented to me by Martin Buchan, the Manchester United captain. What an honour that was. The man who in effect sacked me, Programme Controller Colin Walters, walked by and received boos from most people. That proved I was popular with the staff, at least.

I went to the pub and got very drunk.

I was very proud of my role in helping Piccadilly become one of the great radio stations. I never wanted to leave. We still have reunions, and listeners still contact me, sharing happy memories.

MUSIC WEEK OCTOBER 6, 1979

# BROADCASTING

# Day quits Piccadilly

CO-INCIDING WITH the introduction of new programme schedules, Piccadilly's head of music, Roger Day, has left the station this week.

He has left to work initially as a freelance broadcaster, although he would be interested to listen to any offers from radio stations.

"I enjoy the administration side of the job but I feel I still have something to offer as a presenter," he says. "I felt the time was right to move on and radio has reached a particularly interesting stage with new ILRs soon to come on air. I'm sad to leave Piccadilly because I think it's a great station."

Day also provides an interesting reflection on the current state of the industry from the point of view of a playlist organiser. "I can understand why the record industry is in such a terrible state," he explains, "listening to some of the rubbish they are putting out. They are supposed to be cutting back and yet in one week recently I received 150 records. I thought Christmas had come early."

The main changes at Piccadilly, which have been affected by Day's departure, involve Pete Baker, hosting the breakfast show from 7am to 10am, Phil Wood who will present the morning show from 10am to 1pm, Pete Reeves filling the 1pm to 3pm slot, and Phil Sayer taking Piccadilly through to 6pm. Pete Reeves will get out and about, presenting his show at least

> Edited by
> **DAVID DALTON**

once a month from a live venue. And Phil Sayer's Talkback will include TV and film revues. Evenings will be handled mainly by Mike Shaft, Ray Terret and John Evington who will host Rock Relay on Wednesday and Thursday.

Roger Day can be contacted at 061 499 1894.

# CHAPTER 17

# MANCHESTER UNITED AND ME

As a United supporter from the south, I get all the usual jibes, like "You're a glory seeker" and "Why don't you support a local team?" Well, that was Margate, so I didn't really have an option. My friends all supported London clubs, and, even then, I never followed the herd. I always wanted to be different.

I actually started supporting Wolves as they had a great team under Stan Cullis and were the first team I saw on TV playing FC Dynamo Moscow in 1955. Then I started to read about Manchester United's Busby Babes and liked the idea of young talent being encouraged. Obviously, I couldn't get to see them apart from live on TV. But what cemented it was the Munich disaster. I read about it, and it made me feel very sad about all those young men dying when they should have had glittering futures.

That was it for me, and Manchester United have been my only club ever since. I missed their greatest match of the sixties, the 1968 European Cup Final against Benfica at Wembley. That night, I was on one of my first dates with Jenny.

But when an opportunity to work in Manchester came up, my love for United was a deciding factor in accepting the job offer. The first game I saw was not the best. We were already relegated, and Manchester City were the opposition at Old Trafford. I did, of course, love the atmosphere despite the unhappy ending, with former United forward Denis Law scoring for City. City fans say that was the goal that send us down, but we were already down before that match.

The next season in Division Two was much better, and I attended every home game and many away games. I loved following the lads away from home. I got to know many of the players, and as a result, was invited into the players' lounge after games. They got me tickets for the games, and I got them the latest pop albums and tickets for concerts. Gordon Hill, a winger, was a particular friend. He was quite a cheeky chap. I shall always remember centre back Martin Buchan giving him a clip round the ear for mucking up a pass.

Before my 74-hour marathon broadcast, I went training with the first team as a publicity stunt. That was a favourite day.

Winger Willie Morgan was one of my favourites, and when Tommy Docherty took away the captaincy from him and gave it to Martin Buchan, I had a bit of a go on my radio show. In the pub at lunchtime, I would quite often meet up with the boys after training. The day I made my comments, the players came in and said, "Martin isn't very happy with you." Obviously, he had heard what I'd said. Fortunately, he forgave me, and we became good friends.

One of my favourite memories was after the away game at Southampton when United sealed promotion. We had been at the Slack Alice nightclub, owned by George Best, and were leaving quite early as I had a radio show in the morning. As I got to the entrance, the players were arriving, and they said, "Where do you think you are going? We are going to celebrate promotion! What a party!" When I got home, I passed out on the stairs and had to get a taxi in to work as I was in no state to drive. I doubt it was one of my better programmes, and I had to have a bucket beside me for obvious reasons.

The next season, we were back in the first division, and the boys played some great football and got to the FA Cup Final. I shall always remember the semi-final, driving back to Manchester via the Snake Pass, the roads lined with people cheering as we beat Derby County.

That 1976 final against Southampton was a disappointment, but I was thankful I had at least been to one. The best part was I had managed to get a ticket for Dad, who had never been to the FA Cup Final before. At the end, after Bobby Stokes' offside winning goal, I met up with Dad, who was just ecstatic at being at Wembley as it fulfilled one of his dreams. I wasn't so pleased. I do remember saying we would be back next year to win it.

And my prediction came true. Not many gave United a chance as the opposition was that great Liverpool team of the seventies, who were going for the treble. It was a great day, and we won 2-1. They were known as Tommy Docherty's May Day Marvels, and Piccadilly had special stickers to mark the occasion.

I also played cricket at Stalybridge Cricket club for Manchester United goalkeeper Alex Stepney's testimonial match. I turned out for a showbiz team against United. I was asked to bowl an over, and who should be at the crease but Alex! Unfortunately for him, I bowled him out, which was a great surprise as I'm not really a cricketer. Realising it wouldn't go down well with the huge crowd, I whispered to the umpire, "I think you'd better say it was a no ball!"

I remember in one match, Alex had had a nightmare performance and let in a howler. So on Monday, I played for him on my radio show 'Careless Hands' by Des O'Connor. That lunchtime, I went to a pub and some of the United players were there who had heard the show and told me Alex wasn't very happy with me. But actually, he took it in good spirits.

In 1976, United had a replay in the FA Cup against Wolverhampton Wanderers. I was on the afternoon show, which ended at 18.00, so that didn't give me enough time to get to the game. I got permission to record the last hour of the show but had to keep it a secret from the

Managing Director. Worth it, though, as we won the game 3-2. I even played a dedication for the chaps in the car.

I loved the style of manager Tommy Docherty's Manchester United team. Steve Coppell and Gordon Hill on the wings, Stuart 'Pancho' Pearson and Jimmy Greenhoff up front, a midfield of Lou Macari, Jimmy McIlroy, and Gerry Daly, in defence Jimmy Nicholl, Arthur Albiston, Martin Buchan, Stewart Houston, and Brian Greenhoff, and in goal Alex Stepney. Gordon became a very good friend. Played regular tennis games with him.

Tommy Docherty's reign ended after he had an affair with the wife of the club's physiotherapist. He was a great character and was often a guest on the Piccadilly Radio's phone-ins. His jokes at the expense of City were legendary:

"When I first came here, I asked the way to Old Trafford. I was told, follow the crowds. Next week, City were at home, and I again followed the crowds and ended up at Tesco."

"If City were playing at the bottom of my garden, I wouldn't draw the curtains."

"There are only two teams in Manchester – United and United Reserves."

He did have a good sense of humour. I once went in his office wearing a full-length leather coat, which I was rather proud of. He looked at me and said. "You look like a f***ing wallet."

I also had the honour of meeting the great Sir Matt

Busby. One of my most treasured possessions is a letter from the legend. He thanked me for getting his daughter tickets to see Genesis.

Another treasured moment was when I took Michelle into the Old Trafford ticket office to show the staff there my letter from Sir Matt. Who should be there but Denis Law, who asked if he could hold my daughter. If only I'd had a camera with me. It was a wonderful moment.

Dave Sexton replaced the Doc, and though he was a nice man, the football was not as exciting. United got to another FA Cup Final in 1979, this time against Arsenal. The afternoon before the big match, I presented my programme from the team's hotel in Surrey and interviewed each member of the team. It was one of the highlights of my career.

The final was a disappointment. We were losing 2-0 with six minutes to go, and somehow, we drew level. I actually never saw the Arsenal winner because I was celebrating the equaliser with a friend who was sitting behind me. The next thing I knew, there was a loud groan, and when I turned around the ball was in the back of our net!

One of my big regrets is just before I left Manchester, the ticket office asked if I wanted to buy a season ticket. I turned it down as I didn't think there was much point as I was moving away. It was a stupid decision. But my love for the team never diminishes, particularly the Ferguson years. Sir Alex reminds me of my father.

*Jim Holton*

*Martin Buchan, Club Captain*

Paddy Crerand and Tommy Cavanagh

Me at Old Trafford. Never played a charity game there though, sadly

*A treasured Letter from Sir Matt*

# CHAPTER 18

# BRMB, BIRMINGHAM

After leaving Piccadilly Radio, I was determined to stay in radio and had chats at Hereward Radio Peterborough with managing director Cecilia Garnett, who would be part of my future, and with Radio 210 in Reading, where the interview with MD Neil French Blake was a drinking session in the pub. He told me he was impressed with the way I could hold my drink but didn't think he could afford me. My third meeting was with John Russell at BRMB, and he offered me the evening show. I started with them in October 1979. My first show was 18th October.

My producer was Paul Brown, later to be a big wig at the IBA. On our first meeting, he handed me a bunch of books. When I asked why, he said, "You will be interviewing the authors." My heart sank. From interviewing the biggest pop stars, I was now going to be talking to book writers I'd never heard of about very boring books. At Piccadilly, we believed fun came

# Day moves to BRMB

Radio & Record News 29/10/75

ROGER Day, former head of music at Piccadilly, will present four weekly programmes for BRMB from today (29).

Day will host a two and a half hour programme, Monday to Thursday (19.30 — 22.00) as well as a Sunday morning show from 10.00 to 14.00. Day

Continued on page 6

Record Business 29/10/82 Ins&

## Roger Day moves to BRMB

*From page 2*

describes them as "magazine programmes really, with a lot of art material featured. It's a completely different experience for me and a field I want to know about." Robin Valk, formerly broadcasting in that weekly slot, will host the 22.00 — 02.00 rock show.

Day says his new programmes will help him "prove to people that I can do other things as well. What I like about it is that I can expand my broadcasting experience." Day has a one-year contract with BRMB. As to future ambitions he calmly told us: "eventually I will be a programme director."

ROGER DAY, until recently a presenter and head of music at Piccadilly Radio, has joined BRMB Radio. He will be presenting the station's mid-evening show and Sunday morning show.

# BRMB Radio

What's On 3/11/79

BRMB's new current affairs show "261 Tonight" had a special guest on October 15. Industry secretary, Sir Keith Joseph was interviewed 'live' by news editor Brian Sheppard, directly after his fact finding tour of Midland Industry. Topics ranged from the state of Leyland to public spending cuts. The one hour programme is presented each night at 5.30pm by deputy news editor, Mike Heufield. Beside hard news, it includes sports and feature interviews which have ranged from singing policemen to a man who set a world record for keeping four ferrets down his trousers for ten hours.

## BRMB's New Boy

Squash fanatic, marathon broadcast record holder and real ale enthusiast Roger Day has joined BRMB Radio.

Formerly Head of Music at Piccadilly Radio, Roger will be presenting the mid-evening easy listening programme on weekdays and 'Round The World' on Sunday mornings.

Gloucester born Roger has been in radio since 1966 when he joined pirate radio station Radio England.

Before coming back to the mainland Roger also had spells with Radio's Caroline, Luxembourg and North Sea, so he was already an experienced commercial radio broadcaster before England's ILR network got underway.

When the Manchester based Piccadilly Radio went on air in April 1974, Roger's was the first voice heard.

One of his achievements at Piccadilly was a 74 hour marathon broadcast made in 1975 and still a British record.

Off the air Roger has compered one of the Beach Boys major European tours and (for relaxation) runs himself into the ground playing squash.

And amongst his several other off-duty pursuits Roger says drinking wine and real ale is "one of my more expensive hobbies"   *BRMB*

**24 Hour Radio - 261 metres medium wave   94.8 MHz VHF Stereo**

3-16 NOVEMBER

WHAT'S ON PAGE 15

first, but BRMB was rather like BBC local radio with commercials. I thought I had been hired to liven up the station. Unbelievably, they didn't even have an outside broadcast unit.

It was a very unhappy time for me as my wife, Jenny, and daughter, Michelle, were back in Manchester while the house was sold, and I was staying in Birmingham all week and returning home at weekends. Presenter Ed Doolan, bless him, let me stay at his house. November 4th was a happy day though, when Michelle was christened.

As well as presenting the evening show, I started hosting a Sunday show between 10 am and 2pm.

My first Christmas at BRMB was one to forget. It was Michelle's first Christmas, and I was working both Christmas Eve and Christmas Day. On Christmas Eve, a day I love, I was on air from 8pm till 1am and didn't get home till 2am, passing Santa Claus on the way! On Christmas Day, I was back in at 6pm and on air till 10pm. I managed to spend the day at home but couldn't drink and had to leave for work after lunch.

It shows how different things were at BRMB because my memories from 1980 are pretty scarce. I worked with some great broadcasters there, most of all Les Ross, who really should have been on national radio. I want to give a special mention for Brian Savin, who was the first voice on BRMB. He gets my award for knowing more about me than me! Yes, he is a Roger Day anorak!

In April 1980, at last we sold our house in Heald Green, but the house we wanted to buy in Hall Green fell through. We were forced to put our furniture in storage until we found a house to buy, and in the meantime rented a place in Solihull. We were reunited as a family.

My disco appearances while at BRMB were few and far between, with my first at Redditch in September.

In November1980, I moved to the drivetime show, 4pm – 7pm, which was much better. There were no authors to interview, and it was more like the radio I was used to. I was also given music responsibilities.

We also moved house, buying a property at Bentley Heath. It wasn't as nice as our house in Heald Green, but it had a much bigger garden.

I spent a lot of time at Reddington's Rare Records, buying lots of great stuff, and managed to complete my collection of every top twenty record since 1955.The owner, Danny Reddington, became a great friend and also my squash opponent. Like me, he hated losing, so it sometimes got bad tempered. Another squash player I teamed up with was Bev Bevan from the Electric Light Orchestra.

In 1981, Bob Hopton took over as programme controller at BMRB, and I got the feeling he wasn't a fan of my broadcasting style. Two years later, 1983, I was proved right, when he took me off weekdays and asked me to present shows on Saturday and Sunday, including the chart show. It was a double whammy as he also took away my head of music duties.

Just as the latest listening figures were published, I was presenting my final afternoon show. I had gained the largest increase in listeners. BRMB's head of sales asked me why I was being taken off. I answered, "Because Bob doesn't like me." Sadly, I've come across so much of that in radio. Ability often means nothing.

While I continued to work for BRMB, I joined a campaign to get a local radio station for the place of my birth – East Kent.

One other highlight from 1983 was an audition I had to replace Noel Edmonds on his Swap Shop TV show. It was ironic as he was my replacement on Radio Luxembourg. Anyway, they obviously thought I had the face for radio as I didn't get it.

**BBC tv**

**BRITISH BROADCASTING CORPORATION**
TELEVISION CENTRE WOOD LANE LONDON W12 7RJ
TELEPHONE 01-743 8000   TELEX: 265781
TELEGRAMS AND CABLES: TELECASTS LONDON TELEX

July 1982

Dear Roger

I must apologise for being such a very long time in getting in touch with you again about our Saturday morning plans. As you can imagine there have been many factors to take into account before inviting anyone to join us and it hasn't been easy to come to a decision. However, our minds are now made up and the programme is cast. I am very sorry that we haven't been able to fit you into our plans and to be sending a disappointing reply after such a lengthy wait.

It was a great pleasure meeting you and both Chris and I would like to send our very best wishes for your future success.

Yours sincerely

Rosemary

Rosemary Gill
Editor

# CHAPTER 19

# RADIO WEST, BRISTOL

continued working at BRMB on weekends, but in January 1983, I was approached by Chris Yates, managing director of Radio West in Bristol, along with his programme controller, Mike Stewart. They offered me the weekday morning show as I told them I'd had enough of presenting breakfast.

It meant I was working seven days a week, and once again I wasn't at home as much as I'd liked to have been. I was living in Bristol during the week and at home at weekends while doing the BRMB programmes. I had no intention of moving the family to Bristol as I knew there would soon be a station in Kent, and then we could all return to my home county.

I enjoyed Radio West. Mike Stewart is one of the nicest people I know, and he was a fan of mine, which helped. My old radio pal, Johnnie Walker, was doing evenings, so it was like old times. I was choosing music and also worked on a new jingle package. I was being appreciated again.

Chef Keith Floyd came on the show, giving cooking tips, and boy, did he like a drink. I was also responsible for hiring Paul Phear for his first radio gig, and I resumed interviewing showbiz stars, including Brian Poole, Sandie Shaw, The Human League, Mary Berry (yes, her), Gerald Harper, Hayley Mills, and Tommy Steele.

On March 27th, I left BRMB and wasn't sorry to leave. Shortly afterwards, Radio West again asked me to present the breakfast show, and I relented, thinking it was a nice compliment. My old friend from Piccadilly and UBN, Pete Reeves, also joined the station.

While in Bristol, the station was approached by Aardman Animations, the people behind Wallace and Gromit, who wanted to make a short cartoon about an early morning DJ. I met them and told them a radio studio is quite boring and not much happens. But they persisted and sat in my studio. Well, the result was fantastic. It was run on Channel 4 and called 'The Early Bird'. It is used as a filler from time to time, and I have lost count of the number of people who mention they had seen it and asked if it was based on me. It's called the Radio DJ and Creature Comforts series.

While in Bristol, some progress was being made towards more local radio stations in Kent. I had an interview with Gerry Zieler, the managing director of Northdown Radio, who were bidding for the West Kent licence. I knew him from the pirate Radio Essex days, and he gave me the job of programme controller. But it would be a long and painful journey to actually get on air in Kent.

# RADIO WEST'S NEW SOUND

### By Nicholas Schoon

RADIO West, the Bristol-based independent radio station, last night announced sweeping programme changes in a bid to stop a slump in their audience.

OUT go most of DJ Johnnie Walker's nightly rock music shows. IN come more news, documentary and feature programmes — including the first ever radio programme for home computer enthusiasts.

Radio West has also signed up popular HTV presenter Annie St John to host a record request programme on Sundays.

## Oldies

Veteran DJ Roger Day, the new head of presentation and music, said: "We probably won't be playing as much new music, but we will be playing more familiar sounds, including lots of oldies."

The new music policy represents a complete break with the ideas of DJ Dave Cash, Radio West's former programme controller.

He quit the job after falling out with managing director Chris Yates, and has now severed all links with the station.

---

ROGER DAY, formerly head of presentation at Birmingham's BRMB, and before that a senior presenter for six years at Manchester's Piccadilly Radio, has joined Radio West as head of music and presentation. He will have a regular daytime programme at Radio West, and will be programming number two to former head of news, now programme controller, Mike Stewart.

*Broadcast*
*28/2/83*

---

Radio News

# Day to run Northdown

DAY: Not commenting until Northdown makes an official statement

ROGER Day is to be the programme controller of Northdown Radio, the Maidstone/Medway ILR station due to open next spring.

Neither Day — currently head of music and presentation at Radio West, nor Northdown consultant chief executive Gerry Zierler is prepared to comment on the appointment.

Day told *Radio News*: "I cannot possibly say anything until an official announcement is made."

At the beginning of this year, Day resigned as head of presentation at BRMB in Birmingham.

## Career

His career in radio has spanned Radio England, Radio Caroline, Radio Luxembourg, Radio North Sea and UBN.

His was the first voice on Piccadilly Radio when it came on-air in 1974.

# CHAPTER 20

# INVICTA RADIO, KENT

By 1984, the new radio licences for Kent were awarded with Northdown Radio, getting the West Kent area and Cecilia Garnett the East Kent area. The trouble was that both stations had trouble raising enough money to launch. Britain was in an economic recession and Centre Radio in Leicester had just gone bust. The answer was for the IBA to get the two companies to join forces and become one station, with bases in Canterbury and Maidstone. However, each company had different ideas about what sort of radio station they wanted. Gerry wanted mostly music and as little what he called 'meaningful or boring speech' as possible, whereas Cecilia wanted the reverse. It was a marriage based in hell.

I had already committed to moving back to Kent, and we had sold the house in Bentley Heath and bought a house in Loose near Maidstone. It was a worrying time, and I was commuting from Maidstone to Bristol every weekend. Part of the deal when the companies merged was that I had to be employed. I was certainly not Cecilia's kind of DJ, so she refused to give me the job of programme controller but instead created a joint management team with me as head of entertainment. It made it sound like a Butlin's holiday camp! David Forsdyke was appointed head of news and information. He had worked for Cecilia at Hereward Radio in Peterborough. Another marriage made in hell.

It was a long, hard slog before the station went to air. The IBA summoned David and I to their HQ in Brompton Road and met Peter Baldwin, the IBA's chief. After our meeting, they sent a letter saying I didn't have the right experience for the position of programme controller. In fact, I had more radio experience than Cecilia and David put together, and probably more experience than Peter Baldwin! I still have the letter.

The trouble was that the IBA was a very stuffy organisation and preferred people with a news background to be in charge of radio stations. Music men like me were thought to be 'not suitable'.

I left Radio West at the end of June and welcomed no more long-distance driving on motorways between work and my family home. While doing the drive, I used to listen to Radio Caroline, which was back on air from the Ross Revenge. Part of me wanted to be involved, but with a family and bills to pay, it wasn't an option.]

So having approved me, Mr Baldwin changed his mind.

Invicta Radio was due to go on air in October 1984,

**IBA** INDEPENDENT BROADCASTING AUTHORITY
70 Brompton Road London sw7 1EY  Tel: 01 584 7011  Telex: 24345

15th August 1983

Dear Gerry,

Thank you for your letter of 9th August.

The IBA has no objection to the appointment of Roger Day as programme controller for Northdown Radio.

Yours sincerely,

P.A.C. Baldwin
Deputy Director of Radio

Gerry Zierler, Esq.,
Northdown Radio plc,
32 Earl Street,
Maidstone,
Kent,
ME14 1ND

ROGER DAY at the desk of COAST AM at Whitstable

A TOUR OF
OUR NEW
STUDIOS

*Open to public scrutiny*

---

70 Brompton Road London . . .

STRICTLY PRIVATE AND CONFIDENTIAL

31st May 1984

Dear Cecilia,

We have had the opportunity to meet Roger Day and David Foedyke as part of the preliminary procedure to your seeking our approval for senior appointments referred to in the contract specification (para 2.28) and in the Chairman's letter of 29th June 1983 to Mr. Stewart.

We have in mind the outline of duties you discussed with us when we met on 25th May 1984. You confirmed that your intentions matched our wishes as you proposed to employ a senior executive in each of your programme centres. One of these executives would be employed full-time in Maidstone and Canterbury respectively. You wished to avoid using the title 'station manager' but we agreed that, for example, the incumbent of the Maidstone post would become the local person to whom the authorities, services and utilities looked as representing 'their' local station on matters of an immediate or parochial nature.

It is our view that Roger Day may be out of his depth both in the creative and the junior management sense. We wholly recognise his affable, personable and presentation qualities. Nevertheless we are concerned that he may not be the right man for this particular task. We are aware that he moved into the area on the understanding that he would be programme controller for Northdown Radio. He would, of course, have been under the close supervision, direction and encouragement of a managing director in the same building.

If you wish to appoint Roger Day to the Maidstone 'detached' job our approval is conditional. We shall wish to review the situation after five months on-air with the option then to give unequivocal approval, continued conditional approval for a further probationary period or to withdraw our approval. You will wish to take this into account when arranging contracts.

If you wished to alter your plans, perhaps by focussing your news operation from Maidstone with David Foedyke as the senior person regularly in post there, we should be pleased to consider any alternative ideas you might have for Roger Day.

*Invicta Maidstone Studio 3*

I am sorry if this letter upsets any decisions you may have tentatively promulgated. I assure you our views are expressed in the best interests of Invicta Sound.

Yours sincerely,

P.A.C. Baldwin
Deputy Director of Radio

Ms. C. Garnett,
Invicta Sound,
15 Station Road East,
Canterbury.
CT1 2RB

and it couldn't have been a worse time. The economy was in the doldrums and the competition for listeners had become intense with the arrival of offshore Laser 558 joining Caroline, and they sounded fantastic. Laser was using the same format as Radio England had in 1966, proving we were ahead of our time.

I began the process of building the on-air team of DJs but was outvoted on many I wanted to recruit. However, I did manage to get Glen Thompsett, Duncan Johnson, Terry Purvis, Carl Conway, Nick Piercey, Baz Reilly, and Pete Tong. Cecilia hired Don Durbridge, who had been with BBC Radio Medway. He was a very good broadcaster but not what I was looking for.

I wanted Steve England to do our jingles, but Cecilia hired David Arnold, the well-respected conductor and musician, who was behind Essex Radio's launch jingle package. She wanted very few vocals and mostly instrumental idents. You can imagine my reaction. The station was to be called Invicta Sound: The Sound of Kent. I have to say, it was a buzz to be in the studio with musicians who had played with classical orchestras, but it wasn't rock and roll.

We went on air at 6am on Monday October 1st, and I can honestly say it was the worst first day I have ever been involved in. The breakfast show, presented by Magnus Carter, was mostly news. He was a lovely man and a fabulous journalist and interviewer, but not what commercial radio should sound like. He was followed by Don Durbridge, again a lovely man but BBC local radio to the core. He even had a producer, which was unheard of in commercial radio (sorry, independent radio, funded by advertisers.) Another news-based programme followed Don, and at 3pm, we split transmitters. I broadcast from Station Road in Canterbury and Andy Grahamme from Earl Street in Maidstone. Our two shows were the best thing all day. We just did what local commercial radio was designed to do. One of Invicta's commercial producers, Paul Veysey, came into the studio after the show and shook my hand. He said, "Thank god somebody knows what they're doing."

But I wasn't feeling happy. I got home and polished off a couple bottles of wine. I thought I'd made the biggest mistake of my life. A few weeks later, we did an outside broadcast from Cecil Square in Margate, and two people turned up. The trouble was nobody knew the station was on air. The launch promotion was basically on milk bottle tops.

I shall always remember a board meeting at Canterbury, where Cecilia had brought in her dog, which was smelly. During the meeting, it dropped a doodoo right by her chair. The smell was atrocious. Instead of removing it, she just lent down and put a piece of paper over the offending turd.

By Christmas, things hadn't improved. The only shows that had any audience was Pete Tong and my Sunday Solid Gold. Needless to say, there was no advertising. Just before Christmas, Cecilia called me in and said, "This isn't working. I want you to leave." I told her I wasn't going anywhere and that I would outlast her. What she didn't know was that I knew Harry Lambert, who owned Adscene, a local free newspaper. He had been pumping money into the station and had told me that her days were numbered. And so they were. But before she went, she removed my management roles and reduced my salary.

Cecilia was sacked at the first board meeting of 1985. Michael Bukht, who had been the programme director of Capital radio in London, came in as Managing Director. I was a bit worried for my future as I'd been turned down for a job at Capital. Also known as Michael Barry, the Crafty Cook chef, he had a big clear out of presenters and staff. He appointed me programme manager, even though we differed about how Invicta should sound. We had quite a few arguments. I found out later from his secretary that Michael actually really respected me because I wasn't a yes man and was the only one who had the guts to stand up to him. Between us, we dramatically improved the station's fortunes.

Here's what the new line-up looked like in April 1985:

6am – 9am Glen Thompsett

9am – 12 Kerry Juby

12 – 3pm Don Durbridge

3pm – 5.30pm Roger Day

5.30pm – 6 pm News Round Up

6pm – 9pm Neil Taylor

9pm – midnight Duncan Johnson

We also changed the station's name from Invicta Sound to Invicta Radio. The split programmes were dropped, and the station sounded much better with the emphasis on music rather than speech. I basically made us sound like radio should sound, and I commissioned a new jingle package from my old friend, Steve England.

Listening to radio on FM was becoming more popular in the mid-eighties, and we tried an experiment. We ran different promos on AM and FM to indicate who listened on what. Michael said that more would be listening on AM. I disagreed. The results proved me right.

In June 1986, Michael hired one of independent radio's most experienced sales directors, Nigel Reeve. He'd worked with Radio Orwell, 2CR Bournemouth, and County Sound, Guildford.

Bad weather is known to help local radio stations put on listeners, and that's what happened in 1987.First, there was the severe winter snow, which just about shut down Kent. Invicta became more focused on information. There was travel disruption, school closures, villages cut off, milk and post deliveries affected. We went to town providing desperately needed information to our listeners, many of whom acted on our information and helped those in need.

We were also at the centre of one of the year's greatest disasters – the sinking of the Herald of Free Enterprise ferry at Zebrugge March 6th. Among the many lives lost were local people, both passengers and crew. We ran information and extended news. Although we were a music station, we had a very good newsroom, with some fantastic journalists. The local BBC station used to monitor us as we were getting local stories first.

Fast forward to October 15th and weather of another kind led to another peak in listening. The hurricane hit Kent very badly, causing widespread power cuts, fallen trees, collapsed buildings, chimneys and roofs blown away, and much more. Thanks to generators, Invicta Radio remained on air with all the information people needed.

The three events established Invicta as a trusted and reliable source of information and news. As a result, our audience grew very quickly.

In 1988, Nigel replaced Michael as managing director, and I continued as programme controller. Michael had certainly improved the station sound, but he wasn't a businessman. Under him, the station was earning good revenue, but it wasn't making a profit. It was over staffed, and there was no control of expenditure. Nigel asked me to trim the broadcasting staff. I must admit, I couldn't sleep the night before I had to give people bad news. I think I was as reasonable as I could be, having experienced myself being sacked in the past. I am a very good programme manager and music scheduler, but that side of management I didn't enjoy.

The revised programme schedule was this:
6am – 9am Glen Thompsett
9am – 12 Terry Purvis
12 – 3pm Paul Chantler

3pm – 5.30pm Roger Day

5.30pm – 6 pm news round up

6pm – 9pm Neil Taylor

9pm – midnight Rod Lucas

midnight – 3am Sarah Ollett

3am – 6am Dave Brown

Our weekend line up was a classic team of radio names – Dave Cash, David Hamilton, Paul Gambaccini, Kid Jensen, and Kerry Juby.

When Glen and Rod left us, we promoted Neil Taylor to breakfast and gave a break at 9pm to one of the most compelling broadcasters of the time, Caesar the Geezer, on evenings. Both Neil and Caesar were a nightmare to manage. Neil had a habit of not playing commercials at the correct time, and Caesar said things he really shouldn't. Both very popular though. They helped propel Invicta to get the largest listener increase of any station in the UK. As a result, the advertising revenue went through the roof.

I also employed some broadcasters who had been broadcasting on Radio Caroline on the Ross Revenge – Peter Phillips, Mark Matthews and Johnny Lewis.

In December 1986, I was summoned to a meeting at the IBA. Nothing unusual in that, except I was the only programmer there. The others were the Managing Directors of the Southeast Commercial stations. I wondered why I was there. Very boring meeting for me, then came any other business. The subject was Laser Radio, who had been off air but were due to return. They and Caroline had been hurting the listening figures of the ILR stations. Obviously, I had been invited for my offshore knowledge. They wanted to know how they could do something about it. They certainly didn't like my reply. I said the best way to beat them was to sound better than they did. The notes of the meeting, which according to them never took place (good job I kept the minutes), are amazing. According to the DTI, I talked to Laser on ship to shore (not true), and I was to find out who supplied the ship (I didn't). They said an employee had been blind-folded and taken to a meeting with Laser staff. I was to get a copy of a recording of the meeting (I didn't) and have no proof the meeting took place. There was even talk of blocking the frequency, just like in 1970. Nothing ever happened as Laser failed to establish and went off air. A blind eye was turned to Caroline.

URGENT                                    28th November 1986

You will, perhaps, have read about the likely
re-emergence of Radio Laser as an unauthorised
broadcasting station anchored outside UK territorial
waters. The m.v. 'Communicator' left port having
been 'sold on', we believe, to a non-UK
organisation. You will recall that Mr. Anderson,
who purchased the vessel from the Admiralty Marshal,
was under an obligation not to sell the ship for
broadcasting purposes.

We remain extremely concerned on behalf of our
47 radio contractors at the possible reappearance of
this potential source of cheap competition. During
the year ended 31st March 1986 our hard-pressed
companies paid the copyright bodies nearly
£7 million; the 'pirates' pay nothing. Our
contractors work to union-negotiated rates of pay;
unauthorised stations have no such agreement. Under
the Broadcasting Act 1981 the ILR stations meet
public service broadcasting obligations of news and
information (e.g. the current campaign on AIDS)
while the pirates avoid any such duty.

suppression of an operation which is in contravention
of International Telecommunications Union Article 30
Section I/2665. May I urge you, despite all your
other commitments, to arrange for priority to be
given to clearing up what I understand to be a
significant backlog of prosecutions under the
Marine Broadcasting (Offences) Act 1967. This would
act as a deterrent to those contemplating an
imminent wave of activity; it would also clear the
decks for any new prosecutions to be dealt with
expeditiously.

                    JOHN WHITNEY

Sir Thomas Hetherington, KCB, CBE, TD, QC,
Director of Public Prosecutions,
4/12 Queen Anne's Gate,
London.  SW1H 9AZ.

cc: Q. Thomas, Esq., Home Office
    A. Nieduszynski, Esq., Dept. of Trade and
                                    Industry

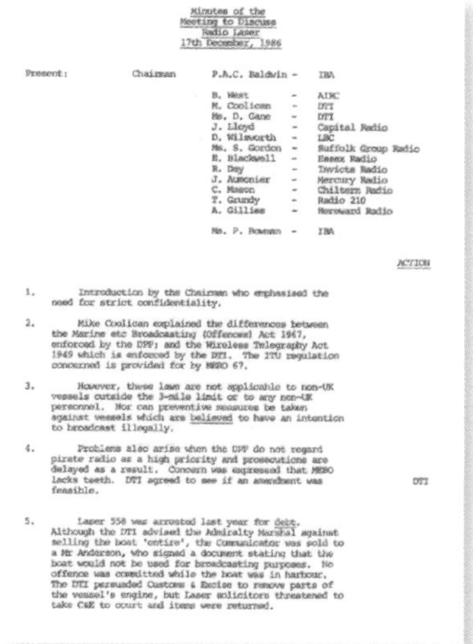

Minutes of the
Meeting to Discuss
Radio Laser
17th December, 1986

| Present: | Chairman | P.A.C. Baldwin - | IBA |
|---|---|---|---|
| | | B. West - | AIRC |
| | | M. Coolican - | DTI |
| | | Ms. D. Gane - | DTI |
| | | J. Lloyd - | Capital Radio |
| | | D. Wilsworth - | LBC |
| | | Ms. S. Gordon - | Suffolk Group Radio |
| | | E. Blackwell - | Essex Radio |
| | | R. Day - | Invicta Radio |
| | | J. Aumonier - | Mercury Radio |
| | | C. Mason - | Chiltern Radio |
| | | T. Grundy - | Radio 210 |
| | | A. Gillies - | Hereward Radio |
| | | Ms. P. Bowman - | IBA |

ACTION

1. Introduction by the Chairman who emphasised the need for strict confidentiality.

2. Mike Coolican explained the differences between the Marine etc Broadcasting (Offences) Act 1967, enforced by the DPP; and the Wireless Telegraphy Act 1949 which is enforced by the DTI. The ITU regulation concerned is provided for by MRRO 67.

3. However, these laws are not applicable to non-UK vessels outside the 3-mile limit or to any non-UK personnel. Nor can preventive measures be taken against vessels which are believed to have an intention to broadcast illegally.

4. Problems also arise when the DPP do not regard pirate radio as a high priority and prosecutions are delayed as a result. Concern was expressed that MRRO lacks teeth. DTI agreed to see if an amendment was feasible. — DTI

5. Laser 558 was arrested last year for debt. Although the DTI advised the Admiralty Marshal against selling the boat 'entire', the Communicator was sold to a Mr Anderson, who signed a document stating that the boat would not be used for broadcasting purposes. No offence was committed while the boat was in harbour. The DTI persuaded Customs & Excise to remove parts of the vessel's engine, but Laser solicitors threatened to take C&E to court and items were returned.

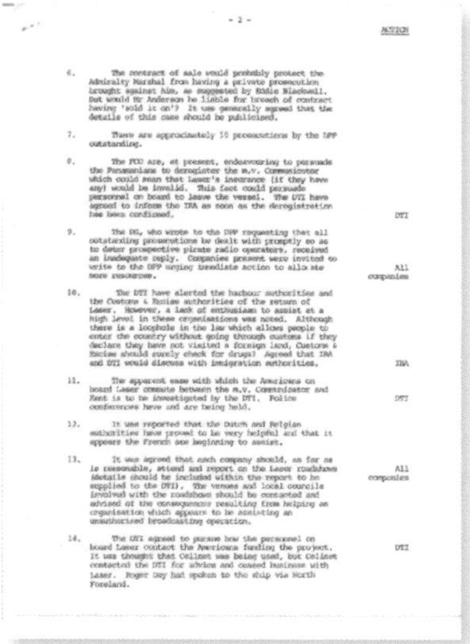

- 2 -

ACTION

6. The contract of sale would probably protect the Admiralty Marshal from having a private prosecution brought against him, as suggested by Eddie Blackwell. But would Mr Anderson be liable for breach of contract having 'sold it on'? It was generally agreed that the details of this case should be publicised.

7. There are approximately 16 prosecutions by the DPP outstanding.

8. The FCO are, at present, endeavouring to persuade the Panamanians to deregister the m.v. Communicator which could mean that Laser's insurance (if they have any) would be invalid. This fact could persuade personnel on board to leave the vessel. The DTI have agreed to inform the IBA as soon as the deregistration has been confirmed. — DTI

9. The DG, who wrote to the DPP requesting that all outstanding prosecutions be dealt with promptly so as to deter prospective pirate radio operators, received an inadequate reply. Companies present were invited to write to the DPP urging immediate action to allocate more resources. — All companies

10. The DTI have alerted the harbour authorities and the Customs & Excise authorities of the return of Laser. However, a lack of enthusiasm to assist at a high level in these organisations was noted. Although there is a loophole in the law which allows people to enter the country without going through customs if they declare they have not visited a foreign land, Customs & Excise should surely check for drugs? Agreed that IBA and DTI would discuss with immigration authorities. — IBA

11. The apparent ease with which the Americans on board Laser commute between the m.v. Communicator and Kent is to be investigated by the DTI. Police conferences have and are being held. — DTI

12. It was reported that the Dutch and Belgian authorities have proved to be very helpful and that it appears the French are beginning to assist.

13. It was agreed that each company should, as far as is reasonable, attend and report on the Laser roadshows (details should be included within the report to be supplied to the DTI). The venues and local councils involved with the roadshows should be contacted and advised of the consequences resulting from helping an organisation which appears to be assisting an unauthorised broadcasting operation. — All companies

14. The DTI agreed to pursue how the personnel on board Laser contact the Americans funding the project. It was thought that Cellnet was being used, but Cellnet contacted the DTI for advice and ceased business with Laser. Roger Day had spoken to the ship via North Foreland. — DTI

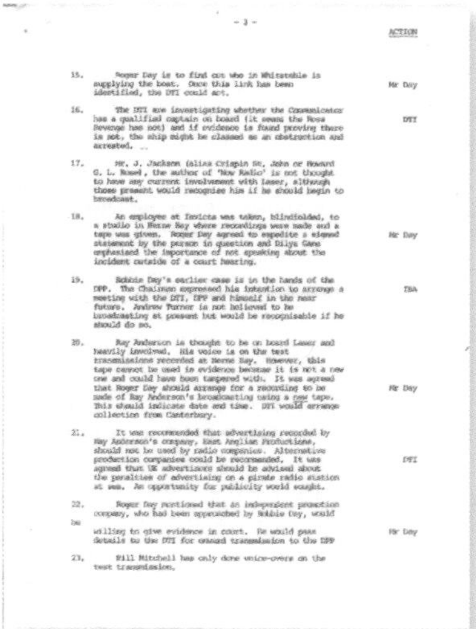

- 3 -

ACTION

15. Roger Day is to find out who in Whitstable is supplying the boat. Once this link has been identified, the DTI could act. — Mr Day

16. The DTI are investigating whether the Communicator has a qualified captain on board (it seems the Ross Revenge has not) and if evidence is found proving there is not, the ship might be classed as an obstruction and arrested. — DTI

17. Mr. J. Jackson (alias Crispin St. John or Howard G. L. Rose), the author of 'New Radio' is not thought to have any current involvement with Laser, although those present would recognise him if he should begin to broadcast.

18. An employee at Invicta was taken, blindfolded, to a studio in Herne Bay where recordings were made and a tape was given. Roger Day agreed to expedite a signed statement by the person in question and Dilys Gane emphasised the importance of not speaking about the incident outside of a court hearing. — Mr Day

19. Robbie Day's earlier case is in the hands of the DPP. The Chairman expressed his intention to arrange a meeting with the DTI, DPP and himself in the near future. Andrew Turner is not believed to be broadcasting at present but would be recognisable if he should do so. — IBA

20. Ray Anderson is thought to be on board Laser and heavily involved. His voice is on the test transmissions recorded at Herne Bay. However, this tape cannot be used in evidence because it is not a new one and could have been tampered with. It was agreed that Roger Day should arrange for a recording to be made of Ray Anderson's broadcasting using a new tape. This should indicate date and time. DTI would arrange collection from Canterbury. — Mr Day

21. It was recommended that advertising recorded by Ray Anderson's company, East Anglian Productions, should not be used by radio companies. Alternative production companies could be recommended. It was agreed that UK advertisers should be advised about the penalties of advertising on a pirate radio station at sea. An opportunity for publicity would sought. — DTI

22. Roger Day mentioned that an independent promotion company, who had been approached by Robbie Day, would be willing to give evidence in court. He would pass details to the DTI for onward transmission to the DPP — Mr Day

23. Bill Mitchell has only done voice-overs on the test transmission.

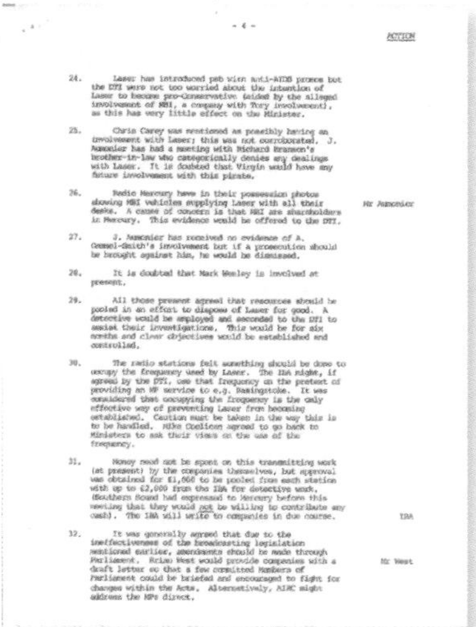

- 4 -

ACTION

24. Laser has introduced pub wien anti-AIDS promos but the DTI were not too worried about the intention of Laser to become pro-Conservative (aided by the alleged involvement of MBI, a company with Tory involvement), as this has very little effect on the Minister.

25. Chris Carey was mentioned as possibly having an involvement with Laser; this was not corroborated. J. Aumonier has had a meeting with Richard Branson's brother-in-law who categorically denies any dealings with Laser. It is doubted that Virgin would have any future involvement with this pirate.

26. Radio Mercury have in their possession photos showing MBI vehicles supplying Laser with all their desks. A cause of concern is that MBI are shareholders in Mercury. This evidence would be offered to the DTI. — Mr Aumonier

27. J. Aumonier has received no evidence of A. Cemmel-Smith's involvement but if a prosecution should be brought against him, he would be dismissed.

28. It is doubted that Mark Wesley is involved at present.

29. All those present agreed that resources should be pooled in an effort to dispose of Laser for good. A detective would be employed and seconded to the DTI to assist their investigations. This would be for six months and clear objectives would be established and controlled.

30. The radio stations felt something should be done to occupy the frequency used by Laser. The IBA might, if agreed by the DTI, use that frequency on the pretext of providing an MF service to e.g. Basingstoke. It was considered that occupying the frequency is the only effective way of preventing Laser from becoming established. Caution must be taken in the way this is to be handled. Mike Coolican agreed to go back to Ministers to ask their views on the use of the frequency.

31. Money need not be spent on this transmitting work (at present) by the companies themselves, but approval was obtained for £1,000 to be pooled from each station with up to £2,000 from the IBA for detective work. (Southern Sound had expressed to Mercury before this meeting that they would not be willing to contribute any cash). The IBA will write to companies in due course. — IBA

32. It was generally agreed that due to the ineffectiveness of the broadcasting legislation mentioned earlier, amendments should be made through Parliament. Brian West would provide companies with a draft letter so that a few committed Members of Parliament could be briefed and encouraged to fight for changes within the Acts. Alternatively, AIRC might address the MPs direct. — Mr West

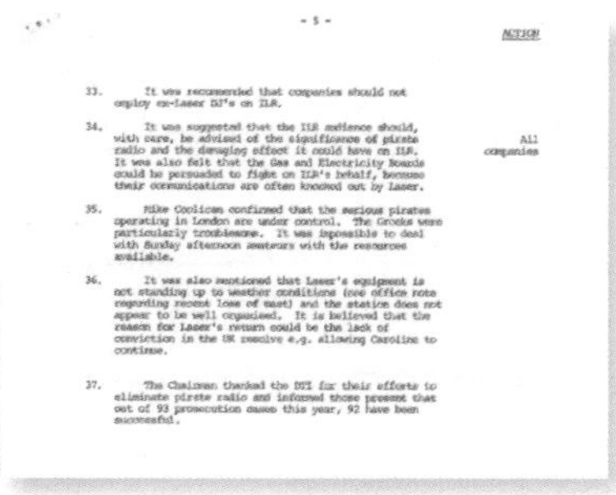

- 5 -

ACTION

33. It was recommended that companies should not employ ex-Laser DJ's on ILR.

34. It was suggested that the ILR audience should, with care, be advised of the significance of pirate radio and the damaging effect it could have on ILR. It was also felt that the Gas and Electricity Boards could be persuaded to fight on ILR's behalf, because their communications are often knocked out by Laser. — All companies

35. Mike Coolican confirmed that the serious pirates operating in London are under control. The Greeks were particularly troublesome. It was impossible to deal with Sunday afternoon amateurs with the resources available.

36. It was also mentioned that Laser's equipment is not standing up to weather conditions (see office note regarding recent loss of mast) and the station does not appear to be well organised. It is believed that the reason for Laser's return could be the lack of conviction in the UK resolve e.g. allowing Caroline to continue.

37. The Chairman thanked the DTI for their efforts to eliminate pirate radio and informed those present that out of 93 prosecution cases this year, 92 have been successful.

*Minutes of the IBA meeting. Regarding items 15, 18, 20, and22, I did nothing of course, and 18 was not true.*

There was a big change in 1988. The monopolies commission said the needletime restrictions should be abolished and there would be no limit on the amount of records stations could play. Up until then, radio stations were limited to nine hours of commercial records. The rest had to be filled with live sessions, library music, and speech. I actually think it was the return of Radio Caroline and Laser that made the authorities reform the ridiculous restrictions. It was a turning point in UK Radio.

In March 1989, there was more change. The Home Office told independent local radio stations that they must offer a different service on each frequency. BBC local radio stations continued offering the same programmes on both FM and AM, apart from football commentaries, which they split. But on independent local radio, we were in effect setting up a whole new radio station. In Kent, Invicta became Invicta FM. It broadcast from Invicta's studios in Canterbury. Invicta set up Coast AM, which broadcast from Earl Street in Maidstone. It was handy for me as I lived in Maidstone.

It was also about this time that the IBA disappeared and was replaced by the Radio Authority. It marked the beginning of the end of local radio as it began to allow owners of local radio stations to buy up others. Groups emerged and stations began to share programming. Then, some of the programming started to be recorded and many radio shows were no longer live. It was very sad.

Here was the Coast AM launch schedule:

6am – 10am Bob Mower

10am – 2pm Geoff Allen

2pm – 6pm Roger Day

6pm – midnight Tony Peters

Midnight – 6am Robbie Frawley

On Monday October the 8th 1991, I held one of the best discos I'd ever staged. It was to celebrate 25 years since I'd appeared on Southern TV's Pop the Question. The venue was the same – the Winter Gardens, Margate. There was a guest appearance by The Fortunes. It was a magical evening.

In 1991, it was all change at Invicta. The radio station board announced that it was closing its two bases in Canterbury and Maidstone and moving to purpose-built studios on an industrial estate near the Thanet Way.

I was made director of programmes as the station was at its peak audience figures and bringing in more revenue than any station in the south of England. The board thought now was the time to expand and wanted to have talks with neighbouring Southern Sound, which covered Sussex and Hampshire, about a merger. At the same time, they wanted to launch Invicta on the stock exchange. They brought in an American radio expert, and I use the word 'expert' loosely. He was like Larry Tremaine mark two. He replaced me as programme director, leaving me with little influence and demoting me to a presenter only on Invicta's AM service. They expected Invicta to be the senior partner with Southern Sound, as our audiences and revenue were higher. Sadly, it didn't work out like that, and Southern Sound won the battle.

On Christmas Eve, managing director Rory McLeod and his new programme controller called a staff meeting. They presented their structure of the plans for the new company on a spreadsheet. I looked and realised my name was missing. I wasn't surprised. I asked to see them in private. Basically, I told them I had been in radio long enough to know what they're up to and that I was on the way out. They replied that they couldn't possibly replace somebody of my talent and experience. My response was, "Look, just be straight with me. I wasn't on the proposed new structure, so be honest, as I want to start looking for another job before there is a rush." Their answer was bullshit.

Two days into 1992, Rory called another staff meeting, this time accompanied by an accountant from Southern Sound. I warned the staff beforehand that it was a redundancy day. When they asked me how I knew, I told them I'd been there before.

We were called in, one by one. When my turn came, I started the conversation, saying, "Before we start, you didn't give me enough notice to have my solicitor with me, so I'll be recording our interview." That put the wind up them, and they flatly refused. I replied, "Well, we either put it on record or I'll come back when my legal man can be with me." Reluctantly, they agreed to me recording it. It was the usual nonsense of how things were worse than they first thought, which was of course rubbish as Invicta was more than paying its way, unlike Southern Sound. The ace I had was my contract, which had a termination clause of one year. Their offer fell far short, so I ended the meeting, telling them they would hear from my legal people. I cleared my desk and headed home.

The outcome wasn't as I had hoped. My lawyer told me although I had a good case, I had to be prepared to lose and then face their costs. I couldn't afford such a gamble, so I had to accept their compromise offer. I was heartbroken to leave Invicta as it had always been my dream to programme and present on a radio station in my home county. I'm very proud of how it sounded. The Laser 558 DJs apparently used to call Invicta the onshore pirate. That was a compliment indeed.

## Monday 8th October
# ROGER DAY'S

## 25th Anniversary Show
at
## Winter Gardens, Margate
## 7·30pm – 12·00pm
featuring
# THE FORTUNES
plus Sixties Disco          Tickets £5

ME8 — Holsome Week ending Friday 9TH OCTOBER 1992. For Editorial telephone (0622) 694200. Advertising Sales Maidstone (0622) 679017

Roger Day has spent 25 years bringing the music to the people. In the Sixties, he broadcast from the pirate ship Radio Caroline, keeping a generation of pop fans tuned in to the latest hits. Now he is controller and presenter on the commercial Kent station Coast AM and at Margate's Winter Gardens on Monday, he will be looking back on 25 years in an anniversary show CAROL DAVIES talks to the man behind the mike about his early freewheeling days.

# The beat goes on for the music man

THEY called him Twiggy in the Sixties when he ruled the airwaves on the pirate ship Radio Caroline.

Now more of a slender bough than a twig, Roger Day is still crazy about music after all these years, and on Sunday celebrates his 25th anniversary in broadcasting.

As programme controller and presenter on the commercial Kent station Coast AM, Roger still looks back with enormous affection to the early days when bringing pop music to the nation meant risking seasickness, at best, or imprisonment, at worst.

The record-mad lad was known as Jukebox Joe at Chatham House school in Thanet, with all of his paper round money being spent on buying hit singles.

It came as no surprise to learn that his first pop purchases, Peter Gunn by Duane Eddy and Dream Lover by Bobby Darin, still enjoy a spin on Coast's turntables from time to time.

His parents' house on Margate sea front became a magnet for local teenagers, with the Dansette record player hardly cooling down between parties.

When he left school, he trained as an accountant at Pfizer's, in Richborough, but spent his evenings working as a DJ in local clubs.

"My first booking was at Dreamland ballroom, and I was so nervous my knees were knocking," he said. "My head was completely empty, but as soon as I picked up the mike, words just spilled out. To this day I don't know what I said, but I got another booking, so it must have been OK."

It was so OK that he soon gathered a mob of fans who turned up wherever he went, and at the age of 20 was offered a job on the pirate ship Radio England.

"My parents were marvellous about it and gave me a lot of support, but my boss at Pfizer's looked as if I had stabbed him in the chest," said Roger.

"What about security and your pension?" he said, but that was the last thing on my mind."

From Radio England, Roger joined the hugely popular Radio Caroline, with shipmates Dave Lee Travis and Johnny Walker.

The romance of the quest to bring pop to the people might be hard to understand for today's youth, with a whole wavebond of stations to choose from.

MID SEASON MID SEASON
Carpet

---

# DJ celebrates 25 years at turntable

*Showbiz*
**AURIOL LUCKHURST**

WHAT have 60s band The Fortunes and Coast AM radio presenter Roger Day got in common?

They both appeared in a Southern TV programme at the Winter Gardens, Margate, on October 8, 1965. The Fortunes were the star guests on Pop The Question and Roger was a guest panellist.

He was an accountant in Sandwich at the time but was a keen radio listener and was becoming very knowledgeable about pop music.

A friend had sent in his name as a possible participant on the show without his knowledge and the surprise became the turning point in his life.

A former colleague, who had become the manager of the Winter Gardens ballroom, saw the programme. Remembering that Roger had once told him he'd like to be a disc jockey, he offered him a part-time spot as his DJ.

Roger said of his dream break: "I was very shy and reserved in those days but I accepted and once I got started I found it all came naturally."

## Seaborne station

Roger's next move was to pirate radio, which was having great success in Radios Caroline and London. He sought an interview and was given a job with Radio England.

The seaborne station went under for financial reasons but its demise opened another door for Roger, because he was offered a job with Radio Caroline, which he accepted.

A year later pirate radio stations were made illegal and after Caroline was forced off the airwaves Roger moved to Radio Luxembourg for six months.

Then, he was offered the chance to compere a Beach Boys tour. It turned out to be a wonderful one-off job, which included an appearance at the London Palladium.

At the end of the tour, he got himself a mobile disco and built a substantial following, mainly among students, until 1974, when commercial radio arrived on the scene.

Since then, Roger has worked for Radio Piccadilly, Manchester, BRMB Birmingham and Radio West Bristol.

Now Coast AM's programme controller and afternoon presenter, Roger says he still enjoys his job, 25 years after that fateful show.

Originally from Margate, Roger now lives in Maidstone, with his wife and two children.

Roger and The Fortunes return to the **Winter Gardens**, on Monday.

Many of Roger's friends and former colleagues hope to be at the anniversary show, which includes a 60s disco.

Tickets at £5 and are available from Roger at Coast AM, Maidstone.

# CHAPTER 21

# PIRATE FM, CORNWALL

Word soon got around that I was looking for a gig. The first to call me was Colin Mason, managing director of Chiltern Radio. His first words to me upon meeting him in Dunstable were, "I can't possibly afford to pay you what you have been earning." So that was a wasted trip to Bedfordshire.

Soon after, I got a call from Mike Powell, who I had known at County Sound in Guildford. He told me about a new station he was setting up in Cornwall called Pirate FM and said he'd welcome a chat with me. Well, I certainly liked the name, so it was time to go west. I didn't realise how far it was.

I met up with Mike, and he offered me the breakfast programme. I went back to Kent to discuss it with Jenny, as it would mean me being away from the family again. We decided that I really didn't have an option, as we still had a mortgage and I couldn't afford to be out of work.

I joined up, and it was fun setting up Pirate FM. They

**Your All New Commercial Radio...**

Better Variety...
More Music !

had the latest RCS software with full automation of music. The studios were good and the on-air team strong. We went on air April 3rd 1992. I was dressed in my dinner jacket so I could launch in style. The reaction was instant, as in the southwest they'd been more or less starved of good music radio. They couldn't hear the pirate offshore stations and all they had was the boring, predominantly speech output delivered at a snail's pace by BBC Radio Cornwall.

I was featured on BBC Tomorrow's World to talk about the new revolutionary way of playing music via a computer screen, rather than record decks.

I enjoyed working there, but being so far away from home got to me. At first, I would head back to Kent on Friday after the programme but had to return on Saturday evening as I was on air Sunday morning. After a while, I only did that every other week. The family came down for the summer holiday and other school holidays. I rented a house in Truro and played squash in my spare time, making some new, good friends. I also enjoyed Cornwall's pubs, with their real ale, including my favourite The Real Ale House, which served ale from wooden casks.

## Hoist the 'Jolly Roger'— Twiggy's on the airwaves

From George Williams, 9, Fords Row, Redruth.

Sadly some show little enthusiasm, but I am a serious radio listener of long standing. There is no licence fee needed from us for the new radio station 'Pirate F.M. 102'.

The BBC, although not viable in its present form, will go on . . . We have to pay for it in our T.V. licences under threat from detector vans, computers and nosey "investigators."

**BREEZY**

We now have an up-market, bright and breezy radio station which compares in some respects with Radio Caroline. It will have as one of its D.J.s ("Twiggy") Day (pictured) who was a good Caroline presenter in the 60's.

He was later on Radio Northsea International in 1970. I have a photo of him in my RNI Souvenir book, and wish him well on the new local radio station.

I hope and feel the emphasis will be on more music rather than awful boring talk which is so much featured on dull, lacklustre BBC radio stations. So hoist the 'jolly roger' and anchors aweigh for April 3rd!

## Appeal for stamps from prison group

*Thought I would dress smart for the first show.*

But by Easter 1993, I'd had enough and headed back home.

Shortly after I got home, I got a call from Jazz FM asking if I would be interested in hosting their breakfast programme. I did explain that I knew nothing about Jazz and didn't even like jazz. They said it didn't matter; it was my banter they wanted. So I accepted and started in July 1993, but lasted three months, at which point they sacked me, because yes, you guessed it, I knew nothing about Jazz. You really couldn't make it up.

It was while I was working at Jazz FM that my dear mother succumbed to Alzheimer's. Thankfully, I was with my mother when she died on a Sunday. I still went to work at Jazz on the Monday, and when I asked for some time off for the funeral, the idiot programme controller said he would never have known I'd had such bad news as I sounded the same. I reminded him I was a professional, which clearly he hadn't realised. One good thing about Jazz FM: it was good to work again with Peter Young, who had been at UBN and briefly at Piccadilly Radio.

**RADIO**

**RADIO 1** *VHF 97.6-99.8MHz*
6.0 Mark Goodier. 9.0 Simon Bates. 12.30 Newsbeat. 12.45 Jakki Brambles. 3.0 Steve Wright in the Afternoon. 6.0 News 93. 6.30 Evening Session. 8.30 Glitter and Twisted. 9.0 Out on Blue Six. 10.0 Nicky Campbell. 12.0 (VHF) Bob Harris. 4.0 (VHF) Bruno Brookes.

**RADIO 2** *VHF 88-90.2MHz*
5.0 Martin Kelner. 6.15 Pause for Thought. 7.5 Sarah Kennedy. 9.15 Pause for thought. 9.30 Ken Bruce. 11.30 Jimmy Young. 2.0 Gloria Hunniford. 3.30 Ed Stewart. 5.5 John Dunn. 7.0 Hubert Gregg. 7.30 Alan Dell. 8.30 Big Band Special. 9.0 Humphrey Lyttelton. 10.0 Traditionally British. 10.30 The Jamesons. 12.5 Digby Fairweather. 1.0 Steve Madden. 3.0 Alex Lester.

**RADIO 3** *VHF 90.2-92.4MHz*
6.35 Open University. 7.0 On Air. 9.0 Composer of the Week. 10.0 Musical Encounters. 12.0 Violinist as Composer. 1.5 BBC Lunchtime Concert. 2.10 Lars Vogt. 3.10 The BBC Orchestras. 3.45 Cesar Franck. 4.30 Keyboard à le King. 5.0 In Tune. 7.30 Garland of Song. 8.10 Inherit the Truth. 8.30 EBU Concert. 10.10 Italian Violin Music. 10.45 Mixing It. 11.30 Music Restored. 12.35 Close. 1.0 (Except in Scotland) Night School. 2.30 Night School Extra. 3.0 Close.

**RADIO 4** *VHF 92.4-94.6MHz*
6.0 News. 6.10 Farming Today. 6.25 Prayer for the Day. 6.30 Today. 8.35 The Week on 4. 8.43 Oh Mary, Don't You Cry Anymore. 9.0 News. 9.5 Start the Week. 10.0 (VHF) Inspiration. 10.0 (LW) Daily Service. 10.15 (LW) The Bible. 10.30 Woman's Hour. 11.30 Money Box Live. 12.0 You and Yours. 12.25 Round Britain Quiz. 1.0 The World at One. 1.40 The Archers. 2.0 Roland's Afterlife. 3.15 Whackademics. 3.30 Eureka. 4.0 News. 4.5 Kaleidoscope. 4.45 Short Story: Flashman. 5.0 PM. 6.0 Six O'Clock News. 6.30 The News Quiz. 7.0 News. 7.5 The Archers. 7.20 The Food Programme. 7.45 The Monday Play: Holus Bolus. 9.0 Silkies. 9.15 Kaleidoscope. 9.45 The Financial World Tonight. 10.0 The World Tonight. 10.45 A Book at Bedtime: It All Began with Growcott. 11.9 You Heard It Here First. 11.30 Benny's Boys. 12.0 News. 12.43 (VHF) Close. 12.43 (LW) As World Service.

**RADIO 5** *MW 693kHz/433m*
6.0 World Service. 6.30 Danny Baker's Morning Edition. 9.0 For Schools. 10.25 Johnnie Walker. 12.30 Baby Talk. 1.0 News Update. 1.10 BFBS Worldwide. 2.30 Sportsbeat. 4.30 Five Aside. 6.30

The Green Hornet. 7.15 The Cricket in Times Square. 7.30 Champion Sport. 9.30 X Minus One. 10.10 Fabulous! 12.0 Close.

**CLASSIC FM** *VHF 100-102MHz*
6.0 Nick Bailey. 9.0 Henry Kelly. 12.0 Susannah Simons. 2.0 Lunchtime Concerto. 3.0 Jamie Crick. 6.0 Classic Reports. 7.0 Close Encounters of a Musical Kind. 8.0 Evening Concert. 10.0 Michael Mappin. 1.0 Andre Leon.

**VIRGIN** *MW 1215kHz*
6.0 Russ and Jono's Rock 'n' Roll Breakfast. 10.0 Richard Skinner. 1.0 Kevin Greening. 4.0 Tommy Vance. 7.0 Mitch Johnson. 10.0 Nick Abbot. 2.0 Wendy Lloyd.

**LBC NEWSTALK** *VHF 97.3*
5.30 Dawn Traders. 6.0 Mike Carlton. 9.0 Richard Littlejohn. 12.0 News. 1.0 Frank Bough. 4.0 Angela Rippon. 7.0 Richard Dallyn. 9.0 Robbie Vincent. 1.0 Through the Night.

**LONDON TALKBACK** *MW 1152kHz*
As Newstalk except: 5.30 Douglas Cameron. 9.0 Pete Murray. 1.0 Steve Allen. 3.0 Mike Dickin.

**GLR**
*VHF 94.9 MW 1458kHz/206m*
6.0 Al Clarke. 7.0 Nick Herbert and Sandy Warr. 9.30 Peter Curran. 12.30 London Live. 1.30 Diana

Luke. 5.0 Bill Overton with Lucy Thorpe. 7.30 Simon Barnett. 8.0 (MW) Asian London. 10.30 Lucy Longhurst. 1.0 As World Service.

**CAPITAL RADIO** *VHF 95.8*
5.0 Richard Allinson. 7.0 Chris Tarrant. 10.0 Pat Sharp. 1.0 Mick Brown. 4.0 David Jensen. 7.0 The Way It Is. 7.30 Neil Fox. 10.0 Martin Collins. 1.0 Seymour Segnit.

**CAPITAL GOLD** *MW 1548kHz*
6.0 Tony Blackburn. 9.0 David Hamilton. 12.30 Paul Burnett. 2.0 Kenny Everett. 4.30 Mike Reed. 8.0 Stuart Colman. 10.0 Mike Ahern. 2.0 Bob Stewart.

**JAZZ FM** *VHF 102.2*
6.0 Roger Dev. 10.0 Peter Young. 2.0 Steve Collins. 6.0 Helen Mayhew. 10.0 David Freeman. 2.0 Mark Sebastian.

**KISS** *VHF 100*
7.0 The Dangerous Breakfast. 10.0 Steve Jackson. 1.0 Pete Wardman. 4.0 David Rodigan. 7.0 The Word. 7.15 David Rodigan. 10.0 Jazzie B. 1.0 Daddy Bug. 4.0 Caesar.

**MELODY** *VHF 104.9*
24-hours-a-day easy listening

**SPECTRUM** *MW 558*
5.0 Traders. 8.0 Asian. 10.0 Jewish. 12.0 Greek. 2.0 Spanish. 3.0 Italian. 5.0 Chinese. 8.0 Asian. 10.0 Arabic. 12.0 Persian; Gay; Afro.

**WORLD SERVICE**
*(648kHz/463m)*

275

# CHAPTER 22

# BACK TO MANCHESTER

Four months later, in early 1994, I was invited to return to Piccadilly Radio to present the breakfast programme on their Piccadilly Gold AM station. It was a bit traumatic because, although I was glad to be back on the station, I'd never wanted to leave. I was replacing my old chum Jim Reeve, who was a very popular lad. As a result, I started getting abusive calls from listeners.

This was the Piccadilly Gold schedule:

2am – 6am Bryce Cooke

6am – 9am Roger Day

9am –12 Mike Sweeney

12 –3pm Phil Wood

3pm – 4pm Umberto

4pm – 7pm Dave Ward

7pm – 10pm Pete Reeves

10pm – 2am James Stannage

# CHAPTER 23

# RADIO MERCURY, SURREY

I worked for Piccadilly Gold for nine months. By September, I was getting so homesick, I returned home to Kent and presented the breakfast show at Radio Mercury FM in Reigate for a short time. It was the one of the best located radio stations I've worked at, overlooking a lake. I started there in November and worked through to the following March.

**MERCURY DJ: Roger Day**

## Roger returns to the hotseat

Former pirate radio DJ Roger Day will be replacing Jon Scraggs in the breakfast show hotseat at Radio Mercury.

Roger takes to the mike next Monday (September 26) fresh from a two-year stint on the afternoon show at Manchester's Radio Picadilly.

He originally comes from Surbiton, and sees the move as coming back to his roots. "It'll be just like coming home again," he said.

His career goes back to the heady days of pirate radio, when he was a DJ on Radio Caroline, the sea-bourne station which inspired BBC bosses to launch Radio One.

"It was very exciting - just like being a modern day Robin Hood. We didn't know if we were going to get blown out of the water or not," said Roger.

It was a far cry from his early days as a trainee chartered accountant.

"I found it terminally boring and was always looking for a way out. I ran a mobile disco and happened to meet the right people and that's how I arrived at Caroline," he said.

From there he went went to Radio Luxembourg, Radio North Sea, Piccadilly Radio and BRMB in Birmingham, finding time to host a Beach Boys European tour along the way.

CRAWLEY OBSERVER
September 21st
1994

# CHAPTER 24

# RADIO LICENCE APPLICATIONS

I n January 1995, it was announced that radio licences were to be given for West and East Kent. The West Kent licence was currently owned by Invicta, themselves now owned by Capital Radio.

My old friend from Invicta, Nigel Reeve, reckoned we should get an application in for East Kent. Putting together a radio licence application is a very complicated and exhaustive process. You have to detail plans for programming, funding, financial forecasts, as well as gather local support from 'the pillars of society' in the area.

Our application was perfect, but we didn't get the licence, although we were told we came very close. I told the Radio Authority that the Capital Radio group, who won the licence, would close all local programmes and network all their stations from London. That's exactly what they did eventually. It was soul-destroying, a waste of time, and a mockery of offering local radio licences.

But I got together another application for a Maidstone licence when that was advertised. Again, it was another good application, but it was given to the Kent Messenger newspaper group, which already had other stations in Kent. Once more, I forecast that they would take over every station in Kent and make it one station. The Radio Authority said that couldn't happen, but of course it did.

Some groups bought licences simply as a way of making a quick buck, selling up to a larger group for a big profit. They were more interested in a bulging bank account than a bulging listenership! It is a flawed system, and having professional radio people involved means nothing.

I have been involved with helping many people interested in getting local licences, such as broadcasting on a restricted local licence. The truth of the matter though is we've very few real local radio stations in the commercial sector left. A great pity as that local advertisers can't afford the rates for the bigger stations. It's so different in the USA, where you tell the authority what sort of station you want to set up, and if there is a spare frequency, you are allowed to get on with it.

In 1995, I started doing work for Channel Travel Radio in Folkestone. No music, just reading out travel information for the tunnel. It was definitely the most boring radio job I've had, but it paid the bills. I also started doing relief work at BBC Radio Kent.

In November 1995, I was invited back to Pirate FM for a temporary contract presenting their breakfast show until their new presenter could start. From there, I worked at County Sound in Guildford, where Mike Powell wanted me to present 7am till 12 noon, Monday to Friday, and 1pm till 6pm on a Sunday. I drove there each day from my home in Maidstone and never realised how busy the M25 gets so early in the morning.

While at County Sound, I had a studio built in the loft of my home so I could produce some independent radio shows.

Nigel Reeve formed a management company in the Spring of 2000 called Fusion Radio. Its aim was to buy small radio stations and improve their audiences and income. I accepted his offer of programme director. It didn't really work out as the people who operated the small stations really couldn't grasp our ideas, so that ended in August 2002. Although I was paid well and had a nice company Mercedez car, I wasn't on air much. I am at my happiest in the studio playing great music.

I did continue to work for Nigel on other projects until 2008. He is one of the best salespeople I have worked with.

There was a rather bizarre occurrence during that period. We had organised a promotion for some big advertising agencies, which involved a trip on Eurostar to Paris for lunch. On the way back, we were, shall we say, rather jolly and loud. I was sitting opposite a chap who had the misfortune to listen to our stories. Anyway, he was smiling, and I asked him why. It turned out he was the man who had organised the jamming of RNI. I think I did give him the sharp end of my tongue.

# CHAPTER 25

# SAGA, WEST MIDLANDS

I n 2004, Brian Savin, who I had first worked with at BRMB, asked me to become relief DJ at the station based in Birmingham. I loved my time there. Very soon, I was asked to host afternoons 16.00–19.00, as well as a Saturday Fifties and Sixties show. This had a huge following, getting great audience figures. It was ideal for me, playing a wonderful selection of golden oldies and targeting Saga's well-publicised over-fifties age group. Great team of people there. During the week, I stayed with a good friend, Chris Mould. All that changed when GMG took over in December 2006. They changed the name to Smooth Radio and had a new music policy. It basically became Heart Two.

The BBC had offered me a chance to return to Kent, so I had resigned from the daily show but continued with the Saturday programme. GMG offered me the mid-morning show, which was flattering, but I wasn't going to give up the chance of what had been offered by the BBC.

Just as well as they hired somebody to do a network show soon after. My last show was in November 2007, and my replacement was Chris Tarrant, a wonderful DJ, but they changed the format and lost thousands of listeners. Now of course, it isn't a regional station as it has gone national. Very sad as it was a unique format to an age group that is underserved. Well, it was then, but not now.

# CHAPTER 26

# LONG WAVE MUSIC MAN, ISLE OF MAN

In 2004, I was approached by Paul Rusling, who had worked for Radio Caroline in the seventies and was behind the set-up of Laser Radio. He had formed a company to set up a long wave station from the Isle of Man that would cover the entire UK. I wrote the programming section for his fundraising document, as I was to be the programme director. The IOM government awarded them the licence, but sadly the money for start-up costs couldn't be raised. I thought it was a great idea and thought, at last, I'm going to be on national radio! Little did I know what would happen some years later!

Of course, Radio Caroline North broadcast off the Isle of Man, and the Manx Parliament were forced to carry out the Marine Offences Act against their wishes, so they were very enthusiastic.

**Isle of Man**
**Government**

### Introduction

The Communications Commission ("the Commission") of the Isle of Man Government, acting under the authority of section 2 of the Broadcasting Act, 1993, of Tynwald, invites applications for the running of a Long Wave Radio station on the Isle of Man.

Clearance has been obtained for the use of 279kHz from the Isle of Man with a daytime power of 500 kW. Night-time power is restricted to 10kW at present but the Commission will seek a dispensation to increase this power level before the successful applicant commences broadcasting. (Relevant documentation is attached to these guidance notes). The Commission gives no guarantee regarding the daytime or night-time coverage from this transmitter.

The Commission intends to offer initially a provisional broadcasting licence as a result of this application process. The successful applicant will be required to undertake an environmental impact assessment and obtain the necessary planning permissions before the Commission grants to it a substantive broadcasting licence.

---

**FINANCIAL TIMES** TUESDAY JUNE 29 2004

**WILLIAM HALL**
VIEW FROM THE ISLE OF MAN

## Poptastic news for island's image

The Isle of Man, a rain-swept island in the Irish Sea with about 70,000 inhabitants, has long envied Luxembourg, stuck in the middle of Europe. While both compete in tourism and as offshore financial centres, Luxembourg has had one big advantage – Radio Luxembourg.

Founded in 1933, it grew to be Europe's most successful commercial radio station in the 1950s by broadcasting night-time pop music to a predominantly young English-speaking audience. It was overtaken by "pirate" offshore commercial radio stations serving the UK, such as Radio Caroline, but it did more than anything to raise Luxembourg's international profile to a whole generation of British "babyboomers".

The Isle of Man has been trying for more than 40 years to get its own international radio station. Manx Radio, founded in 1964, was the UK's first commercial radio station. But it serves a local audience, and the UK government repeatedly blocked attempts to establish a powerful international commercial radio station on the Isle of Man because it would be unfair competition for the country's three national commercial radio stations – Classic FM, Virgin and

the European courts in the early 1990s changed the ground rules and the Isle of Man government awarded a 10-year licence to Isle of Man International Broadcasting in 1999 for a new commercial, long-wave radio station serving the UK and Republic of Ireland. After several planning objections, which resulted in the transmitter having to be moved a few miles offshore, the project finally got the go-ahead earlier this year.

Last week, IMIB announced plans to raise £33m for what will be the country's fourth national commercial radio station. It will have a staff of 40 and a new type of "crossed-field antenna" that is a fraction of the size of the 1,000ft masts normally needed for a similarly powerful long-wave radio transmitter.

IMIB's target audience will be adults aged 35 to 55 with a heavy emphasis on women who have a reasonably high level of disposable income. It has recruited 1960s and 1970s pop stars, such as Gene Pitney and Rick Wakeman, to host shows that will compete with Radio 2, the most popular of the BBC's radio channels.

Paul Rusling, a former Radio Caroline disc jockey and IMIB's chief executive, says the new station will need an audience of 2.5m to break even and is hoping eventually to reach 4m.

By contrast, the latest Rajar ratings show that Radio 2 has a 13.0m audience, Classic FM 6.5m, Virgin 2.5m and Talksport 2.1m.

Richard Corkhill, the Isle of Man's chief minister who remembers when Radio Caroline was moored a few miles offshore from his home, is a big fan of the island's new radio station, which has been on the drawing board for 10 years.

"A lot of people thought Luxembourg was a radio station. We do not want people to think our island is just a radio station," says Mr Corkhill. But he is confident it will raise the international profile of an island with a triple A credit rating that will shortly scrap corporation tax to boost an increasingly diversified economy set to grow at 5.5 per cent a year.

"We are a self-governing crown dependency, and we are keen to make sure that we are not forgotten," says Mr Corkhill.

Mr Rusling promises to do his best. While the new station will not be broadcasting a regular diet of Isle of Man news, local announcers will be encouraged to mention the island's good points, including the weather, unless, of course, it is pouring with rain and the island is shrouded in its usual Irish sea mist.

# CHAPTER 27

# RADIO CAROLINE REUNIONS

I n 2003, I decided to organise a reunion for the fortieth anniversary of the first broadcast of Radio Caroline to take place on March 28th 2004. The event just had to be at The Red Lion in Mayfair near Chesterfield Gardens, where all the DJs and staff would meet up. I spent many hours and days contacting many people who had been associated with the station. On the day, I had no idea how many would turn up. The attendance was way above my expectations. When I arrived, Simon Dee was already there. That was very appropriate as he was Radio Caroline's first DJ. It really was a golden moment.

*Simon Dee*

*Ronan & Simon the men who started it all*

*Group Photo of Caroline People*

*The Three Amigos. With the Admiral Robbie Dale and JW*

*Spangles (Chris Cary on the right)*

*My Hero, Ronan*

*Tom Edwards on the left, Paul McKenna second from the right*

I organised a similar event in 2014 but attendance wasn't so good. I guess we were all getting older. But I will continue to organise reunions on the anniversaries of Radio Caroline, starting and ending until the day I die.

Surprisingly, most UK radio stations ignored Radio Caroline's first significant anniversary in 2004. It shocked and disgusted me as without Radio Caroline there wouldn't have been the radio network that had developed. I say most, because one, a BBC one, put together a major celebration of the offshore pirate radio years, and they made me a big part of it!

# CHAPTER 28

# PIRATE BBC ESSEX

To put pirate in the same title as the BBC was beyond cheek really, but quite clever, and when I learned about the plans by the BBC local radio station, BBC Essex, to mark the fortieth anniversary of Radio Caroline's launch, I realised it could be quite special.

The station's programmes director, Tim Gillett, together with presenters Steve Scruton and Ian Wyatt had managed to persuade the BBC Essex boss, Margaret Hyde, that their plan to mark the anniversary with a seven day on-air recreation of 60s offshore radio would be successful, not only for the station, but would get headlines and pull listeners in from around the world. And of course, it was a local anniversary, as the radio ships had been moored off Essex.

Tim put together a playlist of the songs played by the stations in the 60s, many of which hadn't been played since. He limited his playlist to records released before the Marine Offences Act of 1967, with the majority of the records from the 1964 to 1967 period, with a few pre-'64 oldies, which would have been played by Caroline, London, and the others. He also set about trying to find as many of the original pirate pioneer DJs so that it really would be an authentic broadcast anniversary. He didn't do too bad, signing up Mike Ahern, Paul Burnett, Tom Edwards, Ian Damon, Keith Skues, Pete Brady, Dave Cash, and Duncan Johnson.

The master stroke by engineer Chris Woodward and technical producer Tom Warmington was to get the seven-day extravaganza not only broadcast on one of BBC Essex's medium wave frequencies, but on the internet, giving it a potential worldwide audience.

BBC Essex presenter and 60soffshore pirate radio fan Steve Scruton managed to persuade a Harwich-based charity owner of the LV18 lightship to use the vessel as the ship from which Pirate BBC Essex would be broadcast, moored off the coast in Harwich Harbour. Together with Ian Wyatt, they persuaded Steve England to record a jingle package and my old pirate radio pal Duncan Johnson to record the voiceovers.

I and the other presenters lived, ate, and broadcast aboard the LV18 out in Harwich Harbour from the start of Pirate BBC Essex on April 1 2004 until the 7 April. They'd even organised a tender vessel, courtesy of Alan Sage, who used his Harwich to Felixstowe ferry to take us back and forth and bring out scores of 'anoraks' and on-air guests.

I loved it. They really recreated the atmosphere of the 60soffshore stations. How ironic it was that the best pirate radio should come from the BBC. The response from listeners was fantastic, with emails coming in to the LV18 from across the world. Most said what a pity it was that it wasn't permanent as it was so much better than the mainstream gold stations, with their narrow playlists and lack of fun. There is just some magic about broadcasting from a ship that can never be achieved on land.

*Looking out the porthole on the LVI8*

*Paul Burnett*

*Ray Clark and Mike Ahern*

So successful was it that it was repeated three years later in 2007, this time in August, to mark the fortieth anniversary of the end of Radio London and the passing of the Marine Offences Act, when most of the stations were banned by the Labour government.

The presenter line up was even better, with my pirate radio pal Johnnie Walker on board, together with Norman St John and John Kerr flying in from Australia to take park, Gord Cruse coming from Canada, and Keith Hampshire from the USA. The other original 60spresenters to take part were Dave Cash, Keith Skues, Paul Burnett, Mark Wesley, Vince Allen, Steve England, Emperor Rosko, Tom Edwards, Guy Hamilton, Paul Freeman, and Keith Martin

*Roger Day, chatting to engineer, Michael Barrington, and former Radio Caroline presenter, Johnnie Walker. Can you spot the portable loo on deck in the background?*

*Back of Keith Skues and Johnnie Walker*

*On Air*

*10 – 13 August 2009*

Dave Cash, Keith Skues, Norman St. John, Roger Day, Paul Burnett, Vince Allen, Steve England, Johnnie Walker, Emperor Rosko, Mike Ahern, Tom Edwards, Steve Merike, Tony Blackburn, Alan Turner, Keith Skues

Two years later, Pirate BBC Essex was back, this time broadcasting from the same vessel, the LV18, but moored up by Harwich Ha'penny Pier. The three-day broadcast coincided with the release of the film The Boat That Rocked. Of course, the film was nothing like the real thing but did educate younger days were like. I must point out that the scene where a boat load of girls were brought onto the ship is true fiction. In those days, only men were allowed to stay on board. I often get asked which character in the film I was. I always answer, "The good looking one." There is one moment in the movie that really resonated with me. It's when the US DJ says, "These are the best days of our lives." It was so true. I must thank the BBC Essex team for those revivals, as back in 2004, I was beginning to doubt my ability to communicate with listeners. However, the response was so fantastic it reminded me that there were a lot of people who love what I do.

Two other 60's pirate radio celebrations stand out in my memory. One was organised by the Radio Academy at the Sugar Reef in London 2004. Since that date, though, the RA has ignored any repeats, which is sad. The second was on the Thames in 2017 on August 14th when DJs from all the 60's pirate stations assembled on a ship on the Thames in London to celebrate those golden days.

I must pay tribute to Hans Knot, who has organised some great tributes in Holland.

The 2017 PBE probably had the best response. Harwich was packed on August 14th, and the special moment was when we cast the ashes of Dave Cash into the sea from the pier at Harwich. Dave loved those transmissions as much as I did. I also want my ashes spread in the sea 3 miles off Frinton at the position where the Mi Amigo as anchored.

DJs on that day: Johnnie Walker, Tom Edwards, Norman St John, and me.

Sadly, I don't think there will be any more Pirate BBC Essex events. Can you imagine such celebrations for the stations now on air? I think not.

The Pirate radio event in Harwich. The broadcast took place from the LV18 Lightvessel on Harwich Quay, featuring broadcasters Johnny Walker and Ray Clark under the banner Pirate BBC Essex. Pictured is Roger Day. Pictures: GREGG BROWN

*Keith Skues, Neddy Turner, and me talking Pirate Radio at The Electric Palace, Harwich*

*Tom Edwards left and Norman St. John far right*

*On deck at Pirate BBC Essex*

*Pirate hat for an old Pirate*

*Neddy Turner who was an original Caroline DJ when they first started and was on board when the ship sailed to the Isle of Man, I only found out he lived near me in Maidstone a few years ago.*

*Radio Day in Amsterdam, 2014. Nutty Nora top left, who ran Don Allen's Fan Club; Kenny Tosh and Steve Young top right*

*2004 at the Riga Bar, Southend. Rod Allen from the Fortunes who played Caroline, and me with my t-Shirt of my hero*

*Front row right: Tony Prince, next to the Child Scientist Patrick Starling, the engineer*

## CHAPTER 29

# BBC LOCAL RADIO IN THE SOUTH

I n September 2006, I was contacted by Paul Leaper, the managing editor of BBC Radio Kent, asking if I was interested in taking over the 7pm – 10pm evening programme, shared with Radios Surrey, Sussex, Solent, Hampshire, Isle of Wight, Oxford, and Berkshire. I was to be given free music choice and allowed to invite guests from the music industry. I jumped at the chance to come back home to Kent and started on January 1st 2007. He also gave me Sunday afternoons on BBC Radio Kent. What with that and still hosting a Saturday show at Saga in the Midlands with 50sand 60smusic, I was now on the radio seven days a week.

My BBC regional evening show featured one hour each night of specialised music. On Mondays was Songs From the Shows with Phil Molyneux; it was jazz on Tuesdays, Geoff Wall with folk music on Wednesdays, country music on Thursdays with Steve Cherelle, and on Fridays we featured big band and swing with Grant James.

week ending December 31, 2006     For

**FACE FOR RADIO: Roger Day, in the chair at BBC Radio Kent**

# Over to the Beeb for a veteran DJ

IT'S been a long time coming, but after a 40-year career in commercial radio, Margate-born presenter Roger Day has signed his first ever BBC contract and will become the new voice of weekday evenings on Radio Kent.

By **JAMIE McGINNES**
jamie.mcginnes@kosmedia.co.uk

After a long career in commercial radio that's included slots presenting radio stations such as the legendary Radio Luxembourg, Radio Caroline and the 1960s favourite Swinging Radio England, Roger is finally coming home.

For the past two years, the 60-year-old has been working on Saga Radio in the West Midlands and will be joining BBC Radio Kent tomorrow on New Year's Day.

### Passion

Paul Leaper, BBC Kent's managing editor said: "Roger brings together a love for Kent, a love of music and a real passion for making great radio."

Roger originally trained as an accountant, but soon began working in ballrooms around the South East. It wasn't long before he joined one of the many pirate ships broadcasting off the coast of England and thus began a radio career that's taken him across the UK. In the 1970s he helped take Manchester's Piccadilly Radio to number one in the ratings. In the 1980s he wrote Invicta's application to win it the first commercial radio licence for Kent and in the 1990s he helped launch a new radio station in Cornwall.

He said: "Being born and bred in Kent, it's great to be back broadcasting across the county I love. In fact, the family lives here so it's a chance for us all to be together again. I hope they're ready for that."

Roger's is known for having an encyclopaedic knowledge of music and he owns every Top 10 single released since 1955. He also claims to be the UK's biggest Beach Boy fan – and has even introduced them on stage – so has told viewers to expect plenty of the Californian group's tunes among a mix of classic tracks from the past four decades.

"The new show is all about bringing together the music and the listeners," said Roger. "I'll bring along the music and the guests. Hopefully the listeners will add in their memories and thoughts."

Roger Day can be heard Monday to Friday, 7-10pm starting from January 1. He replaces Charlie Crocker who is moving to Southampton to present on Radio Kent's sister station BBC Radio Solent.

The latest news updated daily
www.kentnews.co.uk

---

There was so much support for the output from the BBC, so different on commercial radio, where you were mostly left to get on with it. I know the Beeb takes some flack, but there are some really talented people there who just want to create great radio. I believe working there improved my performance.

Here's a complete list of all the guests who came on my evening show:

Peter Tork – The Monkees; Jon Lord – Deep Purple, Bonnie Tyler (always call her Blodwyn!), Marty Wilde, Graham Gouldman, Spencer Davis, Dennis Loccoriere – Dr Hook, Jack Savoretti, Dave Berry, Dave Dee, Judy Tzuke, John Walker – Walker Brothers, Ruby Turner, Les Holroyd

– Barclay James Harvest, Paul Layton – New Seekers, Susan Maughan, Chip Hawkes – The Tremeloes, Alexander O'Neal, Tony Hadley, Bob Harris, Curtis Stigers, Crystal Gayle, Cutting Crew, Ralph McTell, Rita Coolidge, Charlie Dore, Chas Hodges Barry Ryan, Elkie Brooks, Colin Blunstone, Roger Chapman, Joan Armatrading, Billy Ocean, John Illsley– Dire Straits (he played Romeo & Juliet live in the studio), Pete Langford – The Barron Knights, Dave Cousins – The Strawbs, Les Reed, Zoot Money, Andy McCluskey – OMD, Mary Weiss – The Shangri-Las, Dave Bartram –Showaddywaddy, Nana Mouskouri, Herbie Flowers, Sally Oldfield, Dean Friedman, Chris Squires – Yes, Julie Felix, David Marks – an original Beach Boy, Humphrey Lyttelton, Suzi Quatro, Tom McGuiness, Otis Williams – The Temptations, Roy Wood, Siouxsie Sioux, Dave Mason – Traffic, Dale Hawkins, The Proclaimers, Bobby Elliot, and Tony Hicks – The Hollies, Joe Brown, Fish –Marilion, Katie Melua, Jools Holland, Rod Argent, Bev Bevan – The Move and ELO, Frank Allen – The Searchers, Terry Dene, Marti Pellow, Paul Carrack, Mari Wilson, Bruce Foxton and Rick Butler – Jam, Vince Eager, Alison Moyet, Geno Washington, Chas Jankel – The Blockheads, Paul Young, Russ Mael – Sparks, Jona Lewie, Kenny Jones – The Faces, Jimmy James, Ranking Roger, Paul Anka, Barrie Masters – Eddie and The Hot Rods, Eric Stewart – The Mindbenders and 10cc, Bobby Smith – The Detroit Spinners, Mike Berry, Kenny G, Ray Philips – The Nashville Teens, Jeff Wayne, Roland Gift – Fine Young Cannibals, Hugh Cornwell – The Stranglers,

Raul Malo – The Mavericks, Chas Smash – Madness, George Kooymans – Golden Earring, Rowetta – Happy Mondays, Moya Brenna – Clannad, Chris Difford– Squeeze, Eddie Amoo– Real Thing, Marianne Faithfull, Kim Carnes, Chris De Burgh, Chris Farlowe, Alistair McGowan.

Ian Gillan– Deep Purple, Roger McGuinn – The Byrds, Dorian Gray, Joe Bonamassa, Ernest Borgnine, Christopher Cross, Joe Satriani, Snowy White, Gerry Marsden, Mike Batt, Al Stewart, Jimmy Pursey – Sham 69, Linda Lewis, Kiki Dee, Ray Sawyer – Doctor Hook, Paul Jones, Mica Paris, Captain Sensible, Michael McDonald, Tommy Allsup – The Crickets, Mike Peters – The Alarm, Jim Diamond, Merrill Osmond,Judith Durham – The Seekers, Ali Campbell, Ade Edmonson, Florence and The Machine, Toploader (played live), Ray Davies, Neil Hannon – Divine Comedy, Leo Lyons – Ten Years After, Hamish Stuart – Average White Band, Bobby Gee – Bucks Fizz, John Mayall, Des O'Connor, Iain Mathews, Mick Green – The Pirates and The Dakotas, Ian Anderson, Kenny Ball, Chris Barber, Acker Bilk, Joey Tempest – Europe, Ian Brodie – The Lightning Seeds, Ray Stiles – Mud, Jan Akkerman– Focus, Clint Boon – The Inspiral Carpets, Terry Reid, Sharon Corr, Klaus Voormann, Manfred Mann, Marc Almond, PJ Proby, Dave Clark, Dom Airey – Deep Purple,  Nick Simper – Deep Purple, The Flowerpot Men, The Pirates, Paul Da Vinci, John McNally – The Searchers, Mick Kaminski – ELO, Violinski, Matt Bianco, Cliff Richard, Hank Marvin, Mike Score – A Flock Of Seagulls, Judy Dyble, David Allen, and Gong, Natalie Imbruglia,

Tony Rivers, Richard Hawley, Chris Jagger, Neil Innes, Mark Knopfler, Michael Bolton, Andy Williams, Beverley Craven, Hazel O'Connor, Steve Hackett, The Beautiful South (played live), Brand New Heavies, Robin Scott – M, Cheryl Baker, Gaz Coombes – Supergrass, Jim McCarty – The Yardbirds, Howard Jones, Howard Kaylan – The Turtles, Jimmy Webb, Westlife, Jim Lea – Slade, Greg Lake, UB40, Todd Rundgren, Keane, Roseanne Cash, Roger Spear – Bonzo Dog Doo Dah Band, Colin Hay –Men At Work, Steve Ellis – The Love Affair, Alice Cooper, Hue and Cry, Gary US Bonds, Mick Jones – Foreigner, Terry Rice Milton – Cupid's Inspiration, Paul Barrere – Little Feat, Neal Schon – Journey, Mick Taylor – The Rolling Stones, Les Mckeown – The Bay City Rollers, Tom Paxton, Timothy B Schmidt – The Eagles, Ian Whitcomb, Brian Poole, Beth Neilson Chapman,  Jennifer Batten – Michael Jackson guitarist, Smokey Robinson, Dan McCafferty – Nazareth, 'Legs' Larry Smith – The Bonzo Dog Doo Dah Band, Andy Fairweather Low, Duke Fakir – The Four Tops, Pauline Black, Judy Collins, Jean Jacques Burnel – The Stranglers, Carlene Carter Cash, John Waite, Pretty Things –played SF Sorrow live, Carly Simon, Boy George, Slash, Rick Lee – Ten Years After, Sandi Thom, Mick Avory – The Kinks, Nik Turner – Hawkwind, Paul Rogers, Paul Hardcastle, Lenny Zakatek– The Alan Parsons Project, James, Alvin Stardust, Rosemary Squires, Don McLean, Del Amitri, Gordon Giltrap, Francis Rossi, Jim Kerr – Simple Minds, Paul Stanley – Kiss, Shakatak, Eddie Philips – The Creation, Ocean Colour Scene, Keane,

Martha Reeves, Roger Taylor – Queen, Jeff Beck, Steve Harley, Wurzels, Katrina, Ian McCulloch – Echo and The Bunnymen, Lotus Eaters, Suzanne Vega, Kelly Rowland – Destiny's Child, Bill Hurd – The Rubettes, Tom McGuiness, Buddy Greco, Candi Staton, Alan Whitehead – Marmalade, Dr John, David Gray, Gary Langan– Art Of Noise, Earth, Wind, and Fire, Sandie Shaw, Steve Miller, Albert Hammond, Dave Stewart, Dave Pegg, Ray McVay, Steve Rowland, Rumer, Randy Bachman, Mumford and Sons, Mike Wilsh – The Four Pennies, Ian Gomm, John Inverdale, Badly Drawn Boy, Paul Heaton and Jacqui Abbott, Beth Neilson–Chapman, Pyschadelic Furs, Verden Allen – Mott The Hoople, Ray Thomas, Plain White Ts, Glen Matlock, A-Ha, Duane Eddy, Sonja Kristina, Stephanie De Sykes, Belinda Carlisle, Huey Lewis, John Coughlan – Status Quo, Paul Carrack, Peter Asher, Elaine Page, Annie Lennox, Tommy James, Belle Stars, Bryan Ferry, Martin Fry –ABC, Kiki Dee, Carol Dekker – T'Pau, Bernie Marsden – Whitesnake, Pete Brown – Cream songwriter, Chrissie Hynde, Steve Lukather – Toto, Geoff Downes, and John Wetton – Asia, Don Fardon, Ben E King, Red Box, Shakin' Stevens, Scott Gorham – Thin Lizzy, Bryn Haworth (played live), Adele, Gilbert O'Sullivan, Nick Heyward, Ray Jackson – Lindisfarne, Patrick Campbell-Lyons – Nirvana, Tony Christie, Nick Rhodes – Duran Duran, Eddi Reader, Andy Kim, Edgar Broughton, Blancmange, Robert Miles, The Dubliners, Robb Royer – Bread, Bobby Harrison – Procol Harum, John Steele – The Animals, Mike Rutherford, Roachford,

John Schroeder – Sounds Orchestral, Billie Davis and Keith Powell, David Paton – Pilot, Mike Scott – The Waterboys, Dee Dee Phelps, Josh Groban, Randy Edelman, Dave Barker and Ansell Collins, K.D. Lang, Joe Elliott – Def Leppard, Barry Manilow, Nick Capaldi, Paul Rodgers, Mari Wilson, Robin Trower, Manfred Mann, Gary Wright, Peter Cox – Go West, Sophie Ellis-Bextor, Tina Charles, John Parr, Vince Clark – Erasure, Russ Sainty, Ray Connolly, Stevie Nicks, Ruby Turner, Little Jimmy Osmond, Mike Sarne, Jack Bruce, Ian McLagan – Faces, Terry Dene, John Fiddler – Medicine Head, Mark Nevin – Fairground Attraction, Randy Crawford, Carol Kaye – session musician on The Beach Boys' Pet Sounds, Barry Blue, Serge Pizzorno– Kasabian, Kenny Thomas, Steve Cropper, Ryan Adams, Nick Lowe, The Thrills, Kid Creole, Chris Spedding, Adam Ant, Wilko Johnson, Roy Harper, Chris Welch, Nigel Kennedy, Bruce Johnston – The Beach Boys, Maisie Williams – Boney M, Thomas Dolby, Bill Wyman, Manic Street Preachers, Charlie Gracie, Bill Nelson –Be Bop Deluxe, Jack Jones, Janice Ian, Peter Frampton, Noddy Holder, Nickelback, Carl Palmer, The Feeling, Francis Rossi, Twiggy (the other one), David Courtney, Jeff Pain 'Dicken'– Mr Big, Seasick Steve, Mick Box – Uriah Heep, John Allison – The Allisons, Keith Altham, Ting Tings, Chris Isaak, Kingsize Taylor, Peter Noone, Tony Hazzard, Jess Conrad, Nanci Griffith, Ray Shulman – Simon Dupree, Clem Cattini, Clodagh Rodgers, David Martin, Dio, Frank Collins –Arrival, Gotye, Cliff Bennett, Kenny Lynch, Gloria Hunniford, Magic Numbers,

Barry Whitman –Hermans Hermits, John Oates, Gary Numan, Peter Hook – New Order, Deborah Bonham (played live), Kate Robbins, Train, Andy Brown – Status Quo and The Herd, Simon May, Garry Christian – The Christians, Alan Price, Francoise Pascal, Pete Staples – The Troggs, Roy Young – Cliff Bennett, Andy Fraser – Free(played live), Roger Laverne – The Tornados, John Lydon, Joe Walsh, Lulu, Big Country, Swing Out Sister, Frankie Valli, Ken Hensley – Uriah Heep, Paul Barrere, and Bill Payne – Little Feat, Dean Ford – Marmalade, Carmel, Rod Lynton – Rupert's People, Pete Waterman, Phillip Goodhand – Tait, John Gustafson – The Big Three and The Merseybeats, Question Mark, Nik Kershaw, Rick Westwood – The Tremeloes, Chris Holland, Eddie Floyd, Dionne Warwick, Larry Graham, Jeff Christie, Jay Aston – Bucks Fizz, Mike Qinn, Bellowhead, Mike D'Abo, Maggie Bell, Ricky Ross, Jim Cregan, Strawberry Alarm Clock, Dickie Harrell – Gene Vincent's drummer, Patrick Olive – Hot Chocolate, Richie Sambora – Bon Jovi, Meatloaf, Charley Pride, Mick Hucknall, Nelson Bragg – Brian Wilson's drummer, Lenny Henry, Andy Powell – Wishbone Ash, Brian May, Suggs, Andy Scott – The Sweet, Chris Andrews, Tanita Tikaram, Jackie De Shannon, Don Powell – Slade, Andy Burrows – Razorlight, Rodger Hodgson – Supertramp, James Warren – Korgis, Al Jardine, Pye Hastings – Caravan, Junior Campbell.

As you can see, I had some great guests and live sessions. My favourite guests were Andy Williams, Stevie Nicks, Joe Walsh, Dion, and Chris Squire of Yes, John

Ilsley of Dire Straits, playing 'Romeo and Juliet' live, The Pretty Things Playing SF Sorrow, and Andy Fraser playing 'All Right Now'.

Two funny moments stand out. One was when I was scheduled to chat to Barry Blue, but my producer, Phil Harrison, got his numbers mixed up, so I started listing the hits Barry had been involved with and then said, "Good evening, Barry." I was somewhat shocked when the answer came back, "I'm Not Barry Blue, but Barry McGuire, who sang Eve of Destruction! Well, of course, I hadn't prepared any notes for interviewing him and had to wing it. Thankfully, I knew enough about him to make it interesting, and to be fair to him, he took it in good spirits.

The other humorous moment was with Verden Allen of Mott The Hoople, who answered every question with "To be perfectly honest with you." Phil and I were in fits. We even took a clip of it and used it for comedy value.

Sadly, at the end of 2012, the weekday evening southern regional show was axed, along with all other BBC regional shows. It was to cut costs, but unless others were paid more, I don't think that was the case. Mark Forrest presented a national show from Yorkshire. The way I found out wasn't ideal. I was on holiday in Portugal with the family. I read about the change on a radio website. My listeners weren't happy and bombarded the BBC with letters of complaint. They also organised a petition that attracted many thousands of supporters. Sadly, it made no difference, but I thank them for the support. For me, it took away the best thing about local content.

# Listener petition to save the Day show

■ **By Chris Yandell**

chris.yandell@dailyecho.co.uk

**OUTRAGED music fans across the south have launched a campaign to prevent popular Radio Solent presenter Roger Day being taken off the air.**

The former Radio Caroline DJ is due to be axed as part of a major cost-cutting drive by the BBC, which is having to slash its budget by 20 per cent.

Regional evening shows on Solent and other stations are being scrapped at the end of the year and replaced by a new national programme.

A message on Roger's website says: "The good news is that BBC local daytime programmes are staying much the same.

"The bad news is that from the end of this year my programme and all the other presenters who host the 7pm-10pm shows on local radio around the country will be replaced by a national programme."

But musician Drew Jaymson has launched an online petition to save the 67-year-old presenter, known as the

**POPULAR DJ:** Roger Day.

"voice of weekday evenings".

Drew said: "The BBC is proposing dramatic cuts to local radio services across England. If they go ahead it could result in many of our favourite programmes being removed, including the Roger Day Evening Show.

"Roger's show is regarded by many recording artists as an important plat-

form to talk about their music and live performances.

"Not only is it excellent fun an informative but he clearly has a love fo all music, which is what's sadly lackin on music shows these days.

"I'm tired of hearing the same song played over and over again on the mor mainstream stations, each one soundin much like the one before, like it's th same track on one continuous loop.

"And that's the kind of thing we will b subjected to if this goes ahead."

Earlier this year BBC director-genera Mark Thompson defended the corpora tion's plans, saying the BBC Trus backed most of the proposals.

"They support the way we have set ou balancing the financial challenge w face with an unwavering commitment t quality programming," he said.

Roger Day – read name Roger Thomas appeared on Southern TV's *Pop Th Question* music quiz in 1965. He joine Radio Caroline two years later befor switching to Radio Luxembourg.

Supporters of the campaign to kee him on the air are being urged to ema Mr Thompson and the controller of BB Radio, David Holdsworth.

---

Although I had been in radio many years before joining the Beeb, I do think they made me a better broadcaster. There are great people working there who love radio. I had some great producers, some of whom went on to work in national radio.

I was left hosting a Sunday evening show across the south, but I was determined to continue hosting a daily show. So thanks to the internet and a home studio, I started Uncool Radio. I got the name after a chat with Francis Rossi of Status Quo, who struggled to get plays on radio as they were viewed as being uncool. So I thought that if I got a reputation for playing artists regarded as uncool, it could take off. And it has. I still do it, and I get great support from listeners who pay monthly subscriptions to pay for my running costs.

There are a few people who I must thank for helping me set up my studio and internet station, who built the studio (sadly no longer with us), Julia Allen, who actually gave me a new computer, and Terry Purvis, who organised the website and internet connections.

In 2013, I did host the breakfast show on Redstone FM Reigate.

In October 2016, my old friend and colleague Dave Cash died. Dave was the guy who got me into radio. It was a great shock. He used to do a Saturday show at BBC Radio Kent, and I hoped I would replace him on that slot, as well as continuing my Sunday gig. But the station manager had other ideas. I did replace Dave on the Retro Chart Show but lost my Sunday show. I was quite disappointed with that decision as I was struggling financially.

Another sad event was the death of Brian Mathew. I loved his Sounds of the Sixties, and I never missed it. It was a great start to the weekend, early on Saturdays. I thought the treatment of him by management prior to his death was appalling. I had the feeling they wanted him out.

When they moved the sixties show to 6am with Tony Blackburn, I saw an opportunity. I wrote to many radio stations, asking if they would like a weekly sixties show with the spirit of what Brian did. The response was fantastic, and it is transmitted by stations around the UK and Europe.

*My home studio in the loft*

10    Mirror, Thursday, December 19, 2013    surreymirror.co.uk

READY TO ROCK 'N' ROLL:
Roger "Twiggy" Day presents
the breakfast show for
Redstone FM from 7-10am

# This team's a dab hand at rockin' Redhill

## Digital radio station in tune with area

By Michael Davies

DIGITAL radio turned on some new players this week, with three transmitters being officially activated.

Among the new arrivals in the revolution is Redhill-based Redstone FM, which is hoping to bring a local voice back to the town – and draw in nearly 600,000 listeners.

Before Monday's launch, the Mirror spoke to Redstone FM founder and chief executive Des Shepherd, who was at the switch-on, about his ambitions for the station.

"We're bringing local radio back to this part of Surrey," he said.

"That's the thing that's been missing since Radio Mercury disappeared some years ago, so we're bringing a local voice, together with some brilliant music, and we'll be talking to local people about serious subjects. It's very much about giving this area a voice again on the radio, which has been missing for a long time."

One of the unique aspects about Redstone, which will broadcast out of the Belfry shopping centre, is that in the build-up and preparation for the digital debut, much of the work has been carried out by people who are visually impaired.

### Ownership

This has been an instrumental in creating a feeling of ownership among local groups, who will now be given the chance to pioneer on the air, says Mr Shepherd.

And there are no plans for it to be a slow-burning success, with well-known presenter Roger Day drafted in to provide a big name and years of radio experience.

BBC mainstay Mr "Twiggy" Day, who will be presenting the station's breakfast show from 7-10am, said he was looking forward to bringing his A-list contacts to the listeners.

"I'm always excited at a new station. What we'll deliver, you just won't get anywhere else.

"We won't be limited to the same 300 songs that other stations are, that won't be a problem for us because we have a bigger library – and we'll use it.

"We'll try to get as many people in the studio as possible and we'll be trying to get the big names."

With a Christmas schedule currently underway, there are plans for specialist music shows to come in the new year, along with programming designed by the borough's young people.

*The BBC Studio in Tunbridge Wells.*

*Nice tribute to my friend and legend Dave Cash*

# CHAPTER 30

# TOUGH TIMES

In 2015, my radio work had dried up, apart from the one programme at the BBC and the income from the internet show. But it wasn't enough. So I was forced to get a real job. It was difficult to find something as all I am good at is talking and playing records, plus my age was against me. I did get a job driving a van delivering drugs for Boots the chemist to hospitals. Very few people knew what I was doing, as to be honest, I was ashamed to have been in that position. I certainly didn't want my radio friends to know how low I had sunk. That's not to put down the importance of that job. A really good friend did joke that he always knew I'd become a drug dealer.

Health issues also were an issue. In 2012, a squash buddy of mine had died of prostate cancer, and although I had no symptoms, I decided to get checked out and had the blood test. Pretty soon, I got a call from the doctor asking me to have an examination. He said that he thought there was a lump which needed further tests. After a couple of quite unpleasant examinations, I was sat down by the surgeon, who told me I had cancer. As anyone who has received this news will know, it does shock you. I'd never smoked and had kept fit. I just burst into tears and, like many people, believed it was a death sentence. However, he said that they had discovered it early and there was a good chance it could be cured. I was given three options and opted for two months of radiology. Thankfully, the treatment worked. I advise male readers to get checked out, as the earlier they discover any problem the better.

With that sorted, my next health problem was my mobility. For years, I'd had severe pains in my left leg. I thought it was because of playing squash. In 2015, I decided to see a specialist and was told I needed a new hip. One of my better decisions. Thanks to that, I am still paying tennis three days a week. I've given up the squash though as that might not be wise for my replacement hip. In fact, I feel better now than I did twenty years ago! I joined Maidstone Tennis Club and met some great people.

In 2017, my marriage broke up. It was probably my fault as I hadn't taken well to van driving and it was getting me down. I must have been a pain to live with. Jenny had supported me through good and bad times, but I needed to change my life. I wish her nothing but health and happiness for the rest of her life. We have two lovely children as a result of our time together.

Following our breakup, I probably then went through the lowest period of my life. I was renting a room in a shared house in Maidstone. Christmas Day that year, I actually spent the evening alone for the first time in my life, although the wife of Dave Cash did invite me over for lunch. But I didn't see to talk to my children, which really hurt.

# CHAPTER 31

# A NEW BEGINNING

I n 2018, I met Jacky, who had no idea of my history. Like me, she wanted to start again. So in January 2019, we moved to the Costa Blanca, where I thought I might get my radio career going again on one of the ex-pat stations. We live in a place called Benitachell, near Moraira,

I asked the BBC if I could record my weekly programme for four months while I concentrated on writing my biography. Of course, I had no intention of going back. And they continued to let me record.

I've got a little radio studio in what was the garage. I moved all my music collection here. A BBC engineer said the quality was better than when I was in the studio. I did miss doing the programme live, though, and getting instant feedback from listeners.

I soon settled in and made lots of new friends, playing tennis three times a week. It's lovely that not playing because of bad weather is a rarity. There is also a lot of live music in the cafes and bars.

I started a daily programme for Pure Gold here but wasn't happy with the way it was run so moved to Bay Radio, which is the most professional. I hosted a Sunday show and fill in when others are on holiday.

*Bay Radio Costa Blanca*

# CHAPTER 32

# COVID

Like many people, my life changed dramatically when the pandemic arrived. Spain locked down in March just as I was about to celebrate my 75th birthday. Obviously, the planned party was cancelled. Unlike the UK, we were ordered to stay at home and could only go out for food shopping. Everything else shut, and the police made sure everyone stuck to the rules.

Thankfully, I could still do my radio shows from home. I used to take my 600-watt disco speakers onto the balcony every night and play music to the locals on their balconies. It was like Frinton-on-Sea flashing with neighbours flashing their lights.

# CHAPTER 33

# BOOM RADIO

I n June 2020, BBC Radio Kent reorganised their schedules and dropped my weekend chart show. I was shattered by the news as I thought that was the end of my UK radio career. It was an honour to work with some great people. I only wish my parents had been around to hear me on there. They would have been so proud.

Then, on November 13th 2020, I was on my way to a local bar (there is a surprise), and I got a phone call from Phil Riley, who I'd first met when at BRMB Birmingham. Since then, he had carved out a very successful career setting up and managing radio stations. He talked about setting up a national DAB station catering for baby boomers and asked if I would be interested. I replied that I wasn't interested in moving back to the UK. Thankfully, he said that all the DJs would work from home. I naturally accepted.

At first, the plan was for me to host two weekend programmes, but that soon changed to five evening shows as well. We started on February 14th, and the response was fantastic. It's certainly the best radio experience I've known for a long time. It does remind me of the love and loyalty we had on the offshore stations. I am not only hearing from people who have listened to me on the many stations I have worked on but many who have not heard me before.

To be honest, I had fallen out of love with radio, but Boom has restored my enthusiasm. It is a very strong line up of presenters, some of whom I have worked with before, but not all. David Hamilton, Kid Jenson, Les Ross, Graham Dene, and Nicky Horne. Johnnie Walker, DLT, and Pete Murray have also broadcast special programmes. The management team is up there with the best I have worked for. David Lloyd keeps us informed of everything that is happening and the reasons why certain decisions are made. That in itself is a rarity. I have believed for many years that the boomer generation have been ignored, and the audience figures and comments we get are proof of that. Even BBC Radio 2 and BBC local radio, who should be catering for the boomers, don't because of their obsession with getting a younger audience. What I also love at Boom is the huge music library, not the same repetitive formats of most stations. I must pay credit to the music controller, Paul Robey, who is very knowledgeable.

The highlight for me is the Saturday morning sixties My Generation programme. I do try to present it in the spirit of Brian Matthew, who for me did a wonderful sixties show. When the BBC treated him very badly and they replaced him, many people said

I should replace him. That is why I say it is the Brian Matthew appreciation society. This is the kind of station I dreamed about for many years. I always wanted to be on national radio and felt I was good enough, but as they say, the good things are worth waiting for, and I couldn't be happier. I now am on five days a week. As well as Saturday, I'm on Monday to Thursday 18.00–20.00, starting with thirty minutes of Sixties at Six. The audience is getting bigger every day.

*From the left: Les Ross, me, Nicky Horne, Kid Jenson, Diana Luke, Graham Dene, David Lloyd, Jane Markham, John Peters, Rob Whiting. Missing are David Hamilton, Andy Marriot, Derek Webster, Mike Wyer, Rob Jones, Dave Brown, Graham Torrington, Dave Jamieson, Paul Robey, Judy Spiers, Jenny Hanley, and Quinton Howard.*

*Here I am in the Pirate Cove Costa Blanca Boom Radio South*

## Finally

During the Easter Weekend in 2023 I broadcast live from the Ross Revenge the ship that replaced the Mi Amigo in 1984. It was the first time I had broadcast on Caroline live since March 2nd, 1968. It was great fun. There is something magical about broadcasting from a ship. They do monthly broadcasts on 648 the AM frequency and Manx Radio on the Isle of Man; that is why they call it Radio Caroline North. A tribute to the station that broadcast from the Ramsey Bay from 1964 until 1968.

*Approaching the Ross Revenge off the Bradwell Marina*

*In the Studio*

*On deck*

# CHAPTER 34

# MY FAVOURITE THINGS

**Music**

In no particular order, apart from number one:

Beach Boys–Good Vibrations
Beatles–In My Life
Rolling Stones –Sympathy for the Devil
The Who–Won't Get Fooled Again
Peter Frampton–Do You Feel Like I Do?
Moody Blues–Question
Elbow–One Day Like This
AC/DC–Highway to Hell
Queen–These Are the Days of Our Lives
Dusty–Going Back
Eagles–Hotel California
Temptations–Papa Was a Rolling Stone
Elvis–Suspicious Minds
Cliff–Miss You Nights
Ike & Tina Turner–River Deep Mountain High

Byrds–Turn Turn Turn
Harry Chapin–Cats in the Cradle
Fleetwood Mac–The Chain

**Films**

Gladiator
Zulu
Guns of Navarone
Star Wars
James Bond
Gunfight At the Ok Coral
Mission Impossible
Anything Clint Eastwood
Big Country
Pride and the Passion

**TV**

Downton Abbey
Heartbeat
Ready Steady Go
24
Game Of Thrones
Line Of Duty
Shetland
Monty Python
Allo Allo
Only Fools and Horses

# EPILOGUE

Well, that is my story. I hope you found it interesting. I am one of those lucky people who have a job they actually enjoy. I could have earned more money if I had remained an accountant, but I wouldn't have had as much fun or met as many interesting people. Music has always been my first love, as that song goes. I get to share my record collection with the millions of people who have listened to me over the years. I have also said I don't have listeners, just people I invite to my studio to have a chat and listen to some music. If I can list one disappointment, it is that I have never been recognised by the radio industry for my long-serving radio career. After all, no other UK radio DJ can match my record of hosting a daily programme for over 56 years. I have no intention of retiring and will continue as long as people want to listen.

Thanks for supporting me all these years.

If you enjoyed the book, it was about me, Roger Day. If not, it was about Jack Jackson.